VERMON7

CANADA

UNITED STATES
OF AMERICA

ewEngland

Pacific
Ocean

Atlantic
Ocean

MEXICO

N
W   E
S

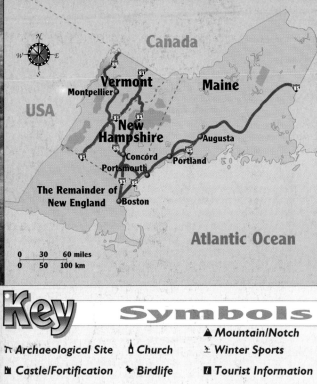

Canada

Vermont
Montpellier

Maine

USA

New
Hampshire

Augusta

Concord

Portland

Portsmouth

The Remainder of
New England

Boston

Atlantic Ocean

0	30	60 miles
0	50	100 km

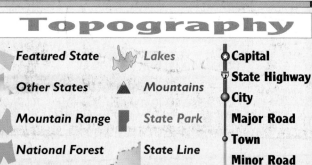

Key Symbols

⛏ Archaeological Site	⛪ Church	▲ Mountain/Notch
🏰 Castle/Fortification	🐦 Birdlife	🎿 Winter Sports
🏛 Building of Interest	🦎 Cave	🈱 Tourist Information
🏛 Museum/Art Gallery	🚂 Railway	* Other Place of Interest
⚓ Water Sports	🚶 Walking	🐟 Aquatic Interest
🐐 Nature/Wildlife Reserve	♣ Parkland or Woodland	🌿 Garden
		🌄 Beautiful View/Natural Phenomenon

Topography

Featured State	Lakes	◉ Capital
Other States	▲ Mountains	🄷 State Highway
Mountain Range	State Park	● City
National Forest	State Line	Major Road
		○ Town
		Minor Road

REGIONAL TRAVELLER

VISITOR'S GUIDE: USA

VERMONT, NEW HAMPSHIRE & MAINE

Don Philpott

MPC®
HUNTER

0668608 04

Published by:
Moorland Publishing Co Ltd,
Moor Farm Road West, Ashbourne,
Derbyshire DE6 1HD England

Published in the USA by:
Hunter Publishing Inc,
300 Raritan Center Parkway, Edison, NJ 08818

ISBN 0 86190 586 5

British Library Cataloguing in Publication Data:
A catalogue record for this book is available from the British Library.

Colour origination by: GA GRAPHICS, Stamford, Lincs. ☎ 01780 56166

Printed in Spain by: GraphyCems

Cover photograph: Vermont Department of Travel & Tourism
(*Jenny Farm, Woodstock, Vermont*)
Page 3: (*Covered Bridge, Vermont*)
Rear cover: Don Philpott (*Ludlow Baptist Church, Vermont*)

The illustrations have been supplied by:
The Greater Boston Convention & Visitors Bureau Inc. pp14, 18, 22, 23, 27;
Vermont Department of Travel & Tourism: pp2, 3, 10, 11, 34, 42, 43, 47,
51 bottom, 54 bottom (Dr John C Weaver), 55, 59, 66 bottom, 67 top
(Robert Bossi), middle (David Brownell), 75 bottom;
Convention & Visitors Bureau of Greater Portland: pp6
Maine Office of Tourism: pp146, 155; remainder by Don Philpott

MPC Production Team:
Editor: Tonya Monk
Designer: Ashley Emery
Cartographer: Mick Usher
Typesetting: Amanda Holdsworth & Stella Porter

CONTENTS

Feature Boxes

Portland, Maine

About This Guide

Although New England is not a large area, there is so much to see and do. Boston, Vermont, New Hampshire and Maine are covered separately, and several itineraries are recommended. Because of the diversity of the different states, their histories are also given separately in their respective chapters.

Getting there: Boston Logan International Airport is the main gateway for visitors flying into New England, and it offers a quick getaway for those driving to other destinations in the region.

After picking up your hire car, follow the exit signs from the airport which is built on a promontory in Boston Harbor. You then have two choices — turn left for the toll tunnels which head for downtown Boston, or right on the Maclennan Highway, depending on your final destination. Note: It helps to remember that Interstate highways with odd numbers ie I-95, run north to south, and Interstates with even numbers run east to west. You will occasionally see an odd numbered Interstate running across country east to west, but this is usually as the road detours round a town or city before returning to its north-south path again.

above: The multi-coloured splendour of the fall in New England

FOR VERMONT

1) Turn left after exiting the airport and take the toll tunnel under the harbour, and then right on to I-93. The Interstate runs into New Hampshire just past the Lawrence turn off. Continue on I-93 to Concord, and then take I-89 west which crosses the border with Vermont just after Lebanon. This route is about 140 miles (225km) to the border.

2) Turn left after exiting the airport and take the toll tunnel under the harbour, then take a left on to I-93 south for just over 1 mile (2km), and turn right to join I-90, the Massachusetts Turnpike. You can then stay on I-90 heading west until Springfield, and then turn north on to I-91 to cross over into Vermont about 15 miles (24km) past the Greenfield turn off. This route is about 160 miles (258km).

A shorter but slightly more complicated version, is to leave I-93 after about $3^1/2$ miles (6km) turn off right to connect with highway 2 and the Concord Turnpike which runs west, through Concord, Leominster to connect with I-91 north which runs into Vermont. This route is about 115 miles (185km).

FOR NEW HAMPSHIRE

Turn left after exiting the airport and take the toll tunnel under the harbour, and then right on to I-93 which runs into New Hampshire just past the Lawrence turn off. This route is about 35 miles (56km) to the border.

FOR MAINE

1) Turn right for the McClennan Highway (Highway 1A) north-east for about 3 miles (5km), and then cross over the intersection onto highway 60 (Squire Road) and follow this north for about 2 miles (3km) to connect with State Highway 1 which runs north to Salem. Just beyond join I-95 which follows the coast north-east via Portsmouth, and then across the border into Maine. It is about 65 miles (105km) to the Maine state border.

2) Turn left after exiting the airport and take the toll tunnel under the harbour, and then turn right on to I-93 which runs north for about 9 miles (14km) to connect with I-95. Turn right on to I-95 and continue into Maine. This route is about 70 miles (113km).

When To Go

Summer and autumn are the best times for sightseeing and mid-September to mid-October the best times for viewing the fall foliage; the winters are long and cold and the heavy snowfalls offer excellent skiing, both downhill and cross country; spring is a great time for avoiding the crowds and enjoying the wide open spaces, especially if you like walking.

What to eat: You will never eat better or fresher seafood. Try the chowder, scallops and lobster. Breakfasts can be huge and will last you all day, but if you do feel hungry there is never a problem with finding somewhere to eat, and again, there is enormous choice from fast food to gourmet fare, and from incredibly good value to astronomic.

Where To Stay

New England is noted for its high standards of accommodation from historic inns and delightful bed and breakfasts, to international hotel chains. Recommended hotels and restaurants to suit all tastes and pockets are given at the end of each section.

Once you have experienced New England, you will want to come back again and again. I hope that this guide will give you the inspiration to visit New England, help you get the most out of your trip, and encourage you to return over and over, because there is something new to discover and enjoy.

Don Philpott

Introduction

Shades of Autumn
in New England

As a tourist destination New England has got it all. It is an area steeped in history, it has spectacular scenery, wonderful food, great hospitality, fascinating attractions and year-round appeal. It is a region noted for its picture-postcard villages with white steepled churches, village greens, Colonial clapboard homesteads and covered bridges. Everywhere one turns, there are reminders both of its great history, and the historic role it played in the founding and growth of the American nation.

New England, however, has even more to offer. It has glorious beaches, lakes, mountains and massive wilderness areas, and of course, huge forests and woodlands which attract visitors in their tens of thousands every autumn because of the spectacular fall foliage colours. New England really is a year round destination. Some of its best kept secrets are its winter sports areas, there are trails to be walked and maple syrup to be processed and tasted in the spring, sea, sun and sand to be enjoyed in the summer, and places to explore in the mild days of autumn.

New England consists of the six states of Massachusetts, Connecticut, Vermont, New Hampshire, Rhode Island and Maine — including five of the original thirteen colonies. Between them they provided the link between the old world and the new, and the spark that ignited revolution and independence.

Since their earliest founding days, the New England states have been known for their political, cultural, educational and artistic traditions. They have produced Presidents and statesmen, are home to some of the nation's finest academic establishments, and have inspired countless artists and writers, with many art colonies.

One of the great pleasures of New England is its size. None of the states are geographically large, yet each is packed with so many things to see and do, that they offer a life time of exploration and discovery. For serious exploration of the countryside you need a car but you will find miles of quiet lanes and byways, and around almost every corner there is a spectacular view or charming scene of yesteryear. If you have more time, you can get out and explore on foot or bike, and in the towns and cities, the historic districts are always best discovered on foot.

If you are interested in fishing, bird spotting, whale watching, fossil hunting or outdoor sports, you will find ample opportunities to keep you busy. If you like shopping, going to the theatre or concerts, you will not be disappointed, and if you appreciate good food and fine hospitality, New England has it all.

New England covers around 66,670sq miles (172,815sq km) and has New York State to the south and south-west, Quebec and New

Brunswick to the north, and the Atlantic Ocean to the east and south-east. Maine accounts for around half the area of New England, while tiny Rhode Island is the nation's smallest state. The mountains of New England are part of the Appalachian Chain, and they like the rest of the countryside, have been shaped and eroded by the glaciers that covered the entire region during the last Ice Age. The melting glaciers and fast flowing rivers also carved out the wide estuaries and natural harbours that helped New England establish its strong maritime base.

The glaciers not only shaped the countryside millions of years ago, but are responsible for how it looks today. The glaciers left little fertile soil in their tracks, and the early settlers found very poor agricultural land. The land was able to sustain trees in their millions, and sheep, and it was their wool and power from the fast flowing rivers, that started the industrial revolution with textile mills. The mills also attracted huge numbers of immigrants which boosted the region's population.

Long before the Pilgrim Fathers stepped ashore in Plymouth in 1620, native American Indians had settled the area and their earliest settlements date back 15,000 years. Many of the region's rivers, mountains and places still have their original Indian names.

Today, New England gives the impression of being a predominantly rural society with little to disturb the peace and calm, but this is misleading. Most people live in towns and cities, and most of these in major conurbations in the south. New England does have major industrial and manufacturing centres; its great charm is that you are just not aware of it.

Boston

History

Settled by the Puritans in 1630, Boston quickly developed into a major port. It was the largest British settlement in North America but fiercely independent. Its reluctance to accept the authority of England, led to its Royal Warrant being withdrawn in 1684, and this signalled the start of unrest which finally culminated in the Revolutionary War. In 1768, because of refusal to pay taxes, British troops occupied Boston and in 1770 they fired on unarmed protesting citizens, killing five in the Boston Massacre. In 1773 Boston citizens, dressed as Indians, dumped three shiploads of tea into the harbour and further acts of resistance triggered the American Revolution in 1775. Boston was besieged by George Washington and in March 1776, the British abandoned the city. Boston grew rapidly in the nineteenth century with surrounding mudflats and marshes reclaimed. This extra land allowed city planners to lay out the many public gardens and wide avenues. Although it remained an impor-

above: The Museum of Fine Arts

tant seaport, Boston became even more important as a commercial and industrial centre. Its success attracted educational, religious and artistic institutions and the Boston Brahmins presided over the city's cultural life from the fashionable Beacon Hill area.

More recently, Boston has become noted as a centre for high technology, education and medicine. There are more than 50 universities and colleges in the area, and more than 500 high-tech companies, as well as world class hospitals and medical research centres.

The great charm of Boston is that despite its growth, it has retained its elegance and character. Huge glass and steel skyscrapers dominate the skyline, but there are still many wonderfully preserved old buildings, such as the 1713 Old State House and the Faneuil Hall. Downtown Boston is still dominated by Boston Common, and the historic districts still boast cobbled streets, gaslights, and marvellous old buildings and, the heart of the city can easily be explored on foot.

Getting Around

Logan International Airport has regular flights from the UK and mainland Europe and connections with the rest of the USA. The airport is across the Inner Harbor in East Boston, and travelling to and from during rush hours can be slow. Public transport is advised as it is quick, convenient and cheap — the combined bus and subway fare is around $1. MassPort operates a free shuttle between the airport terminals and the airport's 'T' subway. Metered taxis are also available, and Logan Express operates a shuttle bus service from Framingham, Braintree and Woburn to Logan daily between 6am and 11pm. A more interesting way to get to and from the airport is to use the Water Shuttle. It operates daily except public holidays, between Logan Dock reached by free airport shuttle bus, and Rowes Wharf, close to the subway by the aquarium.

Greyhound operates from St James Avenue, with links to other major cities ☎ (617) 423-5810. Vermont Transit, uses the same terminal with services throughout New England, New York and Montreal ☎ (802) 864-6811. Trains from the south and west arrive at South Station on Atlantic Avenue, and local services and trains from the north operate from North Station on Causeway Street.

Driving: the main east-west highway into Boston is the Massachusetts Turnpike (I-90) which runs parallel to SR9. The I-93/US1 runs north to connect with the Northeast Expressway, the Southeast Expressway (SR3) runs in from the south, and the I-95/SR125 runs right round the metropolitan area, linking all the main approaches to the city.

Driving in Boston can be awesome. There is no apparent logic to the street lay out in many areas, largely because of the city's piece-meal expansion. It is also too easy to get locked into the one-way system — and often too difficult to escape from it! Rush hour traffic (7.30am-9.30am and 4.30pm-6.30pm) in Boston is also best avoided.

There are street meters downtown but restrictions vary from area to area. There are many parking garages in central Boston, particularly the Auditorium Garage in Dalton Street, Boston Common Garage under the Common via Charles Street, John Hancock Garage in Clarendon Street, and Prudential Garage under the Prudential Tower.

Public Transport: the Massachusetts Bay Transportation Authority (MBTA) provides the efficient public transport service which includes buses, trolleys and subway. The subway which started in 1895 is the nation's oldest. Subway stations are marked with a 'T' and travel is cheap and efficient, except during the rush hours. Each of the four subway lines has its own colour making navigating easy. If spending several days in Boston, get a 3- or 7-day Boston Passport which allows unlimited travel on subway, trolleys and most bus routes.

There are many guided bus, coach, boat and walking tours of Boston. The Old Town Trolley Tours leave from Long Wharf and you can either do the whole tour, or alight at any of the fifteen stops along the way to explore, and then rejoin the tour on a later trolley. Tours leave every 20 minutes daily 9am-dusk May to October, 9am-4pm rest of the year ☎ (617) 269-7010. There are a number of cruises of the harbour, Charles River, coastline and nearby islands leaving from Long Wharf.

There are also many guided walking tours of the city, including the Freedom Trail Tour, Beacon Hill Twilight Tour, North End Tour and Downtown Skyline Tour.

Boston is an easy place to explore on foot, and there are a number of walking tour maps available if you want to explore the city at your leisure, rather than on a guided tour. Details of the Black Heritage Trail can be obtained from the Afro-American Museum, Freedom Trail Information Booth and National Park Visitor Center. There is also a self-guiding 1 mile (2km) walk of the harbour area from the Old State House to the Boston Tea Party ship.

The Freedom Trail Tour

The most popular self-guiding walk is the 3 mile (5km) long Freedom Trail.The walks starts from the information booth on **Tremont Street** beside Boston Common in the heart of the city's downtown. Head north across the Common to the **State House** with its golden dome off Beacon Street, and then take Park Street south which runs along the eastern boundary of the Common to **Park Street Church** on your left. Turn left into Tremont Street to visit the **Granary Burial Ground** on your left. Turn left when you leave the cemetery and then right into School Street with the granite **King's Chapel**, the **statue of Benjamin Franklin** and the **Old City Hall**. On the corner of School and Washington Streets are the **Old Corner Bookstore** and almost opposite, the **Old South Meeting House**. Turn right into Washington Street for two blocks to visit the **National Park Service Visitor Center** and the **Old State House**. The trail continues to the north of the Old State House and on the corner there is a stone circle, which marks the site of the **Boston Massacre**. Cross State and Congress Streets and turn left for **Faneuil Hall**. Then cross North Street and take Union Street to the narrow Marshall Street. At the end of Marshall Street, cross over Black Stone Street and take the pedestrian passageway under the arch leading to the **North End**. Cross over Cross Street, turn left at the corner of Hanover Street, then right into Richmond Street, then left into North Street for **Paul Revere House** on the left. Then turn left on Prince Street, then right back on to Hanover Street to **St Stephen's Church**, past the statue of Paul Revere astride his horse, and the Old North Church behind it. Walk through the mall to visit the church. Then, cross Salem Street, and walk along Hull Street to **Copp's Hill Burial Ground**. Continue downhill along Hull Street then left on Commercial Street to cross the **Charlestown Bridge**. Go through the gate and down the steps to the **Paul Revere Landing Park** and the **Charles River Dam Visitors' Information Center**. Then turn right into Chelsea Street, then right into Chamber Street for Constitution Road which leads to the **Charlestown Navy Yard** and the **USS Constitution**. Then, retrace your route a short way along Constitution Road taking the pedestrian underpass to Chelsea Street. Turn right, and then left into Chestnut Street, then left into Adams Street, then right into Winthrop Street which leads to the **Bunker Hill Monument**. After visiting the site, walk down Monument Avenue to Main Sreet where you can catch any bus marked 'Downtown' to return to your starting point.

US Customs House Tower at dusk

Charles River Basin

Charles River Reservation

Boston

Longf...
Bri

Gibson Ho
Museum

First a
Second C

New England
Historic Genealogical
Society

Institute of
Contemporary
Art

Boylston Street

Boylston Street

Public Library

John Hancock
Observatory

Prudential
Center

Isabella Stewart
Gardner Museum

Boylston Street

Mother Church, the
First Church of
Christ Scientist

Christian Science
Publishing
Society

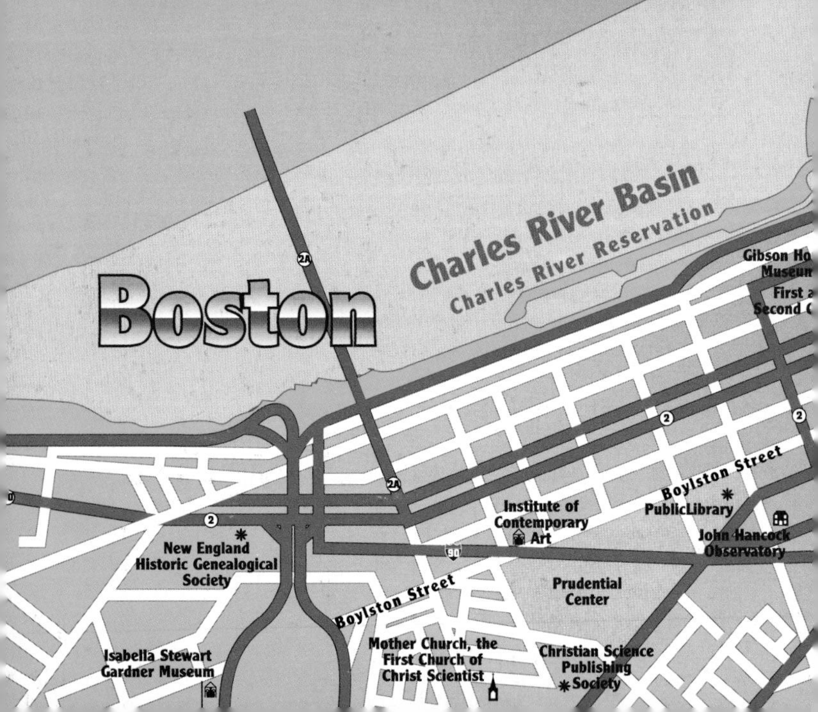

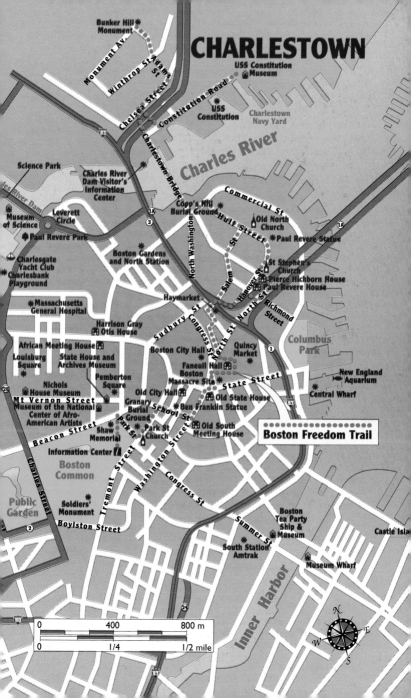

CHARLESTOWN

Bunker Hill Monument

Monument Av.

Winthrop St.

Adams St.

Monument Street

Chelsea Street

USS Constitution Museum

Constitution Road

USS Constitution

Charlestown Navy Yard

Charlestown Bridge

Charles River

Science Park

Charles River Dam Visitor's Information Center

les River Dam

Museum of Science

Leverett Circle

Paul Revere Park

Commercial St.

Copp's Hill Burial Ground

Hull Street

Old North Church

Paul Revere Statue

North Washington

Salem St.

St Stephen's Church

Hanover St.

Pierce Hichborn House

Paul Revere House

Charlesgate Yacht Club

Charlesbank Playground

Boston Gardens and North Station

Haymarket

North St.

Richmond Street

Massachusetts General Hospital

Harrison Gray Otis House

Sudbury St.

Congress Street

Columbus Park

North St.

Quincy Market

African Meeting House

State House and Archives Museum

Boston City Hall

Faneuil Hall

New England Aquarium

Louisburg Square

Pemberton Square

Boston Massacre Site

State Street

Central Wharf

Nichols House Museum

Old City Hall

Old State House

Mt Vernon Street

Museum of the National Center of Afro-American Artists

Granary Burial Ground

School St.

Ben Franklin Statue

Beacon Street

Shaw Memorial

Park St.

Park St. Church

Old South Meeting House

Boston Freedom Trail

Information Center

Boston Common

Washington Street

Congress St

Public Garden

Charles Street

Soldiers' Monument

Boylston Street

Tremont Street

Boston Tea Party Ship & Museum

Summer St.

Castle Isla

South Station Amtrak

Museum Wharf

Inner Harbor

0	400	800 m
0	1/4	1/2 mile

What To See

DOWNTOWN

The **African Meeting House**, at 46 Joy Street, was dedicated in 1806 and the three storey building served for almost 100 years as the centre for black community activities. It is the oldest black church in the USA. It now has changing exhibits about its history and the history of the city's black community. Open: daily 10am-4pm. Admission charge. The **Arnold Arboretum** in Jamaica Plain, is a 265 acre (106 hectare) park with more than 6,000 northern temperate trees arranged by family. Open: daily dawn to dusk. The **Boston Common** is the oldest public park in the country, and was originally designated in 1634 as a cow pasture and training field. Originally it was the location for the punishment stocks, and the British troops gathered here before the Battle of Bunker Hill.

The **Boston National Historic Park** covers seven important sites along the Freedom Trail and the Dorchester Heights Monument in South Boston. The park is an excellent example of cooperation between the public and private sectors, as only the Bunker Hill Monument and Charlestown Navy Yard are federally owned. The other Boston sites — Faneuil Hall, Old North Church, Old South Meeting House, Old State House and Paul Revere House — are owned by the city or private individuals.

The 3 mile (5km) long **Freedom Trail** starts at the information booth on Boston Common taking in the centre of downtown Boston, North End and Bunker Hill. The park's visitor centre is at 15 State Street, opposite the Old State House, and explains the city's history and growth with a 10 minute film. Open: Monday to Friday 8am-6pm, weekends 9am-6pm June to August, Monday to Friday 8am-5pm, weekends 9am-5pm rest of the year. There are free 90 minute walking tours conducted by rangers of the Freedom Trail which leave daily on the half hour between 9.30am and 3pm between mid-June and early September, and daily on the hour between 10am and 3pm May to mid-June and early September to early October, weekends at 10am, 11am, 12noon and 3pm, mid-April to May to early October to November. The **Boston Public Garden**, between Boylston, Charles, Beacon and Arlington Streets, is a landscaped garden with statues and boating on the lake. Open: daily dawn to dusk. Admission free.

The **Boston Public Library**, 666 Boylston Street, has a fine collection of paintings including the mural *The Quest of the Holy Grail* by Edwin Austin Abbey, and works by other famous artists and sculptors. The Wiggin Gallery has changing exhibitions from Rembrandt to contemporary Boston artists. The Research Building in Copley Square was built in 1888 in Italian Renaissance style with inner courtyard and garden. The library opened in 1972 has a collection of rare books and manuscripts. Open: Monday to Thursday 9am-9pm, Friday and Saturday 9am-5pm. Admission free.

The **Boston Tea Party Ship and Museum**, by Congress Street Bridge on Harbor Walk, recreates the historic raid with a full scale replica of the tea party ship. Open: daily 10am-6pm March to mid-December. Admission charge.

The **Bull & Finch Pub**, at 84 Beacon Street, is the bar which inspired the TV series *Cheers*, and fans will recognise the programme's opening sequences shot outside. Open: daily 11.30am-2am. Admission free.

The **Bunker Hill Monument** on Breed's Hill in Monument Square, marks the centre of the battlefield where the Battle of Breeds Hills was fought on 17 June 1775. It is now popularly known as the Battle of Bunker Hill. The 221ft (67m) granite obelisk has a spiral staircase to the top and there is a lodge at the base with a model and exhibits of the battle. Open: daily 9am-4.30pm (lodge to 5pm). Admission free. The 'Whites of their Eyes', is a multimedia presentation which re-enacts the Battle of Bunker Hill, in the Bunker Hill Pavilion, next to the USS Constitution in Charlestown. Open: daily 9.30am-5pm June to August, 9.30am-4pm April, May, September and October. Admission charge. **Castle Island** is in South Boston and stands at the entrance to Boston Inner Harbor. Fort Independence was built in 1801. Admission free. The **Charles River Reservation** extends both sides of the river from the Boston and Cambridge dams to Newton Upper Falls off SR9. The reserve covers almost 1,000 acres (400 hectares) and has cycle and hiking paths, six swimming pools, ice skating rinks, tennis courts, fitness centre and the Hatch Memorial Shell, where concerts are staged from mid-April to mid-October. The **Charles River Dam Visitors' Information Center**, is at the dam off Warren Avenue, and has a 12 minute film on the dam and flood control. Open: daily 9am-3pm. Admission free.

The **Charlestown Navy Yard**, is off I-93 in Charlestown, and covers 30 acres (12 hectares) of the former naval yard. It is part of the Boston National Historic Park. The yard was built in 1800 as one of the country's six naval dockyards, and it served as a repair and supply depot until 1974. It provided ropes for the navy for most of this time and invented the 'ship house' which allowed vessels to be repaired quicker under cover. The US Navy's first purpose built ship of the line, the *USS Independence*, was launched here in 1814.

Downtown skyline from Boston Harbor; home to many hotels, shopping arcades, restaurants and museums around Waterfront Park

The many maritime exhibits include the destroyer *USS Cassin Young,* and the *USS Constitution*, launched in 1797 at Edmund Hartt's shipyard, sited only a short distance from its present berth. It is the oldest commissioned ship in the US Navy and earned the nickname *Old Ironsides* following actions with the British Navy during the War of 1812. The forty-four gun frigate was built of oak and red cedar held together by bolts and copper sheathing made by Paul Revere's foundry. There are guided tours of the ship daily between 9.30am-5.30pm. Admission free. The **USS Constitution Museum**, next to the ship, allows you to command the vessel during a naval engagement, try a hammock and hoist a sail. Craftsmen demonstrate the art of miniature shipbuilding. Open: daily 9am-6pm late June to early September, weekends 9am-5pm April to late June and late September to December. Admission charge. The **Children's Museum of Boston**, on Museum Wharf, off Congress Street, has hands-on displays for fun and learning about science, art and different cultures. Open: daily 10am-5pm (Friday to 9pm) July to early September, Tuesday to Sunday 10am-5pm (Friday 9pm) rest of the year. Admission charge.

The **Christian Science Publishing Society** on the corner of Massachusetts Avenue and Clearway Street, produces the Christian Science Monitor and radio and television programmes. The intriguing Mapparium is a walk through globe which allows you to view the world from inside. Open: Tuesday to Saturday 9.30am-4pm. Admission free. The Multimedia Bible Exhibit, 101 Belvadere Street, has rare Bibles, films of the Holy Land, slide presentations and other audio-visual presentations. Open: Wednesday to Saturday 10am-4pm, Sunday 11.15am-4pm. Admission free.

The **Computer Museum**, Museum Wharf, uses hands-on exhibits to explain the history of computers and how the information revolution affects everyone. Open: daily 10am-6pm mid-June to early September, Tuesday to Sunday 10am-5pm rest of the year. Admission charge.

Faneuil Hall, in Faneuil Square, known as 'the Cradle of Liberty'. The house, capped by its famous grasshopper weather vane, was built in 1742, burned down in 1761, rebuilt 2 years later and expanded in 1805. The second storey meeting room saw many important gatherings during the Revolutionary War. When the British occupied the city, the meeting room was used by the officers as a theatre. It contains many battle paintings and a military museum. There are talks about the house and its history every half hour between 9am and 5pm. The museum is open daily Monday to Friday 10am-4pm. Admission free. The Faneuil Marketplace in-

cludes the Hall and next door nineteenth century **Quincy Market**, ✳
housing more than 125 shops, boutiques, eateries and stalls with
street performers. Open: daily 10am-9pm. The **First and Second** ♦
Church in Boston, Marlborough Street was built in 1972 around the
Gothic steeple, all that remained of the 1868 structure, which in turn
was on the site of an earlier church. Members of its congregation
have included Paul Revere, Ralph Emerson and Henry Thoreau.
Open: by appointment through the church office Monday to Friday
9am-5pm, early September to mid-June ☎ (617) 267-6730.

Fort Warren, on Georges Island is in the Boston Harbor Islands 🏚
State Park, and reached by ferry from Long Wharf. The granite fort
was built between 1834 and 1860 and held Confederate prisoners
during the Civil War. During the Spanish-American War and the
World War I it was an ordnance depot responsible for laying mines
in Boston Harbor. Bay State Cruises offer narrated trips to the fort
daily at 10am, 1pm and 3pm July to early September. The fort is open
daily 10am-5pm July to October. Admission free.

The **Gibson House Museum** at 137 Beacon Street, is in an 1859 🏛
brownstone house with Victorian furnishings, and open for guided
tours Wednesday to Sunday at 1,2 and 3pm May to October, and
weekends at the same time the rest of the year. Admission charge.
The **Government Center** is a 60 acre (24 hectare) urban renewal ✳
project on the site of old Scollay Square, and noted for the stunning
contemporary architecture of the city, state and federal buildings.

The **Granary Burial Ground**, Tremont Street, has the graves of ✳
three of those who signed the Declaration of Independence — John
Hancock, Samuel Adams and Robert Treat Paine — as well as Paul
Revere, Peter Faneuil, the parents of Benjamin Franklin and the
victims of the Boston Massacre. Open: daily 8am-4.30pm. Admission free.

Harrison Gray Otis House, at 141 Cambridge Street, was de- 🏢
signed by Charles Bulfinch and built in 1796 for Otis, Boston's third
mayor. It is furnished in early nineteenth century Federal style, and
is the headquarters of the Society for the Preservation of New
England Antiquities, an organisation that runs twenty-three house
museums throughout New England. Open: Tuesday to Friday
12noon-5pm, Saturday 10am-5pm. Admission charge.

The **Haymarket** is the country's oldest market, and for more than ✳
200 years its stalls have been selling fruit, vegetables and seafood.
The Haymarket area now covers several blocks of Blackstone Street
which is dominated by the statue *Asarotan*, a series of bronze cast-
ings of fruit, vegatables and other produce sold in the market. The
statue's name translated means 'unswept floor'.

Shopping

Boston offers excellent shopping. Main shopping areas are: Copley Place, Huntington Avenue, Dartmouth Street, Quincy Market, Mercants Row and Clinton Street. Downtown Crossing is the town's old shopping area and now a bustling pedestrial precinct which includes Lafayette Square, a new enclosed mall. The stalls at Bull Market are worth browsing through, and the adjoining North and South Markets offer a wide range of goods. Antique hunters should visit Antiques Row on Charles Street, and there are other speciality stores at the Chestnut Hill Mall in Newington, and Harvard Square in Cambridge.

Annual Events

A re-enactment of the Boston Tea Party takes place on 15 December, and Boston's Irish community come out in force for the St Patrick's Day Parade on 17 March, which coincides with Evacuation Day when in 1776, the British abandoned Boston to the Colonists. The Battle of Bunker Hill Celebration is held on 17 June.

Independence Day (4 July) in Boston is celebrated as Harborfest, when the USS Constitution is literally turned round on its moorings to ensure equal weathering. Other activities include a Chowderfest competition, concerts and fireworks.

The Boston International Marathon is held on the third Monday of April, and the womens 6 mile (10km) Tufts Race is held on Downtown streets on Columbus Day. The Head of the Charles Regatta, an international rowing event, takes place on the third Sunday in October.

There are also several ethnic celebrations, such as the Italian Feasts in North End from the last weekend in June to the end of August. The New Year is celebrated with Boston's First Night concerts, entertainments and parades.

Rowing on the Charles River, home of the renowned 'Head of the Charles' regatta

Charles River Boathouse and skyline, a popular boating site as well as a picturesque view of Boston

The **Institute of Contemporary Art**, at 955 Boylston Street, is housed in a nineteenth century police station and has displays on photography, sculpture, architecture and video art. Open: Wednesday to Sunday 12noon-5pm (Wednesday and Thursday to 9pm). Admission charge. The **Isabella Stewart Gardner Museum**, 280 Fenway Street, is in a remarkable building styled on a Venetian palace, with an art collection and Sunday afternoon concerts between September and May. Museum open: Tuesday to Sunday 11am-5pm. Admission charge. The **John Hancock Observatory**, on St James Avenue and Trinity Place, at 740ft (226m) is the tallest building in New England and offers stunning panoramic views. It also houses historical exhibits. Open: Monday to Saturday 9am-10pm, Sunday 10am-10pm May to October, Sunday 12noon-10pm rest of the year. Admission charge.

King's Chapel, on Tremont and School Streets, was built in 1754 on the site of the original 1689 chapel, the first Anglican church in New England, although it later became the first Unitarian Church. Musical recitals are held on Tuesday and Thursday evenings. Open: Tuesday to Saturday 10am-4pm May to October, Tuesday to Friday 10am-2pm, Saturday 10am-4pm rest of the year. Donations. The King's Chapel Burial Ground has the graves of Governor John Winthrop, the Reverend John Cotton and John Davenport, founder of New Haven, Connecticut. Open: daily 9am-4pm. Admission free.

The Mother Church, the First Church of Christ Scientist, off Massachusetts Avenue, is the world headquarters of Christian Science, founded in 1879 by Mary Baker Eddy. The church is topped by an impressive dome. Open: Tuesday to Friday 9.30am-4pm, Sunday 11.30am-2pm. Admission free. The **Museum** at the **John Fitzgerald Kennedy Library**, on the campus of the University of Massachusetts, is a memorial to the 35th President of the United States with personal effects and a 30 minute film about his life and career. Open: daily 9am-5pm. Admission charge. The **Museum of Fine Arts**, 465 Huntington Avenue, is vast with more than 200 galleries and a huge range of exhibits from around the world. The West Wing opened in 1981 houses visiting exhibitions, and was built with granite from the same quarry used to build the original neo-Classical building in 1901. Open: Tuesday to Sunday 10am-4.45pm (Thursday and Friday to 9.45pm). Admission charge. The **Museum of Science**, on the Science Park, has exhibits and hands-on displays on natural history, medicine, physical sciences and astronomy. It includes the Charles Hayden Planetarium with a 45 minute programme about the universe, and the Mugar Omnimax Theater with its four storey high screen with daily one hour film shows. Open: daily 9am-5pm (Friday to 9pm). Admission charge. The **Museum of the National Center of Afro-American Artists**, 300 Walnut Avenue, has exhibits by black American artists in a neo-Gothic mansion made of Roxbury puddingstone and Nova Scotia sandstone. Open: Wednesday to Sunday 1-6pm July and August, Tuesday to Sunday 1-5pm rest of the year. Admission charge.

The **New England Aquarium**, Central Wharf off Atlantic Avenue, has more than 2,000 fish and aquatic animals, a recreated coral reef with tropical fish, sea lions, penguin colony and a hands-on tidal pool. There is a programme of films about marine subjects, and whale watch cruises leave daily between May and mid-October. Open: Monday to Friday 9am-6pm (Wednesday and Thursday to 8pm), weekends 9am-7pm July to early September, Monday to Friday 9am-5pm (Thursday to 8pm), weekends 9am-6pm rest of the year. Admission charge. The **New England Historic Genealogical Society**, Newbury and Clarendon Streets, has a fascinating libary of records and old manuscripts about New England families, often tracing their descendants back to their countries of origin. Open: Tuesday to Saturday 9am-5pm (Wednesday and Thursday to 9pm). Admission and tours free. The **Nichols House Museum**, 55 Mount Vernon Street, is a Federal style house in the heart of Beacon Hill. It was the home of Rose Standish Nichols and reflects the lifestyle of Boston's wealthy upper classes with furnishings from the sixteenth to nineteenth century. Open: Tuesday to Saturday 12noon-5pm May to October, Monday, Wednesday and Saturday 12noon-5pm February to April and November to December. Admission charge. The **Old South Meeting House**, 310 Washington Street, was built in 1729 as a church but was used for many historic town meetings, including those that discussed the Boston Massacre and Boston Tea Party. There is a multimedia presentation tracing the city's 300 year history, and a model of Colonial Boston. Open: daily 9.30am-5pm April to October. Monday to Friday 10am-4pm, weekends 10am-5pm rest of the year. Admission charge. The **Old State House** on Washington Street, built in 1713 on the site of the 1657 Town House, is Boston's oldest public building. The Boston Massacre took place at the east front, the Declaration of Independence was read from the State Street balcony, and in 1780 John Hancock was inaugurated as the State's first governor. The building is managed by the Bostonian Society as a museum of the city's history, and has some fascinating exhibits, including some of the tea salvaged after the Boston Tea Party. Open: daily 9.30am-5pm. Admission charge. **Park Street Church** on Park and Tremont Streets, was built in 1809 and William

World famous artists appear at the Symphony Hall, which is the home of the Boston Pops and Boston Symphony Orchestras. The Boston Ballet Company and the Opera Company of Boston stage performances throughout the year, and the Wang Center for Performing Arts, Tremont Street, also offers ballet and other productions. There are free open air evening concerts in the Hatch Memorial Shell during July, and free chamber concerts and recitals at the Isabella Stewart Gardner Museum. The New England Conservatory of Music also perform free concerts and recitals at various times of the year.

Theatre

Boston's theatres are often used to test plays destined for Broadway. Main theatres are the Colonial on Boylston Street, Shubert and the Wilbur both on Tremont Street. The Boston Repertory Company and the Charles Playhouse both offer contemporary and experimental works, and the Boston Center for the Arts stages plays and art exhibitions. Boston also has several cinemas, and reserved seating is often advisable.

The city is rightly famed for its restaurants and it has some of the world's best seafood restaurants. The menu at Locke-Obers has changed little since it opened in 1875, and the Union Oyster House, in Union Street, was a frequent haunt of Daniel Webster, who was known to eat up to six dozen oysters at a sitting. There are fine eateries in the restored Faneuil Hall and adjoining nineteenth-century warehouses,

Eating Out In Boston

and Quincy Market. Not only is the food excellent, there is a huge range of ethnic cuisines to choose from. North End is noted for its Italian restaurants, and the nearby waterfront area is packed with famous fish restaurants, such as Anthony's Pier 4, and Jimmy's Harborside. There are also many dinner cruises, and international hotels offering world-class cuisine.

Boston is also packed with clubs, pubs and discos such as Boston's Metro in Kenmore Square, and Tam O'Shanter in Brookline. There are comedy clubs, like Stitches on Commonwealth Avenue and the Charles Hotel's Regattabar in Cambridge is famous for its jazz. Local rock bands appear at the Copley Place Marriott's Conservatory.

Lloyd Garrison delivered his first anti-slavery speech here in 1829.
Open: Tuesday to Saturday 9am-3.30pm July and August, rest of the
year by appointment. Admission free ☎ (617) 523-3383.

The **Prudential Center**, between Huntington Avenue and
Boylston Street, was the city's first combined business, civic and
residential development. The 52 storey complex covers 28 acres (11
hectares) and also has shops, restaurants, hotel and covered car
parking for 3,000 vehicles. The Prudential Tower Skywalk is on the
50th floor and offers fabulous panoramic views of the city and
surrounding countryside. The Skywalk is open Monday to Saturday
10am-10pm, Sunday 12noon-10pm. Admission charge. The **Soldiers' Monument** stands on historic Dorchester Heights. George
Washington fortified the heights while laying siege to the city which
was occupied by the British. His action forced the British to abandon
Boston on 17 March 1776. The **State House**, on Beacon Street, has an
imposing façade designed by Charles Bulfinch and virtually unchanged since it was built in 1795. Exhibits include statues, historical
paintings and war relics. When sitting, the legislature meets Monday to Thursday. Open: Monday to Friday 9am-5pm, free guided
tours between 10am-4pm. Admission free. The bronze **Shaw Memorial** by Augustus Saint Gaudens, is opposite the State House.
Colonel Robert Shaw commanded the 54th Massachusetts Regiment, the first black regiment to serve in the Civil War.

The magnificent **Trinity Church** in Copley Square, was built in
1877 in Romanesque-style by Henry Hobson Richardson. The interior was designed by John LaFarge. Open: daily 8am-6pm. There are
guided tours after Sunday morning service and by appointment.
There are free organ recitals at 12.15pm Fridays between September
and June ☎ (617) 536-0944.

NORTH END
North End is the oldest neighbourhood with tiny, colourful streets,
and a large Italian population with many good restuarants and food
stores. There are many summer parades and festivals.

Paul Revere House, 19 North Square, is the oldest house in
Downtown Boston, built around 1680. Paul Revere lived in the
house between 1770 and 1800 and it contains period furnishings and
personal memorabilia. There is a herb garden and a some bells cast
by Paul Revere's foundry in the garden. Open: daily 9.30am-5.15pm
mid-April to October, daily 9.30am-4.15pm rest of the year. Admission charge.

Next door is **Pierce Hichborn House**, 29 North Square. Built in
1711 by glazier Moses Pierce, it is one of the oldest surving Georgian

buildings in the city, and was for a time the home of boatbuilder Nathaniel Hichborn, a cousin of Paul Revere.

North Square is also home of the Seamen's Bethel and the 1838 **Mariner's House**. The Mariner's House provides cheap meals and accommodation for sailors, and the Bethel, were the mariners used to pray, is now a rectory.

Rose Kennedy, matriarch of the Kennedy family, and daughter of John 'Honey Fitz' Fitzgerald, a former Boston mayor and congressman, was born at 4 Garden Court Street.

The **Old North Church** on Salem Street was built in 1723 as Christ Church and is the oldest church in Boston. The new steeple was erected in 1955 replacing one built in 1807 but incorporating much of the original woodwork and the window from which Paul Revere's message was flashed by lanterns. There is a restored 1759 organ, and the church bells first rang in 1744, the oldest peal outside England. Open: daily 9am-5pm. Admission free. A statue of Paul Revere on his horse stands in the Paul Revere Mall behind the church.

St Stephen's Church, on the other side of the shopping area, is built of brick and was designed in Federal-style by Charles Bulfinch, considered America's first native architect. The church has a bell and copper dome case cast by Paul Revere, and it is noted for its interior with pillars, balconies and Palladian windows. The pipe organ dates from the 1830s. The **Copp's Hill Burial Ground**, off Hull and Snow Streets, was the cemetery for Old North Church in the 1600s, and overlooks Boston Harbor atop its small hill. The British positioned their artillery here to bombard Charlestown during the Battle of Bunker Hill. Some of the gravestones bear the scars of the British target practice.

Further Information

Boston offers a wide range of sports and recreation. It is the home of the Boston Red Sox baseball team (☎ 617-267-1700), the New England Patriots football team (☎ 1-800-543-1776), the Boston Bruins — the city's ice hockey team (☎ 617 227-3206), and the Boston Celtics — the city's basketball team (☎ 617 227-3206).

There is year round horse racing at Suffolk Downs in East Boston, and greyhound racing at the Wonderland Dog Track at Revere and Raynham Park. There is boating with boat rentals along the Charles and Mystic Rivers, excellent freshwater and sea fishing, golf, tennis, ice skating and horse riding, with many scenic bridle paths, especially in the Blue Hills Reservation.

Accommodation

The following Hotels (H) and Restaurants ® are recommended. A general price indicator is given: $ inexpensive, $$ medium, $$$ expensive. * denotes an historic inn or hotel.

Aujord'hui ® 200 Boylston St. ☎ (617) 338-4400 $$$
Bay Tower Room ® 60 State St. ☎ (617) 723-1666 $$$
Boston Back Bay Hilton, 40 Dalton St. ☎ (617) 236-1100 $$$
Boston Harbor Hotel, 70 Rowes Wharf. ☎ (617) 439-7000 $$$
Boston Marriott Hotel, 110 Huntington Ave. ☎ (617) 236-5800 $$-$$$
Boston Park Plaza, 64 Arlington St. ☎ (617) 426-2000 $$-$$$
Durgin Park ® 340 Faneuil Hall Marketplace. ☎ (617) 227-2038 $$
***Eliot Hotel**, 370 Commonwealth Ave. ☎ (617) 267-1607 $$-$$$
Four Seasons, 200 Boylston St. ☎ (617) 338-4400 $$$
Hotel le Medidien, 250 Franlin St. ☎ (617) 451-1900 $$$
Howard Johnson Lodge Fenway, 1271 Boylston St. ☎ (617) 267-8300 $-$$
Jasper's ® 240 Commercial St. ☎ (617) 523-1126 $$$
Legal Seafoods ® 5 Cambridge Center. ☎ (617) 864-4444 $$
Midtown Hotel, 220 Huntington Ave. ☎ (617) 262-1000 $-$$
Newbury Guest House B&B, 261 Newbury St. ☎ (617) 437-7666 $$
Parker's Restaurant, 60 School St. ☎ (617) 227-8600 $$$
Ritz-Carlton Boston, 15 Arlington St. ☎ (617) 536-5700 $$$
Parker's Restaurant, 60 School St. ☎ (617) 227-8600 $$$
Westin Hotel Copley Place, 10 Huntington Ave. ☎ (617) 262-9600 $$$

BOSTON OUTSKIRTS
Bartlett
Attitash Marketplace Motel, Route 302. ☎ (603) 374-2509 $
The Villager Motel, US 302. ☎ (603) 374-2742 $
Bedford
**Bedford Village Inn*, 2 Old Bedford Road. ☎ (603) 472-2001 $$-$$$
Bethlehem
**Adair B&B*, Old Littleton Road. ☎ (603) 444-2600 $$-$$$
**The Mulburn Inn B&B*, Main St. ☎ (603) 869-3389 $-$$

Vermont

2

The 'Green Mountain State' is perhaps best known for its maple syrup, red barns, white steepled churches and fabulous fall foliage, but it has something to offer throughout the year, with dramatically different seasons, a wealth of history and historic buildings, and a vast outdoors playground. There are more than one hundred covered bridges, excellent winter ski resorts, and forests and mountains which attract summer walkers and campers. Many millions of people holiday in Vermont each year, and thousands maintain summer and second homes in the state because of its peace and tranquillity.

History

The first settlers were Abenaki Indians who lived by hunting and fishing. In 1609 the French explorer Samuel de Champlain visited the north-western part of the state and Lake Champlain is named after him. The state's name also comes from the French language, although it was given by Connecticut clergyman, the Reverend

---

above: The delightful resort of Woodstock is noted for its well-preserved old homes and village greens

Samuel Peters. Climbing Killington Peak in 1763 he declared the area Vert Mont — *vert* meaning green and *mont* meaning mountain. The first settlement was established by French colonists led by Captain La Mothe who built the Fort Sainte Anne and claimed the Isle la Motte in Lake Champlain in 1666. During the seventeenth and early eighteenth century, Vermont was used by the French as a base for raids into Massachusetts. The Dutch established a settlement in Pownal in 1724 and in the same year, the first English settlement was built at Fort Dummer on the Connecticut River, close to what is now Brattleboro. The outpost was to protect the northern borders of the Massachusetts colony during the French and Indian War. After British victory in 1763, the area was opened up and by 1775 there were about 20,000 settlers. Because Vermont was established as a territory and not a Royal Charter there were constant disputes over the land between New York and New Hampshire. The king ruled in favour of New York who then tried to force the landowners in Vermont to repurchase their holdings. This forced the settlers to form the Green Mountain Boys in 1770, and their successful raid, led by Ethan Allen against Fort Ticonderoga in New York in 1775 was one of the first victories of the American Revolution. On 15 January 1777, fed up with the continuing dispute with England, Vermont declared itself the independent republic of New Connecticut. It later changed its name back to Vermont, and in 1791 they became the fourteenth state to join the Union. The state had the first constitution in the USA to outlaw slavery and to grant universal men's suffrage. The state's growth was halted in the 1830s because of the exodus to the south and mid-west, but it rose dramatically after the railroad arrived in 1848. In 1864 it became the only site north of Pennsylvania to see action during the Civil War, when a band of Confederates raided St Albans from Canada. Vermont's ethnic background is largely English protestant, but there are other important groups, including French Canadians Winooski who came to work in the textile mills around Winooski, Scots in the Caledonia area, Italians in Barre and Spaniards in Barre-Montpelier who brought their quarrying and stone carving skills, Welsh who brought their slate quarrying skills to western Vermont and Poles in Brattleboro. When the railroad reached Vermont in 1848 many Irish immigrants were employed as labourers, and their desendants are represented in many of the towns.

Most of the population, however, is rural with more than two-thirds living in the country or in towns with a population of less than 2,500. Dairying is the main farming activity supplying Boston and urban conurbations in south-eastern New England, with maple syrup and sugar produced throughout the state. John Deere, a native of Vermont, designed the plough and started the worldwide agricultural machinery company that bears his name. Former industries such as textiles and railroad works have been replaced by wood, paper and printing and mining for marble, granite and slate. Barre is one of the world's largest producers of granite. There is a growing computer and electronics manufacturing base, and tourism is now a major year round industry. America's first ski tow was developed at Woodstock in 1934, and the state now has thirty-five developed ski resorts. Vermont's roads are billboard free thanks to a law passed in the 1960s which outlawed them.

Geography

Vermont has Quebec to the north, New Hampshire to the east, Massachusetts to the south and New York state to the west. It is about 151 miles (243km) from north to south, 90 miles (145km) west to east close to its border with Canada, and just over 40 miles (64km) wide in the south bordering Massachusetts. The Connecticut River marks its eastern border with New Hampshire, and the Poultney River and Lake Champlain the western border. Lake Champlain is the largest freshwater lake east of the Great Lakes.

The Green Mountains, part of the Appalachian system, dominate the centre of the state, and the Green Mountain National Forest covers 266,000 acres (106,400 hectares). Mount Mansfield at 4,393ft (1,339m) is Vermont's highest point, and there are more than thirty granite-peaked mountains above 3,500ft (1,067m). Only 15 per cent of the state is flat and fertile, mostly in the Champlain valley. Most of the rivers drain north into Lake Champlain which itself drains into the St Lawrence River via the Richelieu River. Winters tend to be very cold with up to 80 inches of snow in the valleys and up to 110 inches in the mountains. Summers are hot but rarely exceed 90°F (32°C).

Some State Statistics
Area: 9,528sq miles (24,697sq km)
Population: 562,000
Capital: Montpelier
Highest Point: Mount Mansfield 4,393ft (1,339m)
Lowest Point: Lake Champlain 95ft (29m) above sea level
Taxes: 5 per cent statewide sales tax, 8 per cent lodgings and
    food tax, 10 per cent alcohol tax
Nickname: The Green Mountain State
State Tree: Sugar Maple
State Bird: Hermit Thrush
State Animal: Morgan Horse
State Flower: Red Clover

Getting Around

Burlington International Airport is served by a number of major US carriers with links around the country and Burlington Airport Ground Transportation provides interstate services from the airport. The major car hire companies are also based at the airport.

Vermont Transit Lines offers a network of services throughout the state and New England ☎ (802) 864-6811, and Amtrak makes stops at White River Junction, Montpelier, Waterbury and Essex Junction, near Burlington.

The rural nature of Vermont makes getting around slow at times but the stunning scenery makes it worthwhile. There are limited rail and air services and apart from the main interstate highways which generally run north-south, most of the roads are narrow and winding, and often hilly. There are hundreds of miles of scenic drives, and thousands of miles of hiking trails which still offer the best way to explore the countryside. The 270 mile (435km) Long Trail runs the length of the Green Mountains, and inn to inn biking along quiet roads is now a popular pastime.

Vermont divides neatly into three regions — northern, central and southern — and these form the bases for the following tours.

NORTHERN REGION

The Northern Region is an historic location of vast, unspoilt areas, cosmopolitan towns and huge stretches of water.

The tour starts in **Burlington**, on the slopes of Lake Champlain and the largest city in Vermont. It is a major industrial, retail and education centre. It is a main port of entry into the USA from Canada, and the centre for navigation on the lake. The area was first settled in 1775 but most people fled during the Revolution and growth did not start until after the war. Ethan Allen farmed just to the north of the city and is buried in Greenmount Cemetery.

The city's most historic district is on Battery Street, close to the lakeside. Other interesting and old areas include Church, Pearl and Willard Streets, University Green and City Hall Park. The University of Vermont, founded in 1791, overlooks the city. The University's Royal Tyler Theatre presents a summer season of Shakespeare, and the Vermont Mozart Festival is staged between mid-July and early August. Other annual events include the Lake Champlain Fishing Derby in June and July Jazz Festival.

The city makes a good base for exploring the surrounding the area and offers a number of scenic drives, especially I-89 which runs south-east for 95 miles (153km) to White River Junction, and SR116

St Johnsbury

Haskell Free Library & Opera House ✳
Old Stone House Museum
Derby Line
Derby Center
Brownington
Barton
Newport
Glover
Lac Memphremagog
Sugar Mill Farm
Orleans

■ Fairbanks Museum & Planetarium
■ Athenaeum Art Gallery
■ Maple Grove Maple Museum

Bread & Puppet Museum
Goodrich's Sugarhouse
Cabot
Cabot Creamery
Jay
Craftsbury
Graniteville
Long Trail
Fisher Bridge
Wolcott
Rock of Ages
▲ Jay Peak
Morrisville
Barre
Vermont Rug Makers ✳
Morrisville Noyes House Historical Museum
Montpelier ☆
Northfield
Johnson Woollen Mills Factory ✳
Johnson
Madonna Pk. ▲
■ Birds of Vermont Museum
✳ Green Mountain Audubon Nature Center
Enosburg Falls
✳ Highest Point in Vermont
East Fairfield
Smugglers Notch ▲ ▲
Waterbury
Jeffersonville
Mt. Mansfield ▲
Ben & Jerry's IceCream Factory
Waitsfield
Warren
Camels Hump ▲
Underhill
Irasville
Fairfield
The Old Mill Craft Shop ✳
Richmond
Jericho
Old Round Church
Trapp Family Lodge
Stowe
Green Mountain
St Albans Historical Museum
Huntington
St Albans
Rhode Island Corners
National Fores
Swanton
Essex Junction
Bristol
Hinesburg
Burlington
■ Sheldon Museum
Middlebury
Grand Isle
✳ UVM Morgan Horse Farm
New Haven Jct.
Isle La Motte
Hyde Log Cabin ✳

Shelburne
Charlotte
Rokeby Museum
Ferrisburg
Cornwall
St Anne's Shrine
Vermont Wildflower Farm
Vergennes
■ John Strong Dar. Mansion
Addison
Lake Champlain
Basin Harbor
Shoreham

■ Battery Park
🐾 Ethan Allen Homestead
🐾 Ethan Allen Park
■ Robert Hull Fleming Museum

Lake Champlain Maritime Museum
Chimney Point

✳ Vermont Teddy Bear Company
■ Shelburne Museum and Heritage Park

0	5	10	15	20	25	30miles
0		15		30		45km

Vermont

Justin Smith Morrill
Homestead

Montshire
Museum
of Science
Lebanon
Norwich
Strafford
White River Junction
Catamount Brewing Company
American Precision
Museum
Sharon
Quechee
Windsor
Old Stone
Gristmill
Museum
Bellows
Falls
Joseph Smith
Visitor Center
Billing's Farm
and Museum
Old
Constitution
House
Dana House
Woodstock
Old Meeting
House
Santa's
Land
Brattleboro
Museum &
Art Center
Bethel
Sugarbush
Farm
Vermont Country Store
Stellafane
Society
Museum
Rockingham
Springfield
Chester
Grafton
Putney
White River
National Fish Hatchery
Proctorsville
Newfane
Brattleboro
Black River Academy Museum
Joseph Cerniglia
Winery
Plymouth
Ludlow
Townshend
Windham
County
Historical
Society
Museum
Hogback
Mtn.
Crowley Cheese
Factory
Townshend State Forest
Killington/Sherburne
Plymouth Notch
Historic District
Weston
Vermont Country
Store
Jamaica
State Park
Luman Nelson
Museum
Marlboro
Killington Pk.
Guild of Old
Time Crafts
and Industries
Playhouse
Jamaica
Molly Stark
State Park
Shrewsbury
Norman Rockwell
Museum
Rawsonville
Stratton Mtn.
North
River
Winery
Chittenden
Holden
Rutland
Wilson Castle
Vermont Marble Exhibit
Green
Mountains
Mt. Snow
Wilmington
Searsburg
Pittsford
Proctor
Manchester Depot
National
Haystack
Mtn.
Castleton
Federal Fish Hatchery
New England Maple
Museum
Manchester
Center
Forest
Grandma
Moses
Museum
East
Hubbardton
Hildene
Manchester
Norman
Rockwell
Exhibit
Long
Bennington
Bennington
Museum
Orwell
Hubbardton Battlefield
and Museum
Mt. Equinox
Park McCullough House
North Bennington
Old Bennington
Arlington
Trail
Bennington
Battle Monument

Montpelier

Terrace St.
Hubbard
Park
North Street
State
Capitol
Main St.
Supreme
Court
State
State St.
State
Agriculture
Building
Vermont Historical
Society Museum
College St.
Towne
Hill
Road
Vermont
College
T.W. Wood
Art Gallery
Old Country Club Rd.

Northfield St.

0   .5   1 Miles
0   .5   1 km

which runs south for just over 40 miles (64km) to East Middlebury. The city also has good shopping facilities, including the Champlain Mill, a converted nineteenth-century wood mill, which now houses more than thirty speciality shops and eateries. The downtown Church Street Marketplace is a pedestrian precinct with many historic buildings, more than 100 shops and street entertainers.

♣ Battery Park, Pearl Street, is the site of an engagement in 1812 when the US shore battery drove off a force of British vessels on the lake. The park has fine views and summer concerts are held there. Open: daily dawn to dusk.

Ethan Allen Homestead is signposted off the North Avenue beaches exit. The timber house is set in several acres now laid out with gardens and walking trails. There are tours of the house and a presentation about Ethan Allen. Open: Monday to Saturday 10am-5pm, Sunday 1-5pm late June to early September, daily 1-5pm May to late June and early September to early October. Admission charge.

♣ The tower in Ethan Allen Park, on North Avenue, offers good views over the lake and surrounding mountains. Open: Wednesday to Sunday 12noon-8pm May to September.

Robert Hull Fleming Museum, Colchester Avenue on the university campus, was founded in 1876 and has exhibits on art, sculpture, books and prints. Open: Tuesday to Friday 9am-4pm, weekends 1-5pm. Donations.

Spirit of Ethan Allen is a replica of a Mississippi paddleboat offering 90 minute historic lake cruises featuring Revolutionary War battles, plus sunset and dinner cruises. Sailings daily from Perkins Pier ☎ (802) 862-9685 for times.

Drive north on highways 89 or the quieter 2 to Chimney Corner, then take highway 2 to explore Lake Champlain and its island resorts.

Lake Champlain stretches from the Canadian border south for 120 miles (193km) and from just 400 yards (436m) to 12 miles (19km) wide. Two thirds of the lake is in Vermont, and the rest in New York state, except for a small section in Canada. By using the Champlain River, Champlain Canal and Lake and then the Hudson River, it is possible to navigate from New York to Montreal and the Great Lakes, and Lake Champlain accommodates large vessels, many of which operate sightseeing cruises. The lake also has its own 'monster', first sighted by Champlain who described it as being like a serpent, 20ft (6m) long and with the head of a horse. Every so often there are claims of sightings of 'Champ' as he is known locally. Lake Champlain Ferries offer three scenic links between Vermont and

New York — Burington to Port Kent (1 hour), Charlotte to Essex (18 minutes) and Grand Isle to Plattsburgh (12 minutes) ☎ (802) 864-9804.

The lake's islands are very popular during the summer. St Anne's Shrine on **Isle La Motte** is on the site of Forte St Anne, the first settlement in the state, although shortlived. Hyde Log Cabin is by the main road on **Grand Isle**, and is believed to be the oldest log cabin in the country. Built in 1783 is has period rustic furnishings. Open: Wednesday to Sunday 11am-5pm July to early September. Admission charge.

If you island hop on highway 2 you can take highway 78 at Alburg back on to the mainland and **Swanton**. The town is 6 miles (10km) south of the border with Quebec, and has a colourful history which includes smuggling and an incident in 1812 when Vermont ranchers drove cattle across the border and sold them to British troops. The border was also popular earlier in the twentieth century with prohibitionist smugglers. At the end of the seventeenth century French Jesuits with the help of St Francis Indians, built the first chapel in Vermont in Swanton. When the French lost the territory to the English, the Indians dismantled the chapel stone by stone, and rebuilt it in St Hyacinthe in Quebec. The Missiquoi National Wildlife Refuge is to the west off SR78, and covers more than 5,600 acres (2,240 hectares) along the river delta and Lake Champlain. It is an area noted for wildfowl and there is an interpretive trail. Open: daily dawn to dusk.

From Swanton head south on highway 7 to visit **St Albans** and a taste of maple sugar. This histric town is a major distribution and agricultural centre, and the headquarters of the Vermont Central Railway. It has maple syrup and dairy processing industries, and is the venue each April of the Vermont Maple Festival. In the early 1800s it was a notorious centre for smuggling on Lake Champlain and an important link on the underground railway. Later, Henry Ward Beecher described St Albans as 'a place in the midst of a greater variety of scenic beauty than any other I can remember in America'.

St Albans Historical Museum, Church and Bishop Streets, is in the 1863 schoolhouse and has local history exhibits as well as Revolutionary and Civl War relics. The furniture featured in Norman Rockwell's painting *The Family Doctor's Office* is exhibited here and was donated by the doctor who posed for it. Open: Tuesday to Saturday 1-4pm July to September. Admission charge ☎ (802) 527-7933.

The countryside surrounding Peacham is impressive

Take route 36 east out of St Albans for **Fairfield**, birthplace in 1829 of Chester A. Arthur, 21st President of the USA. A replica of his house stands about 5 miles (8km) north-east of town on a well signposted country road. It has exhibits on his life. His father preached in the nearby brick church which houses an exhibition about church architecture in Vermont. From Fairfield head north for route 105 which then runs east following the course of the Missisquoi River to the town of **Enosburg Falls**. In the late nineteenth century the town was noted for all sorts of quack medicines and panaceas, and is now a quiet farming village around central Enosburg Park, producing cheese and dairy products. A dairy festival is held each June. Continue on route 105 through Richford and Stevens Mills. About 18 miles (29km) east of Stevens Mills detour right for **Jay** named after politician John Jay. Nearby Jay Peak and area is known for its winter sports facilities but there is plenty to see and do during the rest of the year, especially hiking and camping in Jay Peak State Forest.

Jay Peak Ski Resort, off SR242, is in the State Forest and has a 60 passenger tramway which climbs 4,000ft (1,219m) to the summit from which there are stunning views across three states and Canada. Open: daily 10am-5pm late June to early September and late September to early October, weekends 10am-5pm mid-September and late October. Admission charge. From Jay return to route 105 east and North Troy, where the road turns south into **Newport**, a major gateway between Canada and the USA which accounts for its name as 'the Border City'. It is on the southern shores of Lake Memphremagog (Indian for 'Beautiful Waters'). To the west is the 3,360ft (1,024m) Owl's Head, named after an Indian chief, and the walk to the summit is worth it for the spectacular views. The granite St Mary's of the Sea church overlooks the town on Prospect Hill. American Maple Products Corporation, on Union and Bluff Roads, is a maple candy factory offering guided tours. A scene setting film is shown first in a converted railway carriage. Open: Monday to Friday 8am-12noon and 12.30-4pm. Admission free.

From Newport detour north on highway 5 to visit **Derby Center** and **Derby Line** with its international opera house. The Haskell Free Library and Opera House, literally straddles the border with the stage in Canada and the 200 seat auditorium in the USA. Performances are staged during the summer. Library open: Tuesday and Wednesday 10am-5pm, Thursday to Saturday 1-5pm (Thursday to 8pm).

Return south on highway 5, detouring east on route 58 for Orleans and then on the country road north to **Brownington**, and the Old

Stone House Museum, off the Derby to Brownington Village Road. It is housed in the four storey granite Athenian Hall, built between 1834 and 1836 by Alexander Twilight, as a school dormitory. It has displays about local history and Americana. Open: daily 11am-5pm July and August, Friday to Tuesday 11am-5pm mid-May and June and September to mid-October. Admission charge.

Return to route 91 and head south for **Barton** where you can visit the Sugar Mill Farm, on SR16 with guided tours of the maple syrup orchard and works, and displays about the history of the industry. In the spring visitors can watch the sap being gathered. Open: daily 8am-8pm. Admission charge.

From Barton, you can take a short detour south on highway 16 for **Glover** noted for the Bread and Puppet Museum, on SR122. It is in an old barn with puppets and props used by the travelling Bread and Puppet Theater founded in 1962. Open daily 10am-6pm May to October. Donations.

Return to Barton and then head south on highway 91 for **St Johnsbury.** The town was named after Saint Jean de Crevecouer, the French consul in New York and close friend of Ethan Allen. Origi-nally called St John, the 'bury' was added at de Crevecouer's sugges-tion to distinguish it from the other towns with the same name. It is the retail, commercial and manufacturing centre of the area known as the Northeast Kingdom, and the town has a wonderful setting at the convergence of three rivers, the Moose, Sleeper and Passumpsic. The town's prosperity was largely thanks to Thaddeus Fairbanks who in 1830 invented the platform scale, and George Cary who came up with the idea of flavouring chewing tobacco with maple sugar. The manufacture of scales and processing of maple sugar are still major industries.

Fairbanks Museum and Planetarium, Main and Prospect Streets, has displays on science, history and the arts and a huge collection of mounted birds and animals. The Northern New England Weather Center is housed there, and a Children's Nature Corner. The museum is open Monday to Saturday 10am-6pm, Sunday 1-5pm July and August, Monday to Saturday 10am-4pm, Sunday 1-5pm rest of the year. The planetarium is open Monday to Saturday 11am and 2pm, Sunday 1.30pm July and August, weekends at 1.30pm rest of the year. Admission charge.

Maple Grove Maple Museum, 1 mile (2km) east on US2 has displays about the history and processing of maple sugar. The maufacturing process is demonstrated in the Old Sugar House and there are guided tours of the Maple Grove Candy Factory. Open: daily 8am-5pm. Admission free.

Maple Syrup

The early settlers learnt from the Indians how to tap and process the maple trees in late winter and early spring for the sweet water. The Indians put the maple sap in hollowed out logs and added stones heated in a fire to boil down the syrup. Today, mass production methods are used to collect and process the sap. Pipes lead from many trees to a single collection point and the juice is then boiled to concentrate the sugar and produce the characteristic colour and flavour. A single mature tree yields about 8 gallons (36 litres) of sap a year and up to 50 gallons (225 litres) of sap are need to produce 1 gallon (4.5 litres) of syrup. There are even grades of maple syrup, the finest being A which is almost clear, to the thicker, heavier C which is usually used for cooking. Although sugar maple trees are common in many parts of North America, the north-east is the only region producing maple syrup and sugar. Vermont is the largest producer in the USA although Quebec produces more annually to make it the largest producer in North America.

Maple syrup, made here at Maple House, is one of New England's most famous exports, a gastronomical treat, and a great souvenir

Burlington's Church Street Marketplace. This is the state's largest city whose waterfront area was praised by Charles Dickens when he visited in the mid-1800's

St Johnsbury Athenaeum Art Gallery, 30 Main Street, is housed in the library. Exhibits concentrate on nineteenth-centry artists of the Hudson River School, and includes Albert Bierstadt's *Domes of Yosemite*. Open: Monday to Friday 10am-5.30pm (to 8pm Monday and Wednesday), Saturday 9.30am-4pm. Donations.

From St Johnsbury take highway 2 west to West Danville, then route 15 north through Walden to connect with route 16 west and Morrisville. On the way you can detour north to take in **Craftsbury**, founded in 1788 by Colonel Ebenezer Crafts. His son became town leader and later Governor of Vermont. It is a typical New England village with charming homes and public buildings around the large green.

Return south to route 15 and follow it west to **Wolcott** and the Fisher Bridge, the the last covered railroad bridge still in use in the state, and one of the few remaining in the country. It has a full length cupola designed to let smoke escape. It was built in 1908 for the St Johnsbury and Lamoille County Railroad and crosses the Lamoille River. It has been reinforced to allow continued use.

Morrisville is south of highway 15 and the Lamoille River, with mountains to the west and south which restricted growth until the arrival of the railroad, and then there was a period of frantic building. This explains why some areas, along Portland Street for instance, are more like a Western boomtown than a typical New England community.

Lamoille Valley Railroad, at the junctions of SR110 and SR15, offers guided train rides along the Lamoille River and through the Green Mountains. One and two hour trips leave daily between 10am and 3.30pm mid-September to mid-October. Admission charge.

Morrisville Noyes House Historical Museum, Main Street, is in a two storey brick mansion built by Jedediah Stafford in the early nineteenth century, with local history exhibits. Open: Wednesday to Saturday 12noon-5pm July to early September. Admission free.

From Morrisville take scenic highway 100 south to **Stowe**, a year round resort area in the Green Mountains, with some of the best skiing in New England, and fabulous scenery in the summer and autumn. Stowe is on the scenic section of the SR100 which runs between Troy and Wilmington. There is a visitor information centre on Main Street. The Mount Mansfield Gondola at the Stowe Mountain Resort carries passengers to the summit daily between 10am and 5pm from late May to early October, and mid-December to Easter. Stowe's annual winter carnival is held in mid-January, and the Sugar Slalom in April.

The Stowe Alpine Slide on SR108 has a chairlift which goes to the top of the slide on Spruce Peak, and passengers can then control the speed of their descent. Open: daily 10am-5pm mid-June to early September, Friday to Sunday 10am-5pm late May to mid-June, weekends 10am-5pm early September to October. Admission charge.

Stowe Recreation Trail, starts at the Stowe Center, and is a 5 mile (8km) scenic walk. The trail is noteworthy because it was the first donated by landowners for public use rather than having to be acquired by the Government. Open: daily round the clock.

Trapp Family Lodge, Luce Hill Road, off Mountain Road, was built in 1942 by Baroness Mara Von Trapp (of *Sound of Music* fame) because it reminded her of the Swiss Alps. The Tyrolean-style buildings are set in 2,000 acres (800 hectares) of forests and alpine meadows, and outdoor concerts are held during the summer. Maria died in 1987 but the lodge is still run by members of her family. Just north of the lodge is a rocky trail to Bingham Falls.

From Stowe take route 108 north-west through Smugglers Notch and past **Mount Mansfield**. The huge mountain is the highest peak in the Green Mountains. It is 4,393ft (1,339m) high, 5 miles (8km) long and 27,613 acres (1,1045 hectares) of the mountain make up the Mount Mansfield State Forest reached by a 4 mile (6km) toll road from Stowe through Smugglers' Notch or Underhill Center. The Stowe Auto Toll Road climbs steeply through forest. The road is very twisting and great caution needs to be taken on both the ascent and descent but the drive is more than rewarded by the views from the top.

From certain positions, the profile of the mountain resembles a human face. There are many trails in the forest including the Long Trail, and the eastern side of the mountain is a wildlife area, while hunting is allowed on the western slopes.

Route 108 continues north to **Jeffersonville**, a year round resort also noted for its antique shops, including the 1829 Antiques House, on route 15 with thirty-five specialist dealers. Bryan Memorial Art Gallery, Main Street, displays work by local and regional artists. Open: daily 11am-5pm April to late October. Admission free.

The Vermont Maple Outlet on route 15 produces maple syrup and a wide range of other speciality foods, including cheese, smoked meats, as well as hand made goods and clothing. Open: daily.

Nearby is the **Smugglers Notch Ski Area**, named because it was a favourite route of smugglers heading for the border during the war in 1812. Madonna, at 3,668ft (1,118m) is noted for its sheer rock faces rising to 2,610ft (796m).

※ You can take the short 10 mile (16km) detour east along route 15 to visit **Johnson** and the Johnson Woollen Mills Factory which has been producing woollen clothing for more than 150 years. The mill shop sells their entire range plus seconds. Open: daily August to March, Monday to Saturday April to July.

※ Vermont Rug Makers Gallery, on route 100c is in a quaint 150-year-old country store by Gihon River, and has a collection of hand made rugs, many by internationally renowned designers. Open: Monday to Saturday 10am-5pm. Admission free.

※ Return to Jeffersonville and continue west, then take route 15 south through Underhill to **Jericho**. The Old Mill Craft Shop is owned by the Jericho Historical Society and is housed in Chittenden Mill, a National Historic Site. Sales of arts and crafts help pay the upkeep of the mill. Open: daily. The next stop on the road is Essex Junction, close to the Champlain Valley Fairgrounds which stage the Champlain Valley Exposition in early September every year.

From Essex Junction take route 117 south-east to **Richmond**. The town is noted for the Old Round Church, a 16-sided polygon which gives it the appearance of being round. Legend has it that sixteen men each built a side and a seventeenth added the belfry. The church dates from 1813 and was restored in 1981. It is still used for special events. Open: Monday to Friday 10am-4pm July to early September, and late September to early October, Saturday 10am-4pm, Sunday 11.30am-4pm May to early July and late October. Donations.

※ From Richmond you can detour south on country roads to **Huntington**, home of the Green Mountain Audubon Nature Center in a 230 acre (92 hectare) reserve with visitor centre and trails. Open: daily dawn to dusk. The Birds of Vermont Museum, Sherman Hollow Road, features a fantastic collection of hand carved birds, each exhibit showing the male and female, as well as nest, eggs and typical habitat. There is also a bird observation area. Open: Wednesday to Monday 10am-4pm May to October, or by appointment. Admission charge ☎ (802) 434-2167. A few miles south is Huntington Center and the Camel's Hump State Park, which covers 16,654 acres (6,662 hectares) and was originally called Le Lion Couchant (Sleeping Lion) by the French. The 4,083ft (1,245m) 'hump' is one of the few remaining undeveloped high peaks in the state, as most have been developed for winter sports. There are a number of trails to the summit and the Long Trail, which runs the length of the state, crosses the peak.

From Richmond take the country road south through Fays Corner and Rhode Island Corners to the east of Lake Irequois, and then

The Fairbanks Museum and Planetarium at St Johnsburg.
The planetarium is the only one in the state open to the public

The Shelburne Museum and heritage park is packed with Americana, with
old buildings, carriages, the 1783 Stagecoach Inn and the Ticonderoga
sidewheeler steamboat

swing west for Mechanicsville and then south to Hinesburg where you take the country road west to **Charlotte**. The town quickly developed in the late eighteenth century on the stage coach route between Burlington and Troy. The historic district east of SR7 has many fine old buildings and three covered bridges, two crossing Lewis Creek in East Charlotte, and the other spanning Holmes Creek north of the Charlotte Ferry.

❋ Visit Vermont Wildflower Farm, on US7, with 6 acres (2 hectares) of wild flower fields and woods, with interpretive self-guiding trail. The gardens also feature plants and herbs used by the Indians for medicines. Open: daily 10am-5pm April to October. Admission charge.

From Charlotte head north on highway 7 for **Shelburne**, settled in 1768 by two German loggers in the valley between the Adirondack Mountains to the west and Green Mountains to the east. The town, later named after the English Earl of Shelburne, has many lovely old eighteenth-century buildings, especially in the downtown shopping area.

❋ Shelburne Farms, west of the town, is a 1,000 acre (400 hectare) estate built in the 1880s as the summer home of Dr William Seward and Lila Vanderbilt Webb. The main house is now an inn and restaurant, while the estate, laid out by Frederick Law Olmsted, designer of New York's Central Park, is a working farm. The estate produces its own cheese and makes furniture. Open: for tours between 9.30am and 3.30pm late May to mid-October. Admission charge.

🏠 Shelburne Museum, on US7, has a fascinating and large collection of old buildings, brought from all over New England and carefully restored and rebuilt on the 45 acre (18 hectare) site. There are farm buildings, jail, schoolhouse, blacksmiths, meeting house, stage-coach inn, lighthouse, apothecary and homes depicting New England life over the centuries, with period furnishings, antiques, tools, toys and paintings. The Electra Havemeyer Webb Memorial has a collection of European furnishings, art and sculpture including works by Goya, Corot, Degas, Monet and Rembrandt, and the Webb Memorial features eminent American artists. The houses are set in landscaped gardens and there are craft demonstrations daily. Open: daily 10am-5pm mid-May to mid-October, guided tours only at 1pm rest of the year. Admission charge.

❋ Vermont Teddy Bear Company, Sherburne Road, offers guided tours showing the manufacturing process. Open: Monday to Saturday 10am-4pm, Sunday 11am-4pm. Admission free. It is then a short drive north back into Burlington.

CENTRAL REGION

This is an area packed with historic buildings and museums, the world's largest granite quarry, the Quechee Gorge, spactacular waterfalls, summer hiking, winter skiing, water sports and great food and drink.

The tour starts in **Rutland**, known as the Marble City because of the huge quarries nearby dating back to the mid-nineteenth century, and many local stone industries. The city, Vermont's second largest although the population is less than 20,000, is in the Otter Creek Valley with the Taconic Mountains to the west and the peaks of Killington, Pico and Shrewsbury, all in the Green Mountains range, to the east. The headquarters of the Green Mountain National Forest are in Rutland and the town is also home of Vermont's oldest continuously published newspaper, the *Rutland Herald*, which was founded in 1794. The annual Vermont State Fair takes place in Rutland in early September. The Norman Rockwell Museum, on US 4, has thousands of pieces of work by the prolific artist and illustrator. Open: daily 9am-6pm. Admission charge.

From Rutland take route 4a west to **Castleton**, a popular resort area around Lake Bomoseen. The town has many fine old buildings, including Zadock Remington's tavern where Ethan Allen and his Green Mountain Boys planned their successful raid on Fort Ticonderoga during the Revolutionary War. Many of the buildings were designed by architect Thomas Reynold Drake who lived in the town from 1807. He favoured grand columns, porticos and Palladian motifs, and these are well preserved on many of the homes. State road 30 offers a scenic drive south to Manchester Center. The Hubbardton Battlefield and Museum, is to the north off US4 at **East Hubbardton**. It is the site of the only Revolutionary War battle fought in Vermont on 7 July 1777 when Colonial troops in retreat from Fort Ticonderoga engaged a force of British and Hessian troops. Open: Wednesday to Sunday 9.30am-5.30pm May to mid-October. Admission charge.

Continue west on route 4a and then take route 22a north to **Orwell**. Towards the southern end of Lake Champlain and settled just before the Revolutionary War by Scotsman John Charter from Montreal, the small town is now the centre for sheep farming in the Champlain Valley. Mount Independence, 6 miles (10km) west off SR73A, has the remains of Revolutionary War fortifications, including the foundations of the blockhouse, stockade, gun batteries and hospital. The 600 acre (240 hectare) site overlooking the lake has a number of walks. Open: daily 9.30am-5.30pm. Admission charge.

*Middlebury
Congregational
church*

*Addison is a small
crossroads town on
the plains leading to
Lake Champlain*

Waitsfield, settled in 1789, is now a major year-round resort area

From Orwell continue north on route 22A to just beyond Shoreham, then take route 74 east to Cornwall, and then route 30 north to **Middlebury**. Founded in 1761 between Salisbury and New Haven, the college town is centred on the green, and is also a year round resort because of the magnificent surrounding countryside.

Middlebury College was established in 1800 and women's education pioneer Emma Hart Willard became principal of the Middlebury Female Academy in 1807. There are changing exhibits in the Christian A. Johnson Memorial Gallery, and and Painter Hall built in 1816, is the oldest college building in Vermont. The college holds an annual winter carnival in the Snow Bowl ski area, and hosts the Bread Loaf Writers' Conference each August. There is excellent walking in the nearby Green Mountain National Forest, and the ranger district office in town has walking guides and maps. Self guiding walking tours of the town's history districts are available from the Addison County Chamber of Commerce, 2 Court Street, Middlebury, VT 05753 ☎ (802) 388-7951.

Sheldon Museum, Park Street, is housed in a 1829 marble merchant's home, with local history exhibits, antiques and paintings. Open: Monday to Friday 10am-5pm Saturday 10am-4pm June to October. Hours vary rest of the year. Admission charge.

❋   UVM Morgan Horse Farm is signposted off SR23. Guided tours of the working farm and ranch that raises Morgan horses, America's first breed of horse, and Vermont's state animal. Open: daily 9am-4pm May to October. Admission charge.

From Middlebury, take route 23 north-west and then route 17 west to **Addison**, a small town in Western Vermont close to Lake Champlain and the New York State border. It was at **Chimney Point**, 8 miles (13km) west of town, on 30 July 1609 that Champlain looked down over the huge lake and gave it his name. A bridge spans the lake connecting the two states and the Chimney Point Tavern and Museum has been restored to depict a late eighteenth century inn.

John Strong Dar Mansion, on SR17, was built in 1795. The two storey brick home has been restored with period furnishings and has a herb garden at the rear. Open: Friday to Monday 10am-5pm mid-May to mid-October. Admission charge.

Continue north to **Vergennes** one of America's oldest cities, and one of the smallest. It was settled in 1766, incorporated in 1788 and today has a population of around 2,600 and covers about 1sq mile (2sq km). The Bixby Memorial Library has a collection of local Indian artifacts.

Ferrisburg is about 3 miles (5km) north of Vergennes on route 22a. The Rokeby Museum, home of author and naturalist Rowland Robinson, has exhibits representing life at the end of the nineteenth century. The Robinson family lived in the house from the 1790s to the 1960s. There are a number of farm buildings in the grounds. Open: Wednesday to Sunday for tours at 11am, 12.30 and 2pm May to October. Admission charge.

Basin Harbor with the Lake Champlain Maritime Museum, is on the lake's eastern shore off Basin Harbor Road, west of Vergennes. The museum tells the history of the lake and area, with nineteenth-century schoolhouse, historic maps and boathouse with maritime exhibits and boats built by locals over the past 150 years. The *Philadelphia* is a full size working replica of Benedict Arnold's gunboat sunk on the lake in 1776. Open: daily 10am-5pm mid-May to mid-October. Admission charge.

Return to Vergennes and take route 7 south to New Haven Junction, and then country roads east through magnificent scenery through Bristol and Lincoln to **Warren**, a small, friendly town with historic buildings, traditional country stores and covered bridges. Granville Gulf State Park covers 1,200 acres (480 hectares) between Warren and Granville on the eastern border of the Green Mountain National Forest, and is disected by the Mad River with the Moss

Glen Falls. There is a 6 mile (10km) scenic drive and the Puddledock Ski Touring Trail. Open: daily 24 hours. Scenic route 100 runs north to **Waitsfield** founded by General Benjamin Wait in 1789, in the Mad River Valley area. Originally an important farming and timber community, Waitsfield is now a leading winter resort area centred around Sugarbush and Mad River Glen. The covered bridge is in the centre of town, and polo is often played on weekends between May and October. There are also good possibilities for hunting, fishing and canoeing nearby.

Continue north to **Waterbury** famous for the Ben and Jerry's Ice Cream Factory, on SR100, with guided tours of the factory. Open: daily 9am-8pm July and August, 9am-5pm rest of the year. Admission charge.

From Waterbury take highway 89 south to **Montpelier**, the state capital. The compact state capital has many fine old buildings and there are splendid views from the 110 acre (44 hectare) Hubbard Park overlooking the Capitol. The city is noted as a centre for insurance companies and granite quarrying industries, and the birthplace of Admiral George Dewey, hero of Manila Bay during the Spanish-American War. There are many nineteenth-century Victorian buildings in Vermont College on East State and College Streets, and maps of the self guiding walking tour of the campus are available from the admission office. There are also guided tours during the academic year.

The Supreme Court building on State Street is made of Barre granite, and the State Office Building opposite is considered a fine example of modern architecture, built in reinforced concrete faced with Vermont marble.

State Capitol, State Street, is also made of Barre granite in Doric style. Built in 1838, it is said to have been modelled on a Greek temple to Theseus. A statue of Ceres, Roman goddess of agriculture, tops the gilded dome, and there is a brass canyon in the portico captured from Hessian troops in 1777 at the Battle of Bennington, and nearby is a marble statue of Ethan Allen. Open: Monday to Friday 8am-4pm, Saturday 11am-2.30pm July to mid-October. Admission free. The State Agriculture Building opposite, has an impressive red brick façade with turrets and arched, convex windows.

T.W. Wood Art Gallery, Vermont College Art Center off E. State Street, stages changing displays of works by New England artists of the nineteenth and twentieth centuries. There is a permanent display of works by Wood. Open: Tuesday to Sunday 12noon-4pm. Admission charge.

Montpelier magnificent State House modelled on the Greek Temple of Theseus with its gold-leaf dome

Montpelier is one of the smallest state capitals in the US but its architecture is stunning, and great pride is taken in its appearance

Horse riding at Strafford

Vintage cars at Barnard

Vermont Historical Society Museum, is in the red brick Pavilion Office Building, State Street, modelled on the Pavilion Hotel demolished in the 1960s. It has displays on the history of Vermont. Open: Tuesday to Friday 9am-4.30pm, Saturday 9am-4pm, Sunday 12noon-4pm. Admission charge.

From Montpelier you can detour north-east on highway 2 and then the country road for **Cabot**, the birthplace of Zerah Colburn, born in 1806 and a mathematical genius able to rapidly multiply two six figure numbers in his head before he could read or write. He became a clergyman and teacher at Norwich University in Northfield. Cabot and neighbouring towns combine each September to celebrate the Northeast Kingdom Foliage Festival.

Cabot Creamery, Main Street offers a chance to visit a working creamery producing butter and cheese. Open: Monday to Saturday 9am-5pm, Sunday 11am-4pm mid-June to early October. Hours vary at other times of the year. Admission charge. **Goodrich's Sugarhouse,** 4 miles (6km) west of junction SR2 and SR15, has guided tours of the production facility. Open: Monday to Saturday 9am-5pm March to January. Admission free.

You can also detour south the 7 miles (11km) to **Northfield**, a college town and winter sports resort, with many well preserved old buildings and four covered bridges. The town has been home of Norwich University since 1866. The university was founded in Norwich in 1819 as the state's military college combining academic and military studies. It moved to Middleton, Connecticut in 1825, back to Norwich in 1829, and finally settled in Northfield. The university museum in White Memorial Chapel displays the history of the university and lists the achievements of its famous old boys, many of whom reached the highest ranks in the military. Open: Monday to Friday 8am-4pm. The Norwich University ski area is off SR12 with chairlifts and rope tow. Guided tours of the campus are available and are conducted from the admissions office in Jackman Hall near the north entrance. The Corps of Cadets stages a march past at 12noon Monday to Friday September to May. There are three covered bridges on Cox Brook Road, and one on Slaughterhouse Road.

On the main tour, from Montpelier take highway 2 east and the route 302 south for **Barre**, world famous as a producer of quality granite mined in the nearby quarries. The industry grew largely because of Scottish and Italian immigrants in the early nineteenth century who brought with them quarrying and stone carving skills. The **Robert Burns Monument** on the high school lawn, carved by local stonemasons, is regarded as one of the finest granite sculptures in the world. Barre granite is favoured because the stone rarely has flaws, and a number of works in the town produce tombstones and other monuments. The Hope Cemetery in Merchant Street, has a huge collection of memorial art from elicately carved small headstones to massive mausoleums.

To visit Rock of Ages in **Graniteville**, follow the signs on the country road which runs south from Barre. This is the chance to visit one of the world's largest granite quarrying enterprises. Quarrying over the last 100 years has produced a huge crater 475ft (145m) deep and covering 55 acres (22 hectares). There is a visitor centre and guided tours of drilling, blasting and stone removal, and an observation platform overlooks the cutting and polishing. Self guiding quarry tours are also available. Open: daily 8.30am-5pm May to mid-October. Admission free.

Take route 14 south through Answorth State Park to its junction with route 89. You can detour the 9 miles (14km) south to beautiful **Sharon**, surrounded by mountains on three sides and nestling in the White River Valley. The small town is noted as the birthplace in 1805 of Joseph Smith, founder of the Mormon church. He lived in the area until he was 11 when his family moved to New York. The Joseph Smith Birthplace Memorial is between Sharon and Royalton. The granite monument marks the site of Smith's birthplace and is set in landscaped surroundings with walking trails. The Joseph Smith Visitor Center has exhibits about his life, and the memorial is noted for its Christmas illuminations from late November. Open: daily 9am-7pm May to October, 9am-5pm rest of the year. Admission free.

Strafford is north-east of Sharon along narrow country roads. The Justin Smith Morrill Homestead on SR132, is a Gothic Revival home built in the mid-nineteenth century by Senator Justin Morrill. His Land Grant College Act signed by President Abraham Lincoln in 1862, paved the way for the nation's higher education system by allowing grants of land to be made for state universities. The house contains period furnishings, family memorabilia, and exhibits about his lengthy political career. Open: Wednesday to Sunday 9.30am-5.30pm May to mid-October. Admission free.

Return to highway 89 and take route 107 west for **Bethel** where you can visit the White River National Fish Hatchery. The visitor centre has displays about the work of the hatchery and the life of the Atlantic salmon which is being re-established in the Connecticut River. Once common, the salmon disappeared from most of New England's rivers in the mid-nineteenth century because of overfishing and dams to provide water power. Open: daily 8am-3pm. Admission free: Continue on route 107 west. You can detour south on route 12 to visit **Barnard**, noted as the place where Vermont's last panther was shot in 1881. The mounted animal is displayed in Montpelier's Vermont Historical Society Museum. The village is now a delightful retreat with summer cottages, many of which have had famous owners. During the 1930s writer Sinclair Lewis and his journalist wife Dorothy Thompson, later an eminent war correspondent, lived at Twin Farms.

Return to the 107 and head west through Gaysville and then turn right on scenic highway 100 which runs along the eastern boundary of the Green Mountain National Forest. There are many side trips which can be made off this route into the huge recreation area, depending on how much time you have.

The Green Mountains and Green Mountain National Forest

This area is the spine of Vermont, running north-south along the length of the state. The highest peaks are in the north with many over 4,000ft (1,219m). The Green Mountain National Forest, with its headquarters in Rutland, covers more than 340,000 acres (136,000 hectares) in two sections, the northern area running from US4 north-east of Rutland to SR17 near Bristol, and the southern area extending from the border with Masachusetts to SR140 near Wallingford. There are six wilderness areas, more than 500 miles (805km) of trails including the long distance Appalachian and Long Trails and Robert Frost National Recreation Trail, wilderness and developed campgrounds and picnic spots. Moosalamoo is a partnership of local communities to promote a 20,000 acre (8,000 hectare) recreation area in the National Forest close to Brandon, Goshen, Leicester, Middlebury, Ripton and Salisbury. The 'moose' sign is used on notice boards which give information about trails, natural features and cultural traditions. For further information contact: Green Mountain National Forest, PO Box 519, Rutland VT 05702 ☎ (802) 773-0300.

After exploring the Green Mountains area, head south on highway 100 to highway 4. Turn right and at Mendon detour north to Chittenden and Holden then west to **Pittsford** and the Federal Fish Hatchery, off US7, which raises Atlantic salmon which are released into Lake Champlain and the Connecticut River. Open: daily 8am-4pm. Admission free. The New England Maple Museum, north on US7, has exhibits on maple syrup production since Indian times, with demonstrations and sampling. Open: daily 8.30am-5.30pm late May to October, 10am-4pm March to late May, November and December. Admission charge.

From Pittsford take highway 7 south to Pittsford Mills and then take the country road to **Proctor**, named after the Governor of Vermont from 1878 to 1880 and founder of the international Vermont Marble Company. The town in Otter Creek Valley has many fine marble buildings and marble sidewalks. The Sutherland Falls, near the centre of the town, provide much of its power. The Vermont Marble Exhibit, Main Street, is the world's largest marble museum, with displays and films about its quarrying, cutting and finishing. There is a resident sculptor and sculpture gallery. Open: daily 9am-5.30pm mid-May to October, Monday to Saturday 9am-4pm rest of the year. Admission charge.

Wilson Castle, West Proctor Road, is an ornate thirty-two room mansion built in 1867 and set in 115 acres (46 hectares) of gardens. It is noted for its English brick and marble façade with arches, turrets, parapet and balcony, hand carved wood panelling and hand painted ceilings with gold leaf, more than eighty stained glass windows and thirteen elaborate fireplaces. It has fine period furnishings and antiques, paintings and sculptures from around the world. There are a number of buildings in the grounds including carriage house, gas house and aviary. Open: daily 9am-6pm late May to late October. Admission charge.

Continue south to Rutland and then take highway 7 south to Pierces Corner and then head east on route 103 detouring off to visit **Shrewsbury**, a tiny village on the North Shrewsbury Road. The steepled church also acts as town hall, and W.E. Pierce Groceries has been run by the same family since 1835, and the brass cash register was bought in 1918. The Meadowsweet Herb Farm, on Mount Holly Road, allows you to learn more about herbs and their uses.

Return to the 103 and continue east to **Ludlow**. During the Civil War the town invented a way of recycling woollen products to overcome the cloth shortage. The Black River Academy Museum is in the High Street. The academy attracted students from throughout New England because of its reputation for academic excellence. The museum displays local history exhibits, manuscripts and old photographs. There is also an exhibit about Calvin Coolidge, who graduated from the academy in 1890. Open: Wednesday to Sunday 12noon-4pm May to early September, weekends 12noon-4pm early September to October. Donations. Crowley Cheese Factory, Healdville Road, claims to be the oldest hand-made cheese factory in the USA. Open: Monday to Friday 8am-4pm. Admission free.

The 300 acre (120 hectare) Camp Plymouth State Park still attracts gold diggers who pan the silty bed of Buffalo Brook. Not much gold is found but it is a great place for walking especially around Echo Lake. **Proctorsville** is 3 miles (5km) east of Ludlow, and you can visit the Joseph Cerniglia Winery on SR103, tour of the winery and enjoy a tasting. Open: daily 10am-5pm. Admission free.

You can also detour south here for **Weston** built on a hill at the northern end of the West River Valley with may well preserved and charming nineteenth-century homes. Guild of Old Time Crafts and Industries, SR100, is a working museum in a converted 1780 sawmill where artists and craftsmen still use the original tools of their trades. Open: Wednesday to Sunday 10am-5pm June to mid-October. Admission free.

Vermont Country Store, SR100, was established in 1890 and still selling items reminiscent of that period. Open: Monday to Saturday 9am-5pm. Admission free.

Weston Playhouse, on the village green, in the converted Congregational Church, which burnt down in 1962 but has been faithfully rebuilt with its original Greek Revival façade. Performances Tuesday to Sunday late June to early September. Admission charge.

Returning to Proctorsville, continue south east on 103 to **Chester**, noted for its many fine buildings and its two historic districts — along Main Street on the green, and North Street's Stone Village, with twenty-five pre-Civil War homes. Then take route 11 east to **Springfield**. The town owed its prosperity to the Black River which powered the many mills built in the eighteenth and nineteenth centuries. Some of the mills still survive along the river, although water power is no longer used. There is an information centre in the restored 1785 one-room Eureka schoolhouse on SR11, close to the 37ft (11m) long cobered bridge built in 1870.

Stellafane Society Museum, Hartness House Inn, Orchard Street, commemorates astronomers and astrology in a five room subterranean complex connected to the inn by a 240ft (73m) tunnel. The complex and tunnel were built by James Hartness, inventor and astronomer and Governor of Vermont between 1920 and 1922. In 1910 he invented the Turret Equatorial Telescope which still operates and stands on the lawn. Open: guided tours daily 6pm. Admission free ☎ (802) 885-2115. Reservations recommended.

Continue east on route 11 until you reach highway 5 which heads north along the western banks of the Connecticut River to **Windsor**. It was here on 8 July 1777 that the constitution of Vermont was adopted after a 6 day meeting. Windsor, still known as the 'Birthplace of Vermont' was used for general assembly meetings until 1805 when Montpelier became the state capital. Windsor was famous during the nineteenth century for innovations, and firearms, the sewing machine, coffee percolator and hydraulic pump were all invented here. The covered bridge over the Connecticut between Windsor and Cornish, New Hampshire, was built in 1866 and is one of the longest in the country. Local handicrafts are displayed in the Cermont State Craft Center on Main Street.

The American Precision Museum, Main Street, has displays of machine tools and firearms, most created in the town. Open: Monday to Friday 9am-5pm, weekends 10am-4pm late May to November. Admission charge.

Old Constitution House, North Main Street is the former tavern where the Constitution was written and agreed in 1777, and now dedicated to the state's history. Open: Wednesday to Sunday 10am-4pm late May to early October. Admission charge.

Stay on highway 5 north and at Hartland take the country road north to **Quechee** and the Quechee Gorge, Vermont's 'Grand Canyon' which is to the west of town. Quechee Gorge has been cut by the Ottauquechee River and the bridge carrying the US4 over it, is 165ft (50m) above the water. There is a 1 mile (2km) trail down to the floor of the gorge.

A covered bridge leads into the small village, which had a mill processing wool from local flocks. The mill is now the name of the shopping area, which includes Simon Pearce Glass, where you can watch glass blowing. The area has many large summer estates with grand mansions.

You can detour east from Quechee along highway 4 and then across to highway 5 from which you can visit **White River Junction**, and the Catamount Brewing Company, South Main Street, which offers tours of the brewey, the history of beer making and sampling. Open: Monday to Saturday 11am-3pm July to October, Saturday 11am-3pm rest of the year. Admission free.

North of White River Junction and close to the Connecticut River is **Norwich**, home of the Montshire Museum of Science, Montshire Road. It has displays on science, technology and natural history,

White River Junction, an important interstate crossing point where the White River runs into the Connecticut River

A covered bridge in the resort of Woodstock

*Killington and Pico,
Vermont's most popular
winter sports area*

including aquariums, live animals and hands-on exhibits. The museum is set in 100 acres (40 hectares) of woodland along the Connecticut River with nature trails. Open: daily 10am-5pm. Admission charge.

※ From Quechee take route 4 west to **Woodstock**, a lovely town built around the green with many fine old buildings. It is now a popular year round resort with winter skiing and summer scenic drives and hiking trails nearby. Water sports and horse riding are also available. Four of the church's bells were cast by Paul Revere at his Boston foundry. There are three covered bridges on US4, one in the centre of town, another 4 miles (6km) east at Taftsville and the third, 3 miles (5km) west. One interesting point is that thanks to a grant from Laurance Rockefeller, power lines are buried so the nineteenth-century landscape has been preserved.

🏠 Billings Farm and Museum, on SR12 combines a modern dairy farm and museum of farming life during the nineteenth century. The farm was established by Frederick Billings, a wealthy lawyer and industrialist, in 1871, who imported a pedigree herd of Jersey cattle from Britain. The museum is housed in four old farm buildings and displays depict the farming year and farm skills. There is also a recreated workshop, kitchen and country store, and restored farm manager's house. Open: daily 10am-5pm May to late October, weekends 10am-4pm November and December. Admission charge.

🏛 Dana House, Elm Street, is the 1807 home of the Woodstock Historical Society with local history exhibits, toys, paintings and furnishings dating from 1740. Open: Monday to Saturday 10am-5pm, Sunday 2-5pm May to October. Admission charge.

※ Sugarbush Farm, Side Road, produces maple syrup and cheese and there are tours of both production processes and tastings. Open: Monday to Friday 7.30am-4pm May to November, hours vary at other times of the year. Admission free.

※ The Vermont Raptor Center, Church Hill Road, has twenty-six species of birds of prey that cannot be released back into the wild because of their injuries. There are also nature trails. Open: Monday to Saturday 10am-4pm year round, and Sundays 10am-4pm May to October. Admission charge.

From Woodstock continue on highway 4 west to route 100A which runs south to **Plymouth**, set in the Green Mountains and the birthplace of Calvin Coolidge. The Vice President was at home on 3 August 1923 when news arrived of President Harding's death, and his father, a notary public, administered the oath of office to his son in the parlour by the light of a kerosene lamp, by which Coolidge became the 30th President of the United States.

Plymouth Notch Historic District, off SR100A, a collection of old ☀
buildings including the home of Calvin Coolidge and his grave, a
visitor centre, the Wilder House and Barn, general store, Plymouth
Cheese Factory and Union Christian Church. Open: daily 9.30am-
5.30pm late May to mid-October. Admission charge.

From Plymouth take highway 100 north to highway 4 and continue north to **Killington**, a year round outdoor recreation area.
Also known as **Sherburne**, it offers downhill skiing in the winter
and summer backpacking. The Killington Music Festival is held
each July and the Mountain Equestrian Festival in mid-July, includes the North American Jumping Championships and the Grand
Prix of Vermont.

Killington Ski and Summer Resort is off US4 in Calvin Coolidge- 🛫
state Forest, with 3 mile (5km) gondola tramway and 1 mile (2km)
long chairlift to the 4,241ft (1,293m) summit of Killington Peak, with
views over five states and Canada. There is a nature trail from the 🏕
summit. Gondola daily: 10am-4pm mid-September to October,
chairlift daily 10am-4pm early June to early October. Admission
charge.

At the Pico Alpine Slide, west on US4, a chairlift carries skiers to
the top of the slide with two runs down. Open: daily 10am-6pm late
June to early September, hours vary rest of the year. Admission
charge.

SOUTHERN REGION

This is an historic, picturesque area from the valleys of the
Berkshires to the majestic Stratton Mountain, which has attracted
vacationers and visitors for more than a hundred years because of its
unspoiled beauty and wealth of attractions. There are charming
towns and villages, museums, great shopping malls and year round
outdoor activity opportunities.

The tour starts in **Brattleboro**, the state's first permanent settle- ☀
ment when Fort Dummer was established by the British in 1724. The
town slogan is 'where Vermont Begins' and it is now the state's main
industrial centre. The 1879 Creamery Covered Bridge is to the west
of the town on route 9. The Molly Stark Trail, named after the wife of
General John Stark, hero of the Battle of Bennington is a 39 mile
(63km) scenic trail which runs from Brattleboro to Bennington.
Brattleboro Museum and Art Center is on Main and Vernon Streets 🏛
in the old Union Railroad Station. It has four galleries on local
history and visual arts. A fifth gallery is devoted to the history of the
Estey Organ Corpporation Open: Tuesday to Sunday 12noon-6pm
May to October. Admission charge.

Brattleboro, site of Vermont's first permanent European settlement in 1724

The ferry boat at Wilmington offers summer cruises in this popular winter ski area

Bennington Battle Monument next to Bennington museum which has the oldest surviving 'Stars and Stripes'

Grandma Moses Museum, Bennington

Dummerston, just to the north, is where Rudyard Kipling lived for 4 years after getting married to Vermont native Carrie Balestier. He called the house Naulakha, and while in residence wrote some of his most famous works, including Captain Courageous, the *Just So Stories* and two of the *Jungle Books*. The house is now a private residence.

The Brooks Memorial Library has changing displays of art and photography , and a children's floor. The scenic SR9 runs west from Brattleboro to Bennington with stunning views of the Hogback Mountain.

Take highway 9 west, and look for the country road which leads to the summit of 2,350ft (716m) Hogback Mountain which is a forested plateau with magnificent views. In the basement of the Hogback Mountain Gift Shop is the Luman Nelson Museum of New England Wildlife, which has thousands of stuffed birds and animals, including extinct species and curiosities. Open: daily.

Back on route 9 head west for **Marlboro**, settled by two families in 1763 neither of which knew the other was there for more a year. Today the small town is home of the Marlboro College and a music school established by pianist Rudolf Serkin. The Marlboro Music Festival is held in July and August each year.

Continue west to **Wilmington** and the Molly Stark State Park, about 2 miles (3km) east of town, which has magnificent stands of maple and birch. It is a good area for spotting beaver and deer, and there is a 2 hour round trip trail which takes in Mount Olga, topped by an abandoned fire tower. The park has several campsites.

North River Winery, SR112S, with guided tours of the mid-nineteenth-century winery and tastings. Open: daily 10am-5pm early May to December, Friday to Sunday 11am-5pm rest of the year. Admission free.

Scenic highway 100 runs north from Wilmington providing access to **Mount Snow**, a popular year round ski resort in the Green Mountains with downhill skiing between early November and early May, and swimming, hiking, mountain biking, boating,fishing, golf and tennis during the rest of the year. The ski area is off SR100 and has around 100 trails and runs served by 24 lifts over a 5 mountain area. There is a sightseeing chairlift to the summit of 3,600ft (1,097m) Mount Snow. Open: Friday and weekends 9am-4pm mid-September to mid-October, weekends 9am-3pm late June to mid-September. Admission charge. Haystack Mountain off Route 100, is another popular ski area, catering especially for families.

Route 9 runs west from Wilmington through Searsburg to **Bennington**, between Mount Anthony in the Taconic range and the

Green Mountains. This beautiful valley town was the scene of the historic Battle of Bennington on 16 August 1777 when General John Stark and his American troops defeated a British force led by General John Burgoyne. The event is celebrated each year in mid-August by the Bennington Battle Day weekend. The town was the first chartered in the state in 1761 but because of raids by the French and Indians, real settlement did not start until 1773. There are three covered bridges, the Silk Road and Papermill Village bridges are on SR67a, and the Bert Henry bridge on Murphy Road. The area is noted for its scenic drives, particularly US7 north to Manchester and SR9 east to Brattleboro. Plays are staged in the Old Everett Castle between April and October, and every August the Composers' Forum is held at Bennington College, featuring chamber music. The County Fair and Antique and Classic Car Show are both held annually in September. Bennington College was founded in 1929 and is now an acknowledged centre of academic excellence and innovation. Jennings Hall, a grand three-storey granite home built in the mid-nineteenth century, is now part of the college campus.

There is downhill and cross country skiing at nearby Lake Paran and Prospect Mountain. The town has many fine old buildings and there are two self-guiding walking tours through the historic districts and homes. Free walking maps are available from the Bennington Area Chamber of Commerce, Veterans Memorial Drive, Bennington VT 05201 ☎ (802) 447-3311.

Bennington Battle Monument, at the end of Monument Drive, was built in 1891 and at the time was the highest battle monument in the world standing 306ft (93m) high. It is still the tallest structure in Vermont, and there are stunning views from the observation chamber reached by lift. A diorama and displays give the story of the battle. Open: daily 9am-5pm, mid-April to October. Admission charge.

Bennington Museum, West Main Street in a vine covered 1855 building, has displays about local history and Americana featuring Bennington pottery, rare glass, uniforms, furniture, toys and the Bennington '76 Stars and Stripes. There are paintings by Grandma Moses plus the Grandma Moses Museum, the adjoining frame schoolhouse, moved from Eagle Bridge in New York, where the artist, who did not start painting until she was 76, went to school. Open: daily 9am-5pm. Admission charge.

Visit Old First Church, Monument Avenue, on the green in Old Bennington Village. The congregation dates from 1762 and the church, built in 1805, is one of the oldest and most beautiful in Vermont. Each of the columns was carved from a single pine tree.

The interior, including the pine box pews and fine plaster and wood ceilings, has been faithfully restored. Open: Monday to Saturday 10am-12noon and 1-4pm. Sunday 1-4pm July to early October, Saturday 10am-12noon and 1-4pm and Sunday 1-4pm rest of the year. Donations.

The Old Burial Ground, next to the church, has the graves of Bennington's founders, five Vermont Governors and poet Robert Frost whose epitaph reads: 'I had a lover's quarrel with the world'.

North Bennington is 5 miles (8km) north-west on route 67A. Park-McCullough House is on West Street. The Victorian mansion was built in 1865 and has period furnishings and family effects. There are formal gardens and a carriage house with carriages and sleighs. The house is also used to stage concerts through the year. Open: daily 10am-4pm late May to October and early to late December. Admission charge.

Take route 67 north to South Shaftsbury and then route 71 north to **Arlington** which was settled in 1763 by Jehiel Hawley, a staunch Loyalist, and known appropriately as Tory Hollow. Because of their open support for the British, when the Green Mountain Boys became active in the area, Isaac Bisco, the town clerk, destroyed all the official records. A British officer visiting the town is said to have carved the scene from his window on to his horn drinking cup, and this was later used as the design for the State Seal. St James Church Cemetery, dating from 1830, has a number of old tombstones with inscriptions bearing testimony to these troubled times. The scenic SR7A is a delightful 11 mile (18km) drive for those heading for Manchester Center. The Norman Rockwell Exhibit, Main Street, is in a nineteenth century church. The artist lived in the town between 1939 and 1953 and several of the local people who modelled for him now act as hosts at the museum which displays hundreds of pieces of his work. Open: daily 9am-5pm May to October, 10am-4pm rest of the year. Admission charge.

Continue north to **Manchester**, a year round resort with Mount Equinox to the west and including Manchester Center and Manchester Depot, and surrounded by scenic areas. Manchester is largely a residential community noted for its elm-lined streets and elegant sidewalks, Manchester Center is the business area and there is excellent skiing in nearby Bromley, Magic Mountain and Stratton.

The American Museum of Fly Fishing, on SR7A and Seminary Avenue, exhibits fishing equipment and tackle used by celebrities and some of the world's greatest fly fishers, including Hemingway, Bing Crosby and several Presidents. Open: daily 10am-4pm April to November, Monday to Friday 10am-4pm rest of the year.

Manchester has been a mountain spa and resort for more than 200 years and has many fine old buildings and estates

Bromley Alpine Slide and Scenic Chairlift, is 6 miles (10km) east on Bromley Mountain, with a chair lift to the summit and sledges down the 1 mile (2km) slide. Open: daily 9.30am-5pm early May to mid-October. Admission charge.

Hildene, on US7A was the summer home of Robert Todd Lincoln, son of Abraham and his descendents until 1975. The Georgian Revival mansion with original furnishings and family memorabilia is set in formal gardens. The house contains a 1,000 pipe Aeolian Organ and there is a slide show in the carriage house about the mansion and Lincoln family. During the winter there is a cross country ski trail. Open: daily 9.30am-4pm mid-May to October. Admission charge.

Mount Equinox, the highest mountain in the Taconic Range.There is a 5 mile (8km) steep, narrow, twisting toll road to the 3,816ft (1,163m) summit and incredible views at the top, including the four large wind turbines on top of neighbouring Little Equinox. Road open: daily 8am-10pm May to November. Toll.

Southern Vermont Art Center, signposted from US7 and West Road, has exhibits by local artists and students, sculpture garden and botany trail. Open: Tuesday to Saturday 10am-5pm, Sunday 12noon-5pm early May to late October. Admission charge.

Take highways 30/11 east through the national forest to Londonderry, and then route 100 south to Rawsonvilla and the gateway to the Stratton Mount recreation and ski area. The **Stratton Resort** offers year round recreation opportunities on Stratton Mountain with skiing in the winter, and hiking, mountain biking and horse back popular in the summer. Golf, tennis, fishing, sailing and swimming are also available. Grout Pond Recreation Area is situated in Stratton township and covers 1,600 acres (640 hectares) of semi-primitive land and a 79 acre (32 hectare) pond, formerly an Indian hunting and fishing ground. There is camping, hiking and it is a good area for spotting beaver, deer, snowshoe hare and many species of bird.

The Stratton Arts Festival is one of the oldest and largest festivals in Vermont and takes place at the Stratton Mountain Base Lodge between mid-September and mid-October.

Highway 100/30 continues south to Jamaica and the Jamaica State Park which covers 690 acres (276 hectares) and is split by the West River. There is a trail along the old railway line that leads to the Ball Mountain Dam, and another to Hamilton Falls.

From highway 100 take the country road east to West Townshend, and the next port of call is **Townshend**, a delightful scenic village and much photographed. The Scott Covered Bridge built in 1870 over the West River was the first in the state to be listed for preservation. It is 276ft (51m) long, one of the longest in the state, and the largest single span at 166ft (51m). Townshend State Forest offers trails to the summit of 1,580ft (482m) Bald Mountain.

Take route 35 north-east cutting across to Saxtons River. From here you can detour on highway 121 north through Cambridgeport to **Grafton**, another picture postcard New England village with well ❄ preserved historic homes, inns, white steepled churches and green. The village grew up in the early 1800s along the post road between Boston and Albany. It had timber and flour mills, tanneries, soapstone quarry, and carriage and sleigh factory. It was also noted for its cheeses. At one time its population reached 1,500, but by the mid-nineteenth century many people had emigrated to the mid West and South. The railroad signalled the end of the post route, and cheap wool imports from Australia forced the closure of the mills. A vigorous renovation programme started in 1963, has restored many of Grafton's fine old buildings, and the village now has a bustling economy with shops, country inns and thriving dairy and sheep industries. The 1801 Old Tavern Inn is packed with antiques and is an old stagecoach inn. It has hosted many famous guests including Kipling and Ralph Waldo Emerson.

Return to Saxtons River and take the country road north to the 103. Turn right for the short drive to **Rockingham**. Old Rockingham ⌂ Meeting House dates from 1787 and is noted for the high pulpit and boxed pews. There are a number of interesting tombstones in the adjoining graveyard. Open: daily 10am-4pm mid-June to early September, and late September to late October. Admission charge.

Vermont Country Store on SR103, opened in the nineteenth cen- ❄ tury as a branch of the Weston store and stocks items reflecting that period. Nearby is an 1872 covered bridge, 1810 gristmill and water wheel. The sculptures are by John Rogers. Open: Monday to Saturday 9am-5pm Sunay 10am-5pm. Admission free.

Continue east to highway 5 and follow it south as it follows the Connecticut River to **Bellows Falls**, and named after the cascade 🔎 originally called the Great Falls. The water is drawn off to power local industry and the flow over the falls can often be reduced to little more than a trickle. In 1792 work started on the nearby canal to allow navigation past the falls for vessels travelling up from the Long Island Sound to Barnet. The canal took 10 years to complete, was the first built in America, and had nine locks which raised steamers and barges over the falls until made redundant by the arrival of the railway in the 1840s. Bellows Falls is also famous as the home of Hetty Green, known as 'the Witch of Wall Street', and in the

1870s reputed to be the world's richest woman. Her home, on the corner of Westminster and School Streets, is now a bank.

Green Mountain Flyer is a 1930s diesel train offering sightseeing rides between Bellows Falls Union Railroad Station in Depot Square and Chester Railroad Station. Trains run daily at 11am and 2pm mid-September to mid-October, Tuesday to Sunday at 11am and 2pm late June to mid-September. Admission charge. The Old Stone Gristmill Museum tells the story of the town's logging history, and there are a number of Indian rock carvings about 50ft (15m) downstream of the Vilas Bridge.

From Bellows Falls continue south to **Putney**, the short lived home of John Humphrey Noyes 'Pefectionists'. The avant garde community, founded in 1838, believed in free love among other things, and were drummed out of town by the arch-conservative citizens. Santa's Land, on US5, with Santa's house, sleigh museum, rides and petting zoo. Open: daily 9.30am-4.30pm May to Christmas Eve. Admission charge.

From Putney you can detour west along country road to **Newfane**, settled in 1774 and everything you expect a New England village to be with wonderful old white clapboard buildings dating back to the 1700s. The Greek Revival Windham County Courthouse, on the green, with its massive pillars, is opposite the 1787 Colonial-style Old Newfane Inn. In 1825 the entire village was moved 2 miles (3km) south to its present site. All the buildings were dismantled and then hauled by oxen to their new locations.

Windham County Historical Society Museum, south of the village green in Main Street, dates from 1825 and has local history exhibits and old maps. The church bell in front of the museum was cast in the early 1800s. Open: Wednesday to Sunday 12noon-5pm June to mid-October. Admission free.

From Newfane or Putney it is 10 miles (16km) south back to Brattleboro.

National, State And Other
Major Recreation Areas

Allis, 487 acres (195 hectares). 5 miles (8km) south of Northfield off SR12, with camping, picknicking and hiking.

Ascutney, 1,984 acres (794 hectares). 3 miles (5km) north-west of Ascutney, with camping, picnicking, hiking and winter sports.

Ball Mountain Dam, off SR100, north-east of Rawsonville, with picnicking, fishing and swimming.

Bomoseen, 2,739 acres (1,096 hectares) in two areas, just north of West Castleton, with nature centre and nature trails, camping, picnicking, hiking, boating, boat rentals, fishing and swimming.

Branbury, 96 acres (38 hectares). 3 miles (5km) east of Salisbury, with camping, picnicking, hiking, boating, boat rentals, fishing, swimming and visitor centre.

Brighton, 152 acres (61 hectares). 2 miles (3km) of Island Pond, with marina, camping, picnicking, hiking, boating, boat rentals, fishing and swimming.

Burton Island, 253 acres (101 hectares). In Lake Champlain, with marina, nature centre, nature trails, camping, picnicking, hiking, boating, boat rentals, fishing, swimming and visitor centre.

Button Bay, 236 acres (94 hectares). 7 miles (11km) west of Vergennes, with nature centre and nature trails, camping, picnicking, hiking, boating, boat rentals, fishing, swimming and visitor centre.

Calvin Coolidge Forest, 16,165 acres (6,466 hectares). 2 miles (3km) north of Plymouth, with camping, picnicking, hiking, fishing and winter sports.

Camp Plymouth, 300 acres (120 hectares) off SR100 north of Ludlow, with picnicking, hiking, boating, boat rentals, fishing and swimming.

Crystal Lake, 16 acres (6 hectares) in Barton, with picnicking, hiking, boating, fishing and swimming.

Elmore, 700 acres (280 hectares) at Elmore, with camping, picnicking, hiking, boating, boat rentals, fishing and swimming.

Emerald Lake, 430 acres (172 hectares) at North Dorset, with camping, picnicking, hiking, boating, boat rentals, fishing, swimming and winter sports.

Fort Dummer, 217 acres (87 hectares). 2 miles (3km) south of Brattleboro, with camping, picnicking and hiking.

Gifford Woods, 114 acres (46 hectares). 2 miles (3km) north of Sherburne, with camping, picnicking, hiking and fishing.

Grand Isle, 226 acres (90 hectares). 5 miles (8km) south of North Hero, with camping, boating, boat rentals, fishing and swimming.

Granville Gulf, 1,200 acres (480 hectares) near Warren, with picnicking, hiking, fishing, winter sports and cross country skiing trails.

Green Mountain National Forest, 340,000 acres (136,000 hectares), with camping, picnicking, hiking, boating, fishing, swimming and winter sports.

Groton Forest, 25,625 acres (102,50 hectares) in nine areas between Montpelier and St. Johnsbury, with camping, picnicking, hiking, boating, boat rentals, fishing and swimming, winter sports, visitor centre and lodging.

Half Moon Pond, 1,570 acres (628 hectares). 11 miles (18km) north west of Rutland, with camping, hiking, boating, boat rentals, fishing and swimming.

Jamaica Park, 690 acres (276 hectares). 1 mile (2km) east of Jamaica, with camping, picknicking, hiking, fishing, swimming and visitor centre.

Kamp Kill Kare, 18 acres (7 hectares) south-west of St Albans, with picnicking, boating, boat rentals, fishing and swimming.

Kingsland Bay, 4 miles (6km) north-west of Ferrisburg, with picnicking, hiking, boating, fishing and swimming.

Knight Point, 54 acres (22 hectares). 3 miles (5km) south of North Hero, with picnicking, boating, fishing and swimming.

Lake Carmi, 482 acres (193 hectares). 3 miles (5km) south of East Franklin, with camping, picnicking, hiking, boating, boat rentals, fishing, swimming, winter sports and lodging.

Lake St Catherine, 117 acres (47 hectares). 3 miles (5km) south of Poultney, with camping, picnicking, hiking, boating, boat rentals, fishing and swimming.

Maidstone, 470 acres (188 hectares) south-west of Bloomfield, with nature trails, camping, picnicking, hiking, boating, boat rentals, fishing, swimming and winter sports.

Molly Stark, 158 acres (63 hectares). 15 miles (24km) west of Brattleboro, with camping, picnicking and hiking.

Mount Mansfield Forest, 27,600 acres (11,040 hectares) near Mount Mansfield, with camping, picnicking, hiking, boating, boat rentals, fishing, swimming and winter sports.

Mount Philo, 650 acres (260 hectares). 14 miles (22km) south of Burlington, with scenic drives, camping and picnicking.

North Hartland Dam, off US5 north of North Hartland, with camping, picnicking, boating and fishing.

North Hero, 400 acres (160 hectares). 8 miles (13km) north of North Hero, with camping, picnicking, boating, boat rentals, fishing and swimming.

Quechee Gorge, 612 acres (245 hectares), 7 miles (11km) west of White River Junction, with camping, picnicking, hiking and fishing.

Sand Bar, 20 acres (8 hectares). 5 miles (8km) north-west of Burlington, with picnicking, boating, boat rentals, fishing and swimming.

Shaftsbury, 100 acres (40 hectares). 10 miles (16km) north of Bennington, with picnicking, boating, boat rentals, fishing and swimming.

Silver Lake, 34 acres (14 hectares). 1 mile (2km) east of Barnard, with camping, picnicking, boating, boat rentals, fishing and swimming.

Stoughton Pond, $1/2$ mile (1km) north-east of Perkinsville, with picnicking, boating, fishing and swimming.

Townshend Forest, 856 acres (342 hectares). 17 miles (27km) north-west of Brattleboro, with camping, picnicking, hiking and fishing.

Townshend Recreation Area, 6 miles (10km) north of Townshend on SR30, with picnicking, hiking, fishing, swimming and hunting.

Union Village Dam, south of Thetford Center on SR132, with picnicking, hiking, fishing, swimming and hunting.

Wilgus, 100 acres (40 hectares). 1 mile (2km) south of Ascutney, with camping, picnicking, hiking, boating, fishing and nature trails.

Woodford, 400 acres (160 hectares). 10 miles (16km) east of Bennington, with camping, picnicking, hiking, boating, boat rentals, fishing and swimming.

Woods Island, 125 acres (50 hectares). 4 miles (6km) north of Burton Island, with camping by permit, picnicking, boating, fishing and swimming.

Wrightsville Dame, 4 miles (6km) north of Montpelier off SR12, with picnicking, boating, fishing and swimming.

Some Suggested Foliage Tours

The Foliage Hotline ☎ 1-800-828-3239 offers 24 hour information on fall foliage conditions from 1 September to 24 October.

Tour 1 (Bennington Region) From Manchester Center
Approximately 104 miles (167km).

Manchester Center to South Shaftsbury via US 7A; South Shaftsbury to North Bennington via Vermont 67; North Bennington to Old Bennington via 67A and Silk Road; Old Bennington to Pownal Center via Bennington and South Stream Road (Morgan Street); Pownal Center to Williamstown, Massachusetts, via US7; Williamstown, Massachusetts, to Searsburg, Vermont, via Route 2, Vermont 100 and Vermont 8; side trip to Somerset Reservoir via unmarked road; Searsburg to Bennington via Vermont 9; Bennington to Manchester Depot via unmarked road through East Arlington, Chiselville and Sunderland. Points of interest along the way: **Arlington**: *Candle Mill Village*; **Bennington**: *Bennington Museum, Vermont State Fish Hatchery*; **Manchester**: *Historic Hildene, South Vermont Art Center*; **Old Bennington**: *Battle Monument*; *Manchester Center*: *The Clock Emporium*; **North Bennington**: *Park-McCullough House*; **Peru**: *Alpine Slide at Bromley*; **Pownal**: *Green Mountain Race Track*, **Shaftsbury**: *Peter Matteson Tavern.*

Tour 2 (Two Rivers Region) From Woodstock
Approximately 130 miles (209km).

Woodstock east via Vermont 4 to Taftsville; right on Vermont 12 to Hartland; right from Vermont 5 to Windsor; right on Vermont 44 through Brownsville to junction Vermont 106; left on Vermont 106 to Felchville; west at Felchville through South Reading to Tyson; north on Vermont 100 through Plymouth Union, West Bridgewater, Sherburne Center, Pittsfield, Stockbridge, Talcville and Rochester; east to Bethel and Vermont 12 via unmarked road; north to Randolph, east on Vermont 66 through Randolph Center to East Randolph; east at East Randolph to Tunbridge and Vermont 110; south through North Tunbridge to Tunbridge; east at Tunbridge to Strafford and South Strafford; south on Vermont 132 to Sharon; south at Sharon to Hewetts Corners and South Pomfret and back to Woodstock. Points of interest along the way: **Sherburne**: *Killington Gondola*; **Strafford**: *Justin Smith Morrill Homestead*; **Plymouth**: *Calvin Coolidge Birthplace, Plymouth Cheese Corporation*; **Woodstock**: *Vermont Institute of Natural Science, Billings Farm and Museum.*

The 'Rock of Ages' granite quarry at Barre is the largest in the world and makes a fascinating visit

Scene from Hyde Park, also known locally as Hide Park because of the old taneries

Tour 3 (Ottauquechee Valley Region) From Woodstock

Approximately 155 miles (250km).

Woodstock to Taftsville; left through covered bridge, then right, through Quechee returning to US4 at Gorge; US411 to White River Junction; White River Junction to East Thetford via US5; East Thetford to Post Mills via Vermont 113; Post Mills to Chelsea via Vermont 113; Chelsea to East Barre via Vermont 110; East Barre to Montpelier via US302; Montpelier to Middlesex via US2; Middlesex to Stockbridge via Vermont 100B and Vermont 100; Stockbridge to junction Vermont 12 via Vermont 107; Vermont 12 to Woodstock. Points of interest along the way: **Barre**: *Rock of Ages Granite Quarries*; **Granville**: *Moss Glen Falls*; **Montpelier**: Vermont *Museum, Vermont Statehouse, Wood Art Gallery*; **Quechee**: *Quechee Gorge*; **Woodstock**: *Billings Farm & Museum, Vermont Institute of Natural Science*.

Tour 4 (Chittenden Region) From Burlington

Approximately 175 miles (282km).

Burlington north on US2 and 7 to junction US2 to Alburg Center via US2; Alburg Center to Swanton via Vermont 78; Swanton to St. Albans via US7; St. Albans to Richford via Vermont 105; Richford to junction Vermont 101 via Vermont 105; Vermont 101 to Troy; Troy to North Hyde Park via Vermont 100; North Hyde Park to Johnson via Vermont 100C; Johnson to Winooski via Vermont 15; Winooski to Burlington via US2 and 7. Points of interest along the way: **Burlington**: *Fleming Museum, University of Vermont*; **Essex Junction**: *Discovery Museum*; **Isle La Motte**: *St Anne's Shrine; Lake Champlain Ferry Crossings*; **Milton**: *Sand Bar Wildlife Refuge*; **Shelburne**: *Shelburne Museum*; **Swanton**: *Missisquoi Wildlife Refuge*.

Tour 5 (Mad River Valley Region) From Middlesex

Approximately 113 miles (182km).

Middlesex to Moretown via Vermont 100B; Moretown to Northfield Falls via unmarked road; Northfield Falls to Roxbury via Vermont 12 and Vermont 12A; Roxbury to East Warren via unmarked road; East Warren to Moretown via unmarked roads; Moretown to Sugarbush Access Road via Vermont 100; return to Vermont 17 via Sugarbush Ski Area and unmarked roads; Vermont 17 west for 8 miles (13km) and north on unmarked roads through Huntington Center and Huntington to Richmond; Richmond to Waterbury via US2; Waterbury to South Duxbury via Vermont 100; South Duxbury to Middlesex via Vermont 100 and Vermont 100B. Points of interest along the way: **Northfield**: *Norwich University Museum*; **Roxbury**: *Vermont State Fish Hatchery*; **Waterbury Center**: *Ben & Jerry's Ice Cream Factory, Cold Hollow Cider Mill*.

Tour 6 (Lamoille Region) From Stowe
Approximately 125 miles (201km).
North on Vermont 100, 2 miles (3km) take left fork (6 miles/10km to stop sign), left 8 miles (13km) to road end, turn right for 1/2 mile (1km) to Johnson; turn right onto Vermont 15, 6 miles (10km) to Vermont 100; turn right and follow Vermont 100 signs to blinker in Morrisville; turn left onto Vermont 12, 6 miles (10km) to Lake Elmore; turn left onto dirt road marked Wolcott; 4 miles (6km) to Vermont 15, turn left for 1 mile (2km), take first right turn 8 miles (13km), turn left just past cemetery to Gulf sign, left again 7 miles (11km) to Eden Mills; left onto Vermont 100, 1 mile (2km); turn right onto Vermont 118 to Vermont 109 to Waterville; turn onto second left in Waterville 5 miles (8km), to Vermont 15, sharp right onto Vermont 15 for 20 miles (32km) to Underhill Flats; left turn to Pleasant Valley Road for 10 miles (16km), right onto paved road 4 miles (6km) to Jeffersonville; right on Vermont 108, 18 miles (29km) to Stowe. Points of interest along the way: **Lake Elmore State Park**; **Stowe**: *Moss Glen & Bingham Falls, Alpine Slide, Mount Mansfield Gondola and Toll Road*; Route 108 through Smugglers' Notch.

Further Information

Green Mountain National Forest

PO Box 519, Rutland, Vermont 05702 ☎ (802) 773-0300.

Sugarbush Chamber of Commerce

PO Box 173, Waitsfield, Vermont 05673 ☎ (802) 496-3409.

Vermont Department of Forests, Parks and Recreation

103 South Main Street, Waterbury, Vermont 05761-0601 ☎ (802) 241-3655.

Vermont Department of Travel and Tourism, 134 State Street, Montpelier, Vermont 05602 ☎ 1-800-VERMONT.

Accommodation

The following Hotels (H) and Restaurants ® are recommended. A general price indicator is given: $ inexpensive, $$ medium, $$$ expensive. * denotes an historic inn or hotel.

Alburg
* *Ransom Bay Inn B&B*, 57 Center Bay Rd. ☎ (802) 796-3399 $
* *Thomas Mott Homestead B&B*, Blue Rock Rd. ☎ (802) 796-3736 $
Ue Olde Graystone B&B, US2. ☎ (802) 796-3911 $

Arlington
* *Arlington Inn*, Route 7A. ☎ (802) 375-6532 $$

Barre
* *Country House Restaurant*, 276 N. Main St. ☎ (802) 476-4282 $$
Hollow Inn, 278 S. Main St. ☎ (802) 479-9313 $$

Bennington
Bennington Station ®, 150 Depot St. ☎ (802) 447-1080 $$
Catamount Motel, 500 South St. ☎ (802) 442-5977 $
Darling Kell's Motel, Route 7 South. ☎ 802) 442-2322 $
* *Four Chimney's Inn*, 21 West Rd. ☎ (802) 447-3500 $$
Paradise Motor Inn, 141 W. Main St. ☎ (802) 442-8351 $-$$
* *South Shire Inn B&B*, 124 Elm St. ☎ (802) 447-3839 $$
Paradise Restaurant, 141 W. Main St. ☎ (802) 442-5418 $$

Brattleboro
Days Inn, Putney Rd. ☎ (802) 254-4583 $

Burlington
Handy's Town House Motel, 1330 Shelburne Rd. ☎ (802) 862-9608 $
Holiday Inn, 1068 Williston Rd. ☎ (802) 863-6363 $$
The Ice House ®, 171 Battery St. ☎ (802) 864-1800 $$
Sweetwaters ®, 120 Church St. ☎ (802) 864-9800 $$
Vermont Pasta Restaurant, 156 Church St. ☎ (802) 658-2575 $$

Chester
* *The Chester House B&B*, Main St. ☎ (802) 875-2205 $
* *Stone Hearth Inn*, SR11. ☎ (802) 875-2525 $-$$

Danby
* *Silas Griffith Inn*, South Main St. ☎ (802) 293-5567 $$

Danville
* *Danville Inn B&B*, Main St. ☎ (802) 684-3484 $
The Creamery ® , Hill St. ☎ (802) 684-3616 $$
* *Raspberry Patch B&B*, Pecham Rd. ☎ (802) 684-3971 $

Dorset
* *Barrows House Inn*, SR30. ☎ (802) 867-4455 $$-$$$
* *Cornucopia of Dorset B&B*, SR30. ☎ (802) 867-5753 $$-$$$
* *Inn at West View Farm*, SR30. ☎ (802) 867-5715 $$

Essex Junction
The Inn at Essex, 70 Essex Way. ☎ (802) 878-1100 $$-$$$
Fairhaven
* *Maplewood Inn B&B*, SR22A south. ☎ (802) 265-8039 $$
* *Vermont Marble Inn*, 121 W. Park Place. ☎ (802) 265-8383 $$-$$$
Grafton
* *Old Tavern*, SR121. ☎ (802) 843-2231 $$-$$$
Killington
Back Behind Saloon Restaurant, West Bridgewater. ☎ (802) 422-9907 $$
The Cascades Lodge, Killington Rd. Off SR4. ☎ (802) 422-3731 $$
Edelweiss Motel & Chalets, US4. ☎ (802) 775-5577 $
Greenbrier Inn, US4. ☎ (802) 775-1575 $$
Grey Bonnet Inn, SR100 North. ☎ (802) 775-2537 $-$$
* *The Vermont Inn*, US4. ☎ (802) 775-0708 $$-$$$
Ludlow
* *Andrie Rose Inn B&B*, 13 Pleasant St. ☎ (802) 228-4846 $$-$$$
Combes Family Inn, SR100. ☎ (802) 228-8799 $-$$
Timber Inn Motel, Main St. ☎ (802) 228-8666 $
Manchester Center
Aspen Motel, SR7A. ☎ (802) 362-2450 $-$$
Barnstead Innstead, SR30. ☎ (802) 362-1619 $-$$
Manchester View Motel, SR7A. ☎ (802) 362-2739 $-$$$
Palmer House Resort Motel, SR7A. ☎ (802) 362-3600 $-$$
Sirloin Saloon, Dept St. ☎ (802) 362-2600 $$
* *Ye Olde Tavern* ®, US7. ☎ (802) 362-3770 $$
Manchester Village
* *Colonade* ®, SR7A. ☎ (802) 362-4700 $$$
* *Reluctant Panther Inn*, West Rd. ☎ (802) 362-2568 $$$
Middlebury
The Middlebury Inn, Court Sq. ☎ (802) 388-4961 $-$$
* *Swift House Inn*, 25 Stewart Lane. ☎ (802) 388-9925 $-$$
Montpelier
* *The Inn at Montpelier*, 147 Main St. ☎ (802) 223-2727 $$
Tubbs Restaurant, 24 Elm St. ☎ (802) 229-9202 $$
Newbury
* *A Century Past B&B*, US5. ☎ (802) 866-3358 $
Newfane
* *Four Columns Inn*, 230 West St. ☎ (802) 365-7713 $$$
Northfield
Northfield Inn, 27 Highland Ave. ☎ (802) 485-8558 $-$$
North Hero
* *North Hero House Inn*, SR2. ☎ (802) 372-8237 $-$$

Perkinsville
* *The Inn at Weathersfield*, SR106. ☎ (802) 263-9217 $$-$$$
Plymouth
Hawk Inn, SR100. ☎ (802) 672-3811 $$-$$$
Proctorsville
* *The Golden Stage Inn*, SR103. ☎ (802) 226-7744 $$-$$$
Quechee
* *Quechee B&B*, 753 Woodstock Rd. ☎ (802) 295-1776 $$
* *Quechee Inn* at Marshland Farm, Club House Rd. ☎ (802) 295-3133
    $$-$$$
Rutland
Best Western Hogge Penny Inn, US4. ☎ (802) 773-3200 $-$$
Holiday Inn, 411 S. Main St. ☎ (802) 775-1911 4-$$
South Station Restaurant, 170 S. Main St. ☎ (802) 775-1736 $$
St Johnsbury
Fairbanks Motor Inn, 32 Western Ave. ☎ (802) 748-5666 $
* *Looking Glass Inn*, SR18. ☎ (802) 748-3052 $
Lincoln Inn ®, 20 Hastings St. ☎ (802) 748-5107 $$
Shelburne
Shelburne Travelodge, 1907 Shelburne Rd. ☎ (802) 985-8037 $
South Burlington
Comfort Inn, 1285 Williston Rd. ☎ (802) 865-3400 $
Pauline's ®, 1834 Shelburne Rd. ☎ (802) 862-1081 $$-$$$
Ramada Inn, 1117 Williston Rd. ☎ (802) 658-0250
Windjammer ®, 1076 Williston Rd. ☎ (802) 862-6585 $$
Springfield
* *Hartness House Inn*, 30 Orchard St. ☎ (802) 885-2115 $$
Stowe
Alpine Motor Lodge, SR108. ☎ (802) 253-7700 $$-$$$
Buccaneer Country Lodge, 3214 Mountain Rd. ☎ (802) 253-4772 $-$$
Butternut Inn at Stowe, 2309 Mountain Rd. ☎ (802) 253-4277 $$
Copperfields Restaurant, Ye Olde England Inn, 433 Mountain Rd.
    ☎ (802) 253-7558 $$
Edson Hill Manor, 1500 Edson Hill Rd. ☎ (802) 253-7371 $$-$$$
Edson Hill Manor Restaurant, Edson Hill Rd. ☎ (802) 253-7371 $$
* *Green Mountain Inn*, Main St. ☎ (802) 253-7301 $$-$$$
Inn at the Brass Lantern B&B, 717 Maple St. ☎ (802) 253-2229 $$
Snowdrift Motel, 2135 Mountain Rd. ☎ (802) 253-7305 $-$$
* *Ten Acres Lodge*, 14 Barrows Rd. ☎ (802) 253-7638 $$

Waitsfield

Inn at Round Basin Farm B&B, E. Warren Rd. ☎ (802) 496-2276 $$-$$$
Mad River Inn B&B, Tremblay Rd. ☎ (802) 496-7900 $-$$
Newtons' 1824 House Inn B&B, SR100. ☎ (802) 496-7555 $$
Tucker Hill Lodge Dining Room, SR17. ☎ (802) 496-3983 $$

Waterbury

Inn at Blush Hill B&B, Blush Hill Rd. ☎ (802) 244-7529 $-$$

West Brattleboro

Dalem's Chalet Motel, 16 South St. ☎ (802) 254-4323 $
Jolly Butcher's Tavern ®, SR9. ☎ (802) 254-6043 $$

West Dover

* *West Dover Inn*, SR100. ☎ (802) 464-5207 $-$$$

West Hartford

* *The Half Penney B&B*, Handy Rd. ☎ (802) 295-6082 $-$$

White River Junction

Comfort Inn, 8 Sykes Ave. ☎ (802) 295-3051 $
Howard Johnson Lodge, US5. ☎ (802) 295-3015 $-$$

Wilmington

Horizon Inn, SR9. ☎ (802) 464-2131 $-$$
* *Nutmeg Inn*, SR9. ☎ (802) 464-3351 $$-$$$
* *The White House Inn*, SR9. ☎ (802) 464-2135 $$-$$$

Woodstock

* *Deer Brook Inn*, SR4. ☎ (802) 672-3713 $-$$
* *Kedron Valley Inn*, SR106. ☎ (802) 457-1473 $$-$$$
* *Lincoln Inn at the Covered Bridge*, US4. ☎ (802) 457-3312 $-$$
Spooner's Restaurant, US4. ☎ (802) 457-1818 $$
* *The Winslow House B&B*, US4. ☎ (802) 457-1820 $-$$
* *The Woodstocker B&B*, 61 River St. ☎ (802) 457-3896 $$

New Hampshire 3

This is the 'Granite State' and the first colony to declare independence from England which has earned it
the right to hold the nation's first presidential primary in election years. New Hampshire has a small coastline but scores of fines beaches both along the Atlantic Ocean and inshore on the hundreds of lakes. There are tremendous year round outdoor activity opportunties from backpacking, camping, fishing and boating during the summer and several excellent winter resort areas.

Above all, there are hundreds of miles of uncrowded roads, more than sixty covered bridges, and scores of delightful old towns, villages and historic sites to explore.

History

Indians have lived in the area for several hundreds years and there are signs that they may have settled here as far back as 2000BC. The dominant Penacook tribe was almost all wiped out by plague in

above: The historic nineteenth-century Thayers Inn, Littleton

1617. The first known European to explore the area was Martin Pring who sailed into the Lower Piscataqua River in 1603, and Algonquian Indians inhabited the area when the first English settlers led by Captain John Mason and Sir Ferdinando Gorges, arrived to found the fishing settlement of Odiorne's Point in 1623 and later that year Dover. The area was divided in 1629 between Mason and Gorges with Mason claiming the area south of the Piscataqua and naming it New Hampshire. During this period, settlements also established at Exeter (1638), and Hampton (1639), and in 1630 the Laconia Company received a Royal land grant and established Strawbery Bank, now Portsmouth. The area came under the control of the Massachusetts Colony in 1641 and although it became a separate crown colony in 1679, boundary disputes with its neighbours and Canada were not finally settled until the Webster Ashburton Treaty of 1842.

New Hampshire was one of the most vigorous supporters of the Revolution. In December 1774 colonists seized the British Fort William and Mary (now Fort Constitution) in New Castle. Weapons captured were later used against the British at the Battle of Bunker Hill. It was the first Colony to declare its independence from Britain by establishing itself as a state in 1776 and issuing its own Declaration of Independence. In 1778, it cast the decisive vote in ratifying the US Constitution. The state has always had political influence, and in 1905 Portsmouth was chosen for the signing of the peace treaty to end the Russo-Japanese war.

In the census of 1790, the state had a population of 141,885 and it has risen every year since, except in 1870 after the Civil War when there was an exodus to the Midwest. Most of the early settlers were English followed by Scots-Irish protestants in 1719 who gave their towns names such as Derry, Antrim and Dublin. Many of their descendants still live in the original family homes. Traditional town meetings are still held annually to determine local government policy. There are also many French Canadian descendants whose forefathers came to work in the mills and factories established immediately after the Civil War. And, in the nineteenth and twentieth centuries there have been waves of immigrants from Central and Eastern Europe. Most of the population is concentrated in the south of the country and more than half live in urban areas. The state's economy formerly reliant on shoemaking, textiles and wool products, is now based on electrical goods and electronic manufacturing, farming, forestry and tourism. Dairy, fruit and vegetable farming are the main agricultural activities, while forests provide timber for wood, paper and pulp as well as maple syrup and sugar, and there is still quarrying for granite. Since the late nineteenth century New Hampshire has been among the top six most industrialised states in the union yet these industries are concentrated in certain areas, leaving an overall impression that it is unspoilt and mostly rural.

Geography

The state covers 9,279sq miles (24,052sq km) and has only a 18 mile (29km) Atlantic Ocean coastline in the south-east. It is bordered by Massachusetts to the south, Vermont on the west, Maine on the east and Quebec to the north. It is 180 miles (290km) north to south and about 90 miles (145km) east to west, and the whole state lies within the Appalachian system. It can be divided into three areas: the White Mountains occupying the northern one third of the state and rising to 6,288ft (1,917m) at Mount Washington; heavily eroded hills and lakes covering the southern two thirds of the state; and the narrow coastal plain along the Atlantic Ocean. The whole state was covered during the last ice age about 10,000 years ago, and glacial erosion largely shaped the landscape seen today.

Some State Statistics
Area: 9,304sq miles (24,116sq km)
Population: 1,109,117
Capital: Concord
Highest Point: Mount Washington 6,288ft (1,917m)
Lowest Point: Sea level
Taxes: There is no state wide sales tax, but an 8 per cent meals and rooms tax
Nickname: The Granite State
State Tree: White Birch
State Bird: Purple Finch
State Animal: White Tail Deer
State Flower: Purple Lilac
State Wildflower: Ladyslipper
State Insect: Lady Bug

Getting Around

Manchester airport is serviced by a number of major US air carriers although Boston is the most convenient international entry point. Concord Trailways operates a bus service across the state linking Boston, Manchester, Concord and smaller towns. Amtrak has a service to Vermont's White River Junction and Bellows Falls on New Hampshire's border, but does not operate in the state.

While interstate highways cross the state, one of the great pleasures of exploring New Hampshire is that you can spend so much time driving on quiet country roads along wonderfully scenic routes. Most of the railroad system has been abandoned although the 6 mile (10km) cog railway on Mount Washington, and the first of its kind, opened in 1869, and still operates during the summer. Buses and highways have taken over from the railway, and many town's have their own small airport or landing strip.

TOUR 1 • THE STATE TOUR

The route to Littleton covers 150 miles (240km). The various other options that are given after have mileages indicated.

This suggested itinerary can be followed in a number of ways depending on the time available. The main tour starts in Manchester and takes in most of the state on a circular route. It can be extended or shortened by following the alternative routes suggested. A second circular tour from Manchester which takes in the south-western corner of the state is also given.

Manchester was originally a logging camp called Derryfield, and the first cotton and wool mills were operating by 1810. Manchester rapidly developed into a major textile centre, especially after 1831 when the ailing Amoskeag Cotton and Woollen Factory was bailed out by Boston Financers and renamed the Amoskeag Manufacturing Company. It became one of the largest mills in the US producing almost 5 million yards of cloth a week and with a workforce of many thousands. By the 1920's old machinery and competition hit production and by 1935 the mills were forced to close. The mills were not abandoned, however, and a group of local businessmen bought them and converted them for other industrial uses, and Manchester is now the state's major industrial centre, as well as its largest city housing almost 10 per cent of New Hampshire's population. The fully restored 1915 Palace Theatre in Hanover Street is famous for its large space and excellent acoustics, and houses the New Hampshire Performing Arts Center. The New Hampshire Symphony, Opera League of New Hampshire, national touring companies and local community groups perform in the theater. General John Stark was born in Derryfield in 1728 and is famous as an Indian fighter. He fought the Abenaki Indians with Major William Rogers and his Rogers' Rangers, considered the forerunner of today's Army Rangers. Stark died in 1822 and is buried in Stark Park, off North River Road and overlooking the river. His childhood home is at 2000 Elm Street.

The Currier Gallery of Art, 192 Orange Street, is in a 1929 Beaux-Arts building modelled on an Italian Renaissance palace. It houses

Hood Museum of Art
Hopkinson Center for the Creative & Performing Arts

Charlestown
Fort at Number Four Living History Museum

St. Gaudens National Historic Site

Horatio Colony Wildlife Preserve
Horatio Colony House Museum

Lebanon
Claremont
Upper Shaker Village
Hanover
Mascoma

Keene
Rhododendron State Park
Newport
Enfield
Dartmouth College
Baker Memorial Library
Webster Cottage

Friendly Farm
Monadnock State Park
Sunapee

Mt Sunapee
Mt Sunapee State Park

Mary Baker Eddy Historic House
Science Center of New Hampshire

Fitzwilliam
Franklin Pierce Home
Dublin

New London
Medicine Wood

Rumney
Hebron

Rindge
Jaffrey
Peterborough Historical Society
Hillsboro
Fox State Forest
Warner
Rollins State Park
Mt Kearsarge
Paradise Point Nature Center
New found Lake
Plymouth
Polar Caves Park
Campton
Covered Bridges

Cathedral of the Pines
Peterborough

Center Sandwich

New Ipswich
Barrett House
Miller State Park

Currier Gallery of Art
Zimmerman House
Lawrence L. Lee Scouting Museum
Manchester Historic Association
Manchester Institute of Arts and Sciences

Daniel Webster's Birthplace
Franklin
Holderness
Squam Lake

Sandwich

Water Valley

Wilton
Frye's Measure Mill
Milford

Concord
Canterbury Center
Loudon
Laconia
Weirs Beach
Meredith

Castle in the Clouds
Moultonborough

Merrimack
Manchester

Shaker Village
New Hampshire International Speedway

Lake Winnipesaukee
Moultonborough Bay

Nashua
Anheuser – Busch Brewery

Pittsfield
Alton

Wolfeboro Center
Ossipee

Robert Frost Farm
Derry
White's Miniature Horse Petting Farm
Lake Wentworth

North Salem
Salem

Hampshire Pewter Co.
Libby Museum
Americana Museum

Museum of Childhood
Wakefield

American Independence Museum
Gilman Garrison House

New Market
Durham
Milton
New Hampshire Farm Museum

Exeter
Hampton Falls
Greenland
Dover
Woodman Institute

Science & Nature Center
Hampton
Newington
Portsmouth

Seabrook
Hampton Beach
North Hampton
Rye
New Castle

Tuck Memorial Museum
Fuller Gardens

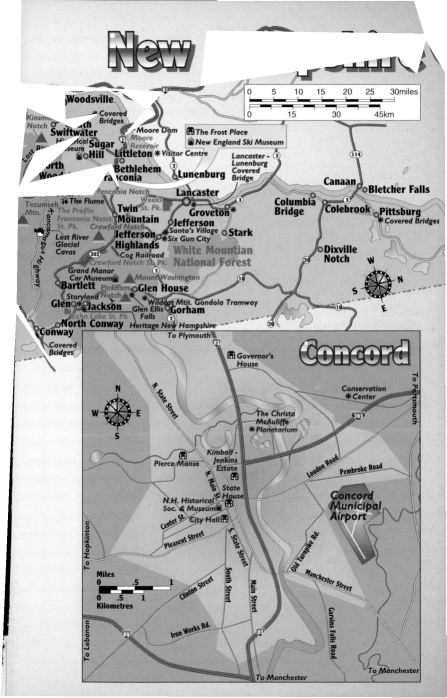

Western European paintings and sculpture from the thirteenth century, as well as American paintings, glass, silver and pewter dating from the eighteenth century. It also has a fine collection of craftsmen-made New Hampshire furniture. Open: Tuesday to Saturday 10am-4pm (to 9pm Thursday), Sunday 1-5pm. Admission free. For Zimmerman House, take the shuttle from the Currier Gallery to tour the grounds and house designed by Frank Lloyd Wright. These small and functional 'Usonian' houses were also noted for their elegance. This one was built for Isadore and Lucille Zimmerman in 1950 and completed in 1952, with original Wright furnishings and the Zimmerman's collection of African, Chinese, pre-Columbian and contemporary European and American sculpture. Open for tours: Thursday, Friday and Sunday afternoon and all day Saturday. Admission charge.

Lawrence L. Lee Scouting Museum, Camp Carpenter on Bodwell Road, has Boy Scout memorabilia dating from the late nineteenth century. The Max Silber Library has scouting periodicals, books and handbooks, including Brailie editions. Hiking and camping facilities are available. Open: daily 10am-4pm, July and August, Saturday 10am-4pm rest of year. Admission free. Manchester Historic Association, 129 Amherst Street has displays on local history, fine and decorative arts, and American Indian artifacts. Exhibits include early firefighting equipment, costumes, firearms and personal items of General John Stark. The library houses the records of the Amoskeag Manufacturing Company as well as maps, photographs and other manuscripts. Open: Tuesday to Friday 9am-4pm, Saturday 10am-4pm. Closed end of August and beginning of September. Admission free.

Manchester Institute of Arts and Sciences on Concord Street has changing exhibits on fine and applied arts, crafts and languages, plus films and concerts. Open: Monday to Saturday 9am-5pm September to June, Monday to Friday 9am-5pm rest of the year. Admission free.

From Manchester drive north on route 93 to **Concord**, capital of the state since 1808. It is a political and commercial hub and a major industrial and distribution centre. A trading post was established in 1660 on the Merrimack River, and in 1697 it was where Hannah Dustin, having been kidnapped by Penacook Indians during a raid on Haverhill in Massachusetts, scalped her sleeping captors and escaped. In 1725 settlers from Haverhill received permission to establish a settlement at Penny Crook, named after the bend in the river, and in 1765 its name was changed to Concord. The settlement prospered, largely because of good relations with the Indians, and it sent strong contingents to fight in the Revolutionary War. A plaque at the corner of Waler and Bouton Streets is where the New Hampshire Constitution was ratified on 21 June 1788. The Concord coach, with its high wheels and springy suspension, was designed here in the early 1800s and its adoption by Wells Fargo and other stage lines helped open up the west. The city has many elegant old houses and there is a charming self guiding walk through the most historic districts with their tree lined streets and parks. Details about the Coach and Eagle self guiding trail are available from the Greater Concord Chamber of Commerce, 244 North Main Street. Concord NH 03301 ☎ (603) 224-2504. The walk starts in Eagle Square marketplace, and buildings that can be seen include the 1734 Reverend Timothy Walker House, 276 North Main Street and the former Eagle Hotel and Tavern (1814-40) at 205 North Main Street now the home of the League of New Hampshire craftsmen.

Christa McAuliffe Planetarium is dedicated to America's first teacher in space who died in the 1986 *Challenger* space shuttle disaster. There is a varied programme and interactive displays. Open: Tuesday to Sunday. Admission charge ☎ (603) 271-7827 for show times.

Conservation Center, 54 Portsmouth Street has displays on energy conservation in the home and workplace, with interpretive nature trail, and cross country ski trail in the winter. Open: Monday to Friday 9am-4.30pm. Trail open: daily dawn to dusk. Admission free.

Kimball-Jenkins Estate, 266 North Main Street is in a 1877 Victorian Gothic mansion, and the home of the Kimball family for more than 200 years. Noted for its high ceilings, carved oak woodwork and panels, and furnishings. Carriage Displays has exhibitions by local artists. Open: Tuesday to Saturday 10am-4pm May to October for tours. Admission charge and reservations required ☎ (603) 225-3932.

The New Hampshire Historical Society and Museum, Park Street, exhibits information on the state's history, old books and manuscripts, arts and crafts, and an original Concord coach. Open: Monday to Friday 9am-4.30pm, weekends 12noon-4.30pm. Donations.

Pierce Manse, 14 Penacook Street, the home between 1842 and 1848 of President Franklin Pierce. The house was originally in Montgomery Street but carefully dismantled and rebuilt on its present site with period furnishings and family memorabilia. Open: Monday to Friday 11am-3pm, mid-June to early September. Admission charge.

State House, Main Street, is the country's oldest state house built in Concord granite and Vermont marble in 1819, with the legislature

Some of the old mills from the nineteenth century when Manchester was the country's major cotton and wool centre

The Manchester Institute of Arts and Sciences has exhibits of fine and applied arts, crafts and languages

Concorde's State House is the oldest in the country still in use. It was built in 1819

Concorde's Memorial Arch was built in 1891 to honour the soldiers and sailors of New Hampshire

still meeting in the original chambers. The neo-Classical building dominates the state house plaza. It is worth reading the many plaques in the plaza detailing historic sites and events. The Memorial Arch was built in 1891 to honour the state's soldiers and sailors. The State House contains almost 200 portraits of the state's most famous residents as well as the Hall of Flags. Four murals by Barry Faulkner adorn the Senate chamber. Open: Monday to Friday 8am-4.30pm. Admission free.

Now head west on 89. **Warner** is about 17 miles (27km) from Concord just to the north of the highway. It is an old farming village with some buildings dating back to the late 1700s, and the home of three state governors. Visit Mount Kearsarge Indian Museum, Kearsarge Mountain Road, with video, displays and artifacts showing the culture and history of the American Indian. Neighbouring Medicine Woods has a walking tour among plants, shrubs and trees used by the Indians for food and medicines. Open: Monday to Saturday 10am-5pm, Sunday 1-5pm May to October, weekends 1-5pm November to late December. Admission charge.

Rollins State Park, is 4 miles (6km) north off SR103. There is a scenic drive up Mount Kearsarge but the final $^1/_2$ mile (1km) to the 2,937ft (895m) summit has to be done on foot. Open: daily 9am-8pm early May to mid-October. Admission charge.

Continue to **New London** with its fine main street with Colonial homes and the brick buildings of Colby-Sawyer College. The town's economy largely relies on the college and the nearby King Ridge ski area. The Barn Playhouse presents a summer season in the refurbished 1820s barn on Main Street.

Continue to Lebanon where you make a short detour north on route 4 to **Enfield**, founded in 1782 by two Shaker brothers from Mount Lebanon, New York. The settlement was in wooded hills close to the eastern shore of Lake Mascoma, and as Enfield, it was one of nineteen Shaker communities throughout the US. In 1792 the village moved to the west side of the lake, and is now part of La Salette Shrine and Center. There were 330 Shakers in Enfield in the 1850s, but numbers declined after the Civil War and the last 10 members moved to the Canterbury community in 1923. La Salette Shrine and Center, SR4A, is a replica of the Marian Shrine of the Blessed Virgin Mary at La Salette, France, with Rosary Pond, Peace Walk and Stations of the Cross. Grounds open: daily 24 hours. Special Christmas lighting mid-December to January. Admission free.

The Shaker Museum at **Lower Shaker Village**, off SR4A is a restored eighteenth-century Enfield Shaker village with self-guiding walking tour, herb and vegetable garden, cemetery, barn, church, mill, 1854 cow barn, laundry, dairy complex and museum with Shaker artifacts. Artists demonstrate Shaker crafts. Open: Monday to Saturday 10am-5pm, Sunday 12noon-5pm, June to mid-October. Saturday 10am-4pm, Sunday 12noon-4pm rest of year. Admission charge.

Return to highway 89 and then take highway 120 north-west to **Hanover** on the Connecticut River. It was chosen by the Reverend Eleazar Wheelock as the home of Dartmouth College, a school to spread Christian education to the Abenaki Indians and other youth. When he arrived the farming village had twenty families. Today Dartmouth College is one of the nation's eight Ivy League institutions and the most northerly. Founded in 1769, the school's first classroom was a log hut built by the Reverend Wheelock in 1770. The campus now boasts many fine Colonial and modern structures, especially on Dartmouth Row with its four classroom buildings, the oldest dating from 1784. The Thompson Arena and the Leverone Fieldhouse was designed by Pier Luigi Nervi noted for his use of arches in building.

Baker Memorial Library on the north end of the Green, is housed in a 1928 Georgian building and contains nearly 2 million volumes and huge murals by Mexican artist Jose Clemenle Orozco telling the story of civilization on the American continents. Open: daily 8am-midnight (library 8am-8pm, murals 8am-5pm during campus holidays). Admission free. Hood Museum of Art, on the south side of the Green, with ancient Asian, European, early American art and silver, Abenaki Indian and African art, and twentieth-century works including Picasso in ten galleries. Open: Tuesday to Saturday 10am-5pm, Sunday 12noon-5pm. Admission free. Hopkinson Center for the Creative and Performing Arts, next to the Hood Museum and Wallace Harrison's prototype for his Metropolitan Opera House in New York. It stages theatre, music, film, art and dance. Building open daily 7.30am-11pm. Admission free ☎ (603) 646-2422 for performance times and prices. Webster Cottage, built in 1780, was the home of Daniel Webster while an undergraduate. Open: Wednesday and weekends 2.30-4.30pm. May to October. Admission free.

Follow highway 10 along the eastern banks of the river through Oxford to Woodsville and the Haverhill-Bath covered bridge on highway 135, a quarter of a mile north of route 302. It was built in 1827 and is the oldest 'authenticated' bridge in the state, spanning the Ammonoosuc River where it runs into the Connecticut River. It is a two span Town lattice design held together with wooden pins. It is 278ft (85m) long and used to be a favourite spot for professional

Enfield, the site of one of the first Shaker settlements on the shores of Lake Mascoma

A self guiding walking tour takes in the twelve historic sites in downtown Littleton

left: Enfield's attractive Lutheran church

salmon fishermen whose catches were salted down and shipped all over the US.

❋ Then take highway 302/10 towards Bath. After about 2 miles (3km) there is a turning off on the right for **Swiftwater** with an 1849 covered bridge spanning the wild Ammonoosuc River. It is 174ft (53m) long and 20ft (6m) wide and has a Paddleford truss with arches added in later years.

Bath is noted for its 400ft (122m) long covered bridge on route 302, built in 1832 and spanning the Ammonoosuc River. The bridge is 24ft (7m) wide with a 4ft (1m) walkway and supported by three stone tiers. Horses were banned for a time for fear that vibrations from their trotting would cause the bridge to collapse.

Keep north and about 5 (8km) miles north of Lisbon you can detour east to visit **Sugar Hill**, formerly a hunting ground of the Abenaki Indians in the middle of the White Mountains. The first settlers farmed but mining and forestry quickly took over. The railroad carried minerals and timber out and visitors in, and by the end of the nineteenth century it was a popular summer resort. Sugar

🏛 Hill Historical Museum has local history exhibits from the time of the first settlers to the present. Displays include blacksmiths, stage-coach tavern kitchen, maps, old photographs and collection of horse drawn vehicles, including a piano box sleigh owned by Bette Davis. Open: Thursday and weekends 1-4pm July to mid-October, or by appointment. Admission charge.

Then continue north to **Littleton**. Before the Civil War Littleton was a station on the branch of the underground railroad that led north to Vermont and Canada, and is now a resort centre and stopover for travellers heading for the White Mountains. The Ammonoosuc River drops 235ft (72m) as it travels through the town. This was harnessed to provide water power for manufacturing industry. The Moore hydro-electric plant on the Connecticut River, 8 miles (13km) west on SR18, now provides the town's power.

❋ There is a visitor centre by the **Moore Reservoir** open: daily 9am-5pm early May to early October. There is a self-guiding walk with free leaflet describing the twelve historic sites along Littleton's Main Street. The leaflet is available Monday to Friday 9am-5pm from the Littleton Area Chamber of Commerce, 141 Main Street, Littleton, NH 03561.

From Littleton there are three options:
Option 1 (95 miles/153km)
To head north, take route 116 through Whitefield to **Lancaster**, a delightful town settled in 1764 with many beautiful old homes. It was the first town in northern New Hampshire, and quickly developed as a trading centre at the confluence of the Israel and Connecticut rivers, with the jagged Pilot Range as a backdrop to the northeast, and Presidential Range to the south-east.

The covered bridge on Mechanic Street was built in 1862 over the Israel River and is 108ft (33m) long. When first built it was forbidden to cross the bridge faster than a walking pace under penalty of a fine. The Lancaster-Lunenburg covered bridge is west of highway 135, 5 miles (8km) west of Lancaster. Built in 1911, it replaced the original washed away by floods in 1905. The 288ft (88m) long bridge was the first toll bridge between South Lancaster, New Hampshire and Lunenburg, Vermont. **Weeks State Park** covers an area of 430 acres (172 hectares) and is 2 miles (3km) south on US3. This was the mountaintop summer home of John Wingate Weeks, former secretary of war and author of the legislation that led to the establishment of the Eastern national forests. The stone and stucco mansion has exhibits and political mementos. There is a stone observation tower giving views of Mount Washington and the Presidential Range to the east and the Green Mountains in Vermont to the west. A free lecture series is held on Thursday evenings during July and August. Open: Wednesday to Sunday 10am-6pm mid-June to early September, weekends 10am-6pm May to mid-June and early September to October. Admission charge.

You can detour east along route 115A to **Jefferson**, a scenic summer resort on the side of Mount Starr King, known locally as Jefferson Hill, with spectacular views. A plaque just west on US2 is to the memory of inventor and pioneer aeronaut Thaddeus S.C. Lowe, born nearby in 1823. During the Civil War he operated a Union balloon force and later invented a number of atmospheric observation and metallurgical processing devices. Santa's Village, 1 mile (2km) north-west on US2, set in woods with ponds, animal enclosures, reindeer, yule log flume, roller coasters, monorail, shows and more. Open: daily 9.30am-6.30pm June to early September, weekends 9.30am-5pm early September to October. Admission charge. **Six Gun City**, on US2, has been reconstructed as a frontier town with thirty-five restored buildings including church, schoolhouse and blacksmiths. The Carriage and Sleigh Museum has more than 100 horse-drawn vehicles and antiques, plus rides and shows.

Groveton covered bridge, one of the many spendid covered bridges in the state

Balsams resort at Dixville Notch looks over Lake Gloriette and 15,000 acres (6,000 hectares) of year-round recreational land

Mount Washington
soars over 6,288ft
(1,917m) to its
snow-capped peak

Moose frequently graze
by the roadside in
summer and are a hazard

The Miniature Diamond B Ranch features miniature animals. Open: daily 9am-6pm mid-June to early September, weekends 9am-5pm early September to October. Admission free. To the south-east is Jefferson Highlands and the gateway to Jefferson Notch.

You can continue north on route 3 from Lancaster. The road runs to **Groveton** with its 136ft (41m) long covered bridge east of route 3 was originally built in 1852 spanning the Upper Ammonoosuc River. The new road was built around it in 1939 to preserve it, and the bridge was rebuilt between 1964 and 1965 and is for passenger only traffic now.

From Groveton there is an 8 mile (13km) detour east on 110 to **Stark**. The covered bridge north-west of highway 110 spans the Upper Ammonoosuc River although when the original was built is not known. It was reconstructed in 1949. It used to be supported by a central pier but during a flood the bridge was swept off. Luckily it got caught in nearby weeds and the townspeople were able to retrieve it but rather than rely on the single central pier, they built a series of arches, which were finally removed in 1954.

Return to route 3 and carry on to North Stratford. About 9 miles (14km) north you reach **Columbia** with a covered bridge west of highway 153. It was built in 1912, and is the most northerly spanning the Connecticut River. It is 148ft (45m) long, and unusual in that the upstream side is open lattice halfway down while the downstream side is fully covered.

Continue to Colebrook. You can continue north the 8 miles (13km) to West Stewartson with Canaan on the opposite banks of the Connecticut River in Vermont, and Beecher Falls to the north on the boundary with Quebec.

About 10 miles (16km) miles north-east of West Stuartstown on highway 3 is **Pittsburg**, the state's most northerly community and once an independent territory called Indian Stream Republic. In the early nineteenth century Canada and the United States engaged in a bitter border dispute which left this area almost ungoverned. In 1832 the settlers had had enough. They set up their own independent republic with its own constitution, courts, council and forty man army. The Webster Ashburton treaty of 1842 resolved the border dispute, and Pittsburg, as the settlement was to be named, because part of the US. A memorial on the common records these unusual events.

There are three remaining covered bridges in Pittsburg. The Pittsburg-Clarksville covered bridge is 1 mile (2km) west of the village. Its date of construction is unknown but at 91ft (28m), it is the longest in the Pittsburg area. The Pittsburg-Happy Corner covered bridge is 1 mile (2km) south of US3 and 6 miles (10km) north-east of the village spanning Perry Stream. It is 86ft (26m) long. The Pittsbury-River Road covered bridge is just over 5 miles (8km) north-east of the village, and with a length of 57ft (17m) is one of the smallest covered bridges in the state.

Return to Colebrook, then take highway 26 to **Dixville Notch**, the most northerly and wildest of the glacially erdoded notches in the White Mountains. Route 26 crosses the north from Colebrook to Errol and offers breathtaking scenery with Lake Gloriette and Cathedral Spires, Cascades, and Table Rock. Most of the area is within the Dixville Notch State Park. Lake Gloriette is home of the Balsams Resort and covers 15,000 acres (6,000 hectares) of recreational land offering year round activities and including the Balsams Wilderness ski area.

Continue to Errol, then south on highway 16 with the **White Mountain National Forest** to the west. This huge 770,000 acre (308,000 hectare) mountainous area is known both for its scenic beauty and outstanding opportunities for outdoor activities. Mount Washington 6,288ft (1,917m) is the tallest peak in the Presidential Range and the tallest mountain in the US north-east. Mounts Adams, Jefferson, Madison and Monroe are all over 5,000ft (1,5254m). Many of the mountains are named after famous Indian chiefs, such as Passaconaway, who united seventeen tribes into the Penacook Confederacy in the mid-1600s. Kancamagus was Passaconaway's grandson, and the last 'sagamore' (great chief) of the Confederacy.

When the first settlers arrived in the White Mountains, the area was inhabited by Indians, notably the Abenaki, Sokosis and Pennacock tribes, and today many of the park's other most famous features still bear their traditional names. Some of these names are Ammonoosuc (Fish-Place), Pemigewasset (Swift Water), Abenaki (Land of the Dawn), Agiochook (Place of the Great Spirit), Connecticut (Long River), Jearsage (High Place), Umbagog (Clear Water), and Waumbek (Snowy Mountains).

The area is noted for its many 'notches', huge passes carved out by ice funnelled between granite-resistant mountains. The national forest, which extends into Maine, is popular year round and can be busy at times. There is excellent skiing in the winter, world class trout fishing in the summer, and a vast 1,200 mile (1,932km) network of hiking trails including a section of the long distance Appalachian Trail which stretches 2,135 miles (3,437km) from Georgia to Maine. Several areas, such as the Great Gulf Wilderness, can only be reached on foot. More than 8sq miles (21sq km) of the park are above the tree line.

Visitor centres at Lincoln, Campton and the Saco Ranger Station in Conway, are generally open daily. For further information contact: White Mountain National Forest, PO Box 638, Laconia NH 03247. There are also ranger stations in Bethlehem, Gorham, Bethel and Plymouth. Both visitor centres and ranger stations have leaflets with maps about hiking in their area, with walks lasting from an hour to all day and all graded according to difficulty.

There are 21 large campgrounds with facilities and accessible by car, and around 60 undeveloped walk-in campsites in the national forest, including Camp 13 off Franconia Brook Trail, Ethan Pond Shelter, Franconia Brook, Garfield Ridge, Hermit Lake Shelters, Liberty Springs, and Mizpah Tentsites.

High temperatures in the summer and low winter temperatures can lead to heat stroke and hypothermia respectively and backpackers should take frequent rests when walking at altitude. Bears can also be a problem in the area, should be avoided, and foodstuffs kept out of their reach and away from your camp.

Mount Washington is in the Presidential Range of the White Mountains, and the north-east's highest peak at 6,288ft (1,917m). The weather at its summit can rival Antarctica, and average annual temperatures are below freezing with an average 15ft (4m) of snow in the winter. The highest wind speed ever recorded was 231 miles per hour (372km per hour) in April 1934. Conditions can change in minutes although summer temperatures can rise to the low 70s and the views from the summit on clear days make the ascent worthwhile.

Mount Washington Auto Road leaves SR16 at Glen House, about 8 miles (13km) south of Gorham. Allow about 45 minutes each way. There are frequent lay-bys with water for overheating engines. Use low gear for both ascent and descent, as the road is very steep with hairpin bends. Campers and trailers are not allowed. There are tours with a 30 minute stay on the summit for those not wishing to drive up. Road open: daily 7.30am-6pm mid-June to early September, hours vary at other times depending on weather.

Sherman Adams Summit Building, named after a former State Governor, offers a 360 degree view of the northern Presidential Range. At the end of the nineteenth century there were so many buildings on the summit, it was known as 'the city among the clouds.' A fire in 1908 destroyed most of the buildings, but the 1853 Top House has been restored. It was the first hotel on Mount Washington, and is one of the oldest mountain buildings in the US. The summit can be reached on foot, by car and by cog railway, and the Summit Building has an information centre and museum with exhibits about the weather, geology and animal and plan life unique to the mountain. Open: daily 8am-8pm. May to early October weather permitting. Museum admission charge.

The Kancamagus Highway on SR112, offers one of the region's most scenic drives. From Conway it takes in the Swift River Valley, Rocky Gorge scenic area, the old logging village of Passaconaway, the Sabbaday Falls (at the end of a 15 minute path) Kancamagus Pass and Pemigewasset Valley. There are many turn offs, picnic spots and campsites along the 34 mile (55km) route, with many hiking trails leading off from it.

There are also many less travelled roads, known as 'Shunpikes" which travel through the forest and are ideal for fall foliage tours, and the White Mountains area boasts twenty-six covered bridges.

Continue south on highway 16 past **Pinkham Notch**. This ice-carved notch on the eastern fringes of the White Mountains runs between the Presidential Range to the west and Mounts Moriah, North Carter and Carter Dome to the east. The notch is named after Joseph Pinkham, who allegedly hauled his possessions on a sledge drawn by pigs. The route that he followed is now the scenic 16 which crosses the pass between Jackson and Gorham. For part of the route the road follows the Ellis River and the Tuckerman Ravine Trail leads past the Glen Ellis Falls and Crystal Cascades. The ravine's west wall is suitable only for the most experienced skiers.

Wildcat Mountain Gondola Tramway, climbs more than 4,000ft (1,219m) from Pinkham Notch to the top of Wildcat Mountain. The ascent takes around 12 minutes and there are spectacular views over the White Mountains from the summit. There are also hiking trails and winter skiing. Open: daily 10am-4.15pm July to early October, weekends 10am-4pm, May to June. Admission charge.

Glen makes a good base for visiting both Franconia and Pinkham notches, and popular year round because of summer walking and winter skiing.

The **Grand Manor Car Museum**, 3 miles (5km) north at SR16 and US302, houses vintage and antique cars and motoring memorabilia. Open: daily 9.30am-5pm June to early September, weekends 9:30am-5pm May and October. Admission charge.

Heritage-New Hampshire, SR16, uses audiovisual techniques to help trace more than 300 years of New Hampshire history, from 1634 with a voyage on a sailing ship to the New World. There is also a simulated train ride through Crawford Notch. Open: daily 9am-6pm mid-June to early September, 9am-5pm mid-May to mid-June and early September to mid-October. Admission charge.

✳ **Storyland**, on SR16 brings children's fairy tales to life with pirate ship, polar coaster and raft rides, African safaris and water flume rides. Open: daily 9am-6pm mid-June to early September, weekend 10am-5pm early September to October. Admission charge. From Glen the route rejoins the main itinerary.

Option 2 (125 miles/201km)
Return to Manchester along scenic highway 3 south back through the White Mountains via **North Woodstock**, a year round resort village offering many scenic drives and hiking trails. This is a good base for exploring Franconia to the north and the Kancamagus Highway with the Lost River Glacial Caves, off route 112. There are trails above and below ground. Open: daily May to late October weather permitting. Admission charge.

✳ You can continue south on highway 3 all the way back to Manchester. This route takes in **Lincoln** at the western end of the Kancamagus Highway, one of the state's most popular scenic drives. With North Woodstock, its sister community across the Pemigewasset River, Lincoln is a popular resort town and base for those exploring the area. The New Hampshire Highland Games, held in mid-September, feature Scottish athletic games, country dancing, pipe bands and competitions. The League of New Hampshire Craftsmen are on route 112 and this and other shops around the state offer a wide range of handmade goods from rocking chairs and sweaters to stained glass and paintings.

✳ **Clark's Trading Post**, 1 mile (2km) north on US3, has the Pemigewasset Hook and Ladder Fire House with old fire fighting equipment, Clark's Museum featuring early cameras, typewriters, guns and toys, the Americana Museum and a number of other attractions, including rides on the White Mountain Central Railroad. Open: daily 9am-5.45pm mid-May to mid-October. Amusements and rides daily 10.30am-4.30pm July to early September, weekends 10.30am-4.30pm May and June and early September to mid-October. Admission charge.

✳ **Hobo Railroad**, off I-93 exit 32 on SR112, offers one hour narrated rides along the Pemigewasset River, and includes a stop at the Swimming Hole Bridge. Trips depart daily at 11am, 1, 3, 5 and 7pm July to early September, daily at 11am and 1pm in June, weekends at 11am and 1pm in May. Admission charge. Allow 2 hours.

♣ **Loon Mountain Park**, off the Kancamagus Highway, is reached by four passenger gondola which climbs 7,000ft (2,134m) to the
🌲 summit, offering spectacular panoramas of the White Mountain National Forest. There are hiking and nature trails, including glacial

caves, in the summer and skiing over the winter. There are pony rides, petting zoo, horseback riding and mountain bike trails. Gondola operates Monday to Saturday 9am-5pm, Sunday 8.30am-5pm. Admission charge.

Whales' Tale Waterpark, US3, has water slides and rides. Open: daily 10am-6pm mid-June to early September. Admission charge.

On the western side of route 3 is **Kinsman Notch** discovered by Asa Kinsman after taking a wrong turn while travelling to take up a land grant at Landaff. Rather than turn back he and his wife and two Woodstock townsmen literally hacked their way through the wooded mountain pass, which runs between Mount Moosilauke and Kinsman Range. The pass was shaped during the last Ice Age. Huge granite boulders on the north face, weakened by ice, crashed down into **Lost River Gorge** forming the high sided narrow passages in which the river gets lost. The river, 6 miles (10km) west of North Woodstock on SR112, is full of giant boulders, and caves and potholes carved by the ice. The largest pothole is 25ft (7m) across and 60ft (18m) deep. The river often disappears underground as it crashes through the gorge, emerging at the bottom to form Paradise Falls. There is a self guiding walk with bridges and ladders, which includes wriggling through the Lemon Squeezer and standing under the Guillotine, an appropriately named rock formation. The cavern trip, which can be by passed, takes about 1 hour, and stout footwear is essential. Open: daily 9am-6pm June to August, 9am-5pm, mid- to end May, September and October. Admission charge.

Lost River Nature Garden has more than 300 labelled varieties of native plants, shrubs, ferns and mosses. Flowers bloom June through September. Open: daily 9am-4.30pm.

You can take the mountain road east from Woodstock to visit **Waterville Valley**, a year round White Mountains resort surrounded by magnificent 4,000ft (1,219m) peaks. There is alpine skiing at Mount Tecumseh and Snow Mountain and many miles of excellent cross country ski trails. Mountain biking, horseback riding, fishing, swimming, boating and hiking are popular summer activities. The town hosts the Waterville Valley Music Festival in July and August with contemporary music and jazz.

The road then runs south to **Campton** which has three covered bridges in the area. The Campton-Blair bridge is the oldest and longest, 2 miles (3km) north of Livermore Falls and built in 1828 across the Pemigewasset River. It is 300ft (91m) long. It is said that the bridge was built after the town doctor was almost drowned trying to cross the river one stormy night. His horse was not so lucky and was washed away. The Campton-Turkey Jim's bridge is $^1/_2$ mile

(1km) east on US3. Built in 1883 it is 60ft (18m) long and crosses West Branch Brook. Its real name is Stevens Bridge, but is better known as Turkey Jim's because it connected an island turkey farm with the mainland. Hundreds of the turkeys drowned in a 1927 flood. Campton-Bump bridge is 1 mile (2km) east at Campton Hollow. Built in 1887 it crosses the Beebe River and is unusual in that it sits on 'horses' rather than stone foundations, and that the clapboards run lengthwise instead of vertically.

From Campton you can make a detour east into the mountains to visit **Center Sandwich**, the main village of the Sandwich region, close to the eastern end of Squam Lake and south of the Sandwich Mountains, and a farming community, crafts centre and tourist area. Poet John Greenleaf Whitter wrote about 'sunset on the Bearcamp', the river between Center Sandwich and North Sandwich. Sandwich Historical Society Museums are at the junctions of SR109 and SR113 in a 1849 house with changing local history exhibits and Americana. The Quimby Barn Museum has a replica of a country store and old farm tools. Open: Tuesday to Saturday 11am-5pm mid-June to September. Donations. You can then take route 109 south to **Moultonborough** at the northern end of Moultonborough Bay, part of Lake Winnipesaukee. The village's star attraction is Castle in the Clouds, on SR171. Built around the beginning of the twentieth century, the mansion is set in the Ossipee Mountains, and there is a self guiding tour covering the castle's history. Tours of the Castle Springs bottling plant are also available. Open: daily 10am-5pm mid-June to early September, daily 10am-4pm early September to mid-October. Weekends 10am-5pm late May to mid-June. Admission charge. You can follow 109 south along the shore of the lake to the popular summer resort of **Wolfeboro.** In 1768 John Wentworth, governor of Massachusetts made history by building a summer home on the lake. It was the first summer home in the US and it established Wolfeboro as a fashionable resort. A plaque in Wentworth State Park, 6 miles (10km) east on SR109, commemorates the house which burned down in 1820. There are now scores of summer houses and estates along the shore of Lake Wentworth and neighbouring Lake Winnipesaukee. There are sightseeing cruises on the lake. The Hampshire Pewter Company, 9 Mill Street, still uses traditional sixteenth century techniques to produce fine pewter ware. Open: tours Monday to Friday 9am-3pm late May to October, and by appointment. Admission free ☎ (603) 569-4944. The Libby Museum on SR109, displays exhibits about the local history and natural history of the town and area, with mounted animals, Indian artifacts, early tools and household effects. Open: Tuesday to Sunday 10am-4pm late May to mid-September. Admission charge. The

Wolfeboro Americana Museum, Main Street, has the 1868 Pleasant ![icon]
Valley Schoolhouse, Firehouse Museum, and Clark House, a Colonial farmhouse with period furnishings. Open: Monday to Saturday
10am-4pm July to early September. Donations. You can then cir-
cumnavigate the lake via Alton and Meredith where you take route

Daniel Webster's Birthplace near Franklin

*The Polar Caves at Plymouth were formed by glacial action more than
14,000 years ago*

25 west for **Holderness** and the Science Center of New Hampshire, junctions of SR3 and SR113, with nature trails and more than a dozen exhibit buildings and live animal enclosures including bears, deer, bobcats, otters and birds of prey in natural habitat settings. Open: daily 9.30am-4.30pm May to October. Admission charge.

From Holderness take route 3 to **Plymouth** with its Polar Caves Park, 5 miles (8km) west on Tenney Mountain Highway. The caves were formed by the ice cap that covered the land around 14,000 years ago. There are paths through the caves and a nature trail through the park which has exotic birds and deer. Open: daily 9am-5pm, May to mid-October. Admission charge.

An interesting detour from Plymouth is take route 25 west to Rumney Depot and then north for just under 2 miles (3km) to **Rumney**, a farming and summer resort community settled in the 1760s along Stinson Brook. The brook, nearby lake and mountain all carry the name of David Stinson, an associate of General John Stark. The Mary Baker Eddy Historic House, Stinson Lake Road, was the home of the founder of Christian Science between 1860 and 1862 who before then lived in nearby North Groton. Open: Tuesday to Saturday 10am-5pm, Sunday 2-5pm May to October. Admission charge. On the return trip turn right at West Plymouth and take the mountain road south past Tenney Mountain 2,310ft (704m) to visit the **Hebron** district around the northern part of Newfound Lake. Hebron's Paradise Point Nature Center, North Shore Road on Newfound Lake, is owned by the Audubon Society. There are live animals, day camp, evening programmes and nature trails on 43 acres (17 hectares). Open: daily 10am-5pm mid-June to early September, weekends 10am-4pm May to mid-June and early September to October. Donations.

Return to route 3 and follow it south 11 miles (18km) to take route 104 east towards Lake Winnipaukee and **Weirs Beach**, a very popular and beautiful resort on Lake Winnipesaukee with yachting, fishing, swimming and other water sports and land-based amusements. The lake's name in Indian means 'Smile of the Great Spirit'. It is the largest lake in the state with a coastline of more than 280 miles (451km) because of its many bays and inlets. Endicott Rock bears marks made by the expedition sent by Governor John Endicott to determine the northern border of the Massachusetts Colony. They actually established the border 3 miles (5km) north of the rock, and this stood until the separation of Massachusetts and New Hampshire in 1740. There are many boat cruises available on the lake leaving from the Weir Beach docks. The *MS Mount Washington* has sailed the lake since 1939 and replaced its namesake launched in

1872 and destroyed by fire in 1939 ☎ (603) 366-5531 for times of sailings.

Take route 3 south-west to **Laconia** at the southern tip of Lake Winnisquam. A land grant to settle the area was issued in 1727 but the first building, a log cabin, was not erected until 1766 because of Sachem Indians. Originally called Meredith Bridge, the settlement did not grow much until the railroad arrived in 1848 when many mills and factories were built, and the town became a trading and manufacturing centre. Paugus Bay and lakes Winnisquam and Opechee extend into Laconia's city limits, offering 'doorstep' opportunities for water sports. **Lake Winnipesaukee**, 5 miles (8km) north, is the largest lake in the state and a major resort centre. Sky Bright offer 20 minute sightseeing flights over the White Mountains and Lake Winnipesaukee ☎ (603) 528-6818, and the headquarters of the White Mountain National Forest is in the town. The Belknap Mill presents plays, recitals, concerts and art exhibitions, and a summer symphony series is sponsored by the New Hampshire Music Festival. Major annual attractions include the World Championship Sled Dog Derby in February, and 230ft (70m) ski jumping competition at the Gunstock ski area.

Gunstock, 7 miles (11km) east on SRllA, is a year-round recreation area with downhill and cross country country skiing in the winter, and around 40 trails and 7 lifts open late November to April. There are horseback rides, hiking trails and camping facilities from mid-May to early October.

Continue west on route 3 to **Franklin**, originally part of Salisbury, but incorporated as a town in 1828 and named after Benjamin Franklin. It prospered as a milling and industrial community using water power from the Pemigewasset and Winnipesaukee rivers. On the corner of Central and Dearborn Streets, there is a boulder with a glacier caused depression, which was further deepened by Penacook Indians and settlers grinding corn. Another boulder is carved with a shad, a fish plentiful in the Winnipesaukee River until the dam was built. There is a bust of Daniel Webster in front of the 1820 Congregational church. The citizens wanted to name the town after their famous son, a US Secretary of State, but there was already another town called Webster, so they opted for Franklin instead. The bust was sculpted by Daniel Chester French, sculptor of the seated Abraham Lincoln in the Lincoln Memorial in Washington, D.C.

Daniel Webster's Birthplace off SR127 can be visited. He was born here in 1782. It has period antiques and memorabilia. Open: daily 10am-6pm late June to early September, weekends 10am-6pm early September to October, rest of the year by appointment. Admission charge ☎ (603) 934-5057.

From Franklin and head south for about 12 miles (19km) and then
take route 132 east through **Canterbury Center** to visit the Canterbury Shaker Village, one of New England's few remaining Shaker
communities, established in 1792 and now preserved as a museum
with twenty-five restored buildings. The farming colony was famous for its tools, textiles and elegant Shaker furniture. Guides in
costume conduct tours and artisans continue to practice the Shaker
skills of carpentry, box making and weaving. There is a nature trail
around the herb gardens and early irrigation ponds. Open: Monday
to Saturday 10am-5pm, Sunday 12noon-5pm May to October, Friday and Saturday 10am-5pm, Sunday 12noon-5pm April, November and December. Admission charge. Allow 2-3 hours.

You can then head south on the country road from the Shaker
Village to visit **Loudon** and the New Hampshire International
Speedway, on SR106, which seats 60,000 and hosts the IndyCar 200
and Winston Cup 300 as well SCAA National and NASCAR stock
car races. Open: daily for racing and watching practice, 8am-5pm
April to November. Admission charge.

If you like animals, there is a further detour east from Loudon on
route 129 to Loudon Center and then south to **Pittsfield** and White's
Miniature Horse Petting Farm, South Pittsfield Road, with miniature horses, donkeys, pygmy goats and other animals that can be
petted. Open: daily 10am-5pm May to September. Admission
charge.

From either Pittsfield or Loudon return west to the main highway
and continue south through Concord back to Manchester.

Option 3 (140 miles/225km)
Continue the main itinerary from Littleton by heading east the 3
miles (5km) to Bethlehem, and then south to Franconia and the
spectacular Franconia Notch. **Franconia** is a year round resort with
plenty of accommodation and a good base for exploring the White
Mountains. The Frost Place, SR116, is the house poet Robert Frost
bought in 1915 after returning from England. It has his memorabilia,
including signed first editions of all of his books. There is a self-
guiding tour of the 1859 farm house and nature trail. A poet is in
residence during the summer and gives readings in the old barn. A
Festival of Poetry is held late July and early August. Open: Wednesday to Monay 1-5pm July to early October, weekends 1-5pm May to
June. Admission charge.

The New England Ski Museum, by the Cannon Mountain Aerial
Tramway 11, exhibits art and a video on the history of Nordic and
Alpine skiing. Open: Thursday to Tuesday 12noon-5pm late May to
mid-October, and late December to March. Admission free.

Franconia Notch is the most famous mountain gap in the East. The huge gap between the massive Kinsman and Franconia ranges was carved out by the ice cap, and is noted for its spectacular beauty. The US3 crosses the gap from Echo Lake, south-west of Twin Mountain, to Lincoln. By the mid-nineteenth century it had become a favourite tourist destination and grand hotels were built to accommodate the visitors. The hotels have long since gone, but the area continues to attract large number of visitors to enjoy the area's beauty and the many outdoor activity opportunities in Franconia Notch State Park. The Lincoln-Flume covered bridge is east of US3 in the state park, built, it is thought, around 1886 across the Pemigewasset River. It is for foot traffic only. The Lincoln-Sentinel Pine covered bridge is a little further along, and was built in 1939 for visitors wanting to cross the Flume.

The Basin, reached by a path from US3 north of the Flume, is a deep glacial pothole, 20ft (6m) across, at the foot of a waterfall. Its sides have been polished smooth by sand, stones and water. The Pemigewasset River then runs through the Baby Flume, a smaller version of the well-known gorge ☎ (603) 745-8391. **Cannon Mountain Aerial Tramway 11**, $^1/_2$ mile (1km) north of the Profile, runs between Valley Station and the top of Cannon Mountain. The 80-passenger cars make the vertical 2,022ft (616m) ascent in 5 minutes, and from the Summit Observation Platform there are fabulous mountain views. There are a number of trails. Open: daily 9am-7pm July to early September, 9am-4.30pm mid-May to end of June. Admission charge.

Echo Lake is at the northern end of the notch and bounded by mountains on three sides. It gets its name from for its special acoustic qualities. The lake is the largest in the notch and offers swimming, boating and fishing. Beach admission charge.

The Flume, at the southern end of the notch, is a gorge almost 800ft (244m) along the side of Mount Liberty. A stream crashes in a series of waterfalls and pools between its granite walls up to 90ft (27m) high. There is a free bus for part of the way and then a 2 mile (3km) hike to the gorge. Although the path in the gorge is good it is steep in places. There are two covered bridges in the Flume. Open: daily 9am-4:30pm mid-May to late October. Admission charge.

The Profile (also called the Old Man of the Mountains and the Great Stone Face) is 1,200ft (366m) above Profile Lake, formerly known in as The Old Man's Wash Bowl. The 40ft (12m) high 'head' on the mountainside is made up of five ledges. The Profile is best seen from the eastern shore of the lake between 10am and sunset.

The main route continues north on highway 3 through Twin Mountain to **Bretton Woods**, a fashionable resort since 1902 when the Mount Washington Hotel opened. The European-style resort was popular as a summer European-style spa with the wealthy during the depression and up to fifty trains, many with private railcars, arrived daily. In July 1944 the hotel was the venue for the World Monetary Fund Conference which set the gold standard at $35 an ounce in a move which helped stabilise the post war economy. The room in which the conference was held is now a small museum which is open daily. Today the town is a year round resort offering summer hiking, golf and many other activities, and winter skiing.

Mount Washington Cog Railway is north of town and clearly signposted. It was the first mountain climbing railway in the world and celebrated its 125th anniversary in 1994. The beautiful 3 hour round trip takes in the summit of Mount Washington (6,288ft/1,917m), the tallest peak in the north-eastern states. Trains depart daily on the hour between 8am-4pm late July to early September, operating times between May and late July and early September to October vary. Admission charge.

The huge 'notch' of **Crawford Notch** was caused by glaciers during the last Ice Age. The glacier's progress was blocked by the granite mountain peaks so it forced its way through the software rocks of the pass carving out the notch which runs from Bartlett in the south to Saco Lake in the north. This is steep wooded mountain land and the drive through the valley on US302 which follows the Saco River is spectacular. To the west is Willey Mountain and to the east Mount Webster with Mount Jackson (4,052ft/1,235m) beyond. This is the southernmost peak of the Presidential range. This steep area is prone to landslides and in 1826 one slip engulfed the fleeing Willey family after whom the mountain is now named. The Willey homestead escaped unscathed and is now part of the Crawford Notch State Park. The notch was discovered by Timothy Nash in 1771 while on a hunting trip. He was promised a land grant if he could travel through the pass with a horse. It is claimed that the route was so steep that Nash and companions only succeeded by hauling the horse up and down the cliff faces by rope. The discovery of the pass and the subsequent roads through it allowed the northern part of the state to be opened up for settlement. The 200ft (61m) Arethusa Falls, are just over 1 mile (2km) off the US302 along a well marked but steep path. Silver and Flume Cascdes are to the west of the road at the northern end of the notch. The Silver Cascades tumble more than 1,100ft (335m) down the steep slopes of Mount Webster.

Continue to **Bartlett**, a year round outdoor recreation centre set in spectacular mountains, with Bear Mountain to the south, Mount Carrigan to the west and Mount Parker to the north. William Stark and a number of other men were given a land grant after fighting in the French and Indian War, settled here and Bartlett was incorporated in 1790. There is a wonderful drive through Bear Notch to the Kancamagus Highway. Bartlett covered bridge is west of route 302, ✳ just over 4 miles (6km) east of town over the Saco River. It was closed to traffic when the road bypassed it in 1939, and is now privately owned and houses an antique and gift shop.

Attitash Alpine Slide, on US302, has alpine slides, scenic chairlift, waterslides, horseback riding and pony rides and golf driving range. Open: daily 10am-6pm mid-June to early September, weekends 10am-5pm mid-May to mid-June early September to October. Admission charge.

Glen is at the junctions of 302 and 16 which runs north. Just north of Glen is **Jackson**, a charming mountain village in the White Mountain National Forest offering a wide range of year-round recreational opportunities. There are more than 93 miles (150km) of cross-country and alpine ski trails which are available on Attitash, ⃕ Black and Wildcat mountains. Trails are usually open from mid-November to April. There is also horseback riding, sleigh rides, ice skating and golf. The Jackson covered bridge is also known as the 'Honeymoon Bridge', and was built in 1876 over the Ellis River. It is ✳ 138ft (42m) long and was repaired and widened in 1939. Nestlenook Farm, Dinsmore Road, offers year-round recreational activities, with cross country skiing and hiking along the Ellis River, ice skating on Emerald Lake with sleigh rides, horse-drawn trolley rides and horseriding on the 65 acre (26 hectare) Victorian estate. The reindeer in Emerald Forest can be hand fed. Open: grounds 9am-5pm (sleigh rides and skating often continue until 10pm). Admission free.

From Glen take the 302 south to **North Conway**. It is said that ✳ artist Benjamin Champney was so impressed with the view of Mount Washington from the town's main street that he set up his easel in the middle of the road in August 1850 and painted the scene. Since then, the mountain and the area's many other scenic spots, including Thompson's Falls have been attracting arts and sightseers. The sale of reproductions of Champney's landscapes also promoted the beauty of the Granite State worldwide. Today, North Conway is the commercial centre for the Mount Washington Valley recreation area which attracts visitors year round. It has good shopping along Main Street, restaurants, nightlife, arts and crafts,

The covered bridge is one of the many attractions in North Conway, which is the centre of the Mount Washington Valley recreation area

The North Conway Scenic Railroad offers delightful trips into Mount Washington Valley

and the Mount Washington Valley Theater Company which stages a summer season. In early September the White Mountain Jazz and Blues Crafts Festival is held, while the World Championship Mud Bowl, a football tournament, is held in mid-September. Conway Scenic Railroad, on SR16 and US302, offers a one hour narrated ride along the Saco River to Conway through the Mount Washington valley, on track laid in the early 1870s. The station was built in 1874. Round trips leave daily at 10am, 12noon, 2 and 4pm (also Tuesday to Thursday and Saturday 6.30pm July and August) June to October, weekends 12noon and 2pm November and December. Admission charge. **Echo Lake State Park**, Westside Road, has 396 acres (158 hectares) with scenic drive to Cathedral Ledge, 700ft (213m) above the valley, and walking trails. Open: daily 9am-8pm mid-June to early September, weekends 9am-8pm mid-May to mid-June. Admission charge.

Conway 3 miles (5km) south, has three covered bridges in the area. The Conway-Swift covered bridge was built in 1850 is 144ft (44m) long and spans the Swift River. The structure was washed away in floods in 1869 but rebuilt the same year. About $^1/_2$ mile (1km) north of the village is a second covered bridge over the Saco River. Built in 1890 it is 240ft (73m) long and the arches were a later addition. This is the third bridge on the site and for foot traffic only. The Albany bridge is 6 miles (10km) west of the village in the White Mountain National Forest. It was built in 1857 over the Swift River, but almost immediately destroyed by a sandstorm. The present bridge was built in 1858 and is 136ft long (41m).

Russell Colbath Historic House, 12 miles (19km) from Conway, was built in 1830 by one of the area's first settlers. Open: daily 8-4.30pm mid-June to September, Wednesday to Sunday 8am-4.30pm rest of the year. The Passaconaway Historic Site has an interpretive centre, and is open daily 9am-5pm late May to August, Friday to Sunday 9am-5pm early May, September and October. Admission free.

Continue south on route 16 through Center Ossipee to **Wakefield** with its Museum of Childhood, Wakefield Corner. It has a huge collection of dolls and toys dating from the mid-nineteenth century, as well as an 1890 one room school house with original desks and equipment, and a collection of sledges. Open: Monday and Wednesday to Saturday 11am-4pm, Sunday 1-4pm late May to late October. Admission charge.

Take highway 16 south for about 12 miles (19km) and visit **Milton** to the east of the main highway. Visit the New Hampshire Farm Museum, on SR125, based around Jones Farm, the best preserved collection of connected farm structures in the state. The buildings were built over 200 years and reflect a number of architectural styles. The Plummer Homestead is a living-history farm depicting late nineteenth-century farm life. Old Time Farm Day, the second Saturday in August, features more than sixty artisans demonstrating rural skills. Open: Tuesday to Saturday 10am-4pm, Sunday 12noon-4pm mid-June to early September, Saturday 10am-4pm, Sunday 12noon-4pm late September to October. Admission charge.

Then continue south through Rochester and then detour east on route 4 to visit **Dover**, the oldest permanent settlement in the sate, established in 1623 as a fishing and fur trading centre at Pomeroy Cove, now called Dover Point, and independent until 1642 when it became part of the Massachusetts Bay Colony. By the end of the century the settlement had grown so large that further expansion was impossible, and it moved to its present site. Industrial growth started after the water power of the Cocheco Falls had been harnessed, with sawmills and flour mills largely taking over from fishing and farming, and after the 1812 war, cotton mills predominated. The downtown and waterfront areas have many fine restored Colonial and Victorian properties.

Woodman Institute, Central Avenue, is housed in three buildings, the oldest being the 1675 hand-hewn Dame Garrison House with original furnishings. Note the small round windows from which settlers could fire at attacking Indians. The 1818 Woodman House has natural history artifacts and Penacook exhibits, and the 1813 Hale House was home to abolitionist Senator John P. Hale from 1840 to 1873, and has historical exhibits. Open: Tuesday to Saturday 2-5pm April to January. Donations.

Return to route 125, head south for about 6 miles (10km) and then make the short detour west on route 4 to visit **Durham**, which was settled in 1635 and originally part of Dover but incorporated as a town in its own right in 1732. Noted as the home of Revolutionary War hero Major General John Sullivan, and three-time governor of New Hampshire. A plaque marks the site of the meeting house where Sullivan and his band are said to have stored the gunpowder taken after their raid on the British Fort William and Mary in New Castle in 1774. The British sent a frigate to get their powder back but the water was too shallow for it to sail beyond Portsmouth. In 1893 the College of Agriculture and Mechanical Arts—later to be came the University of New Hampshire—was moved from Hanover to Durham. Today Durham is very much a university town, with the Paul Creative Arts Center a focus for cultural events, and the campus nature reserve a relaxing area to stroll in.

Retrace your route to the main road and head south, turning off after about 5 miles (8km) to visit **Newington**, a sprawling community between Great Bay and the Piscataqua River, with well-manicured farms, historic buildings and scenic views in all directions. Now a commercial and industrial centre, the town has two large shopping areas and several good restaurants. The nearby water and shoreline make this is one of the richest areas for birdlife in the country, and Great Bay has been designated a National Estuarine Research Reserve. In 1987, the 110 acre (44 hectare) Newington Center Historic District was placed on the National Register of Historic Places. It includes the ancient cemetery, parade ground and the state's old meeting house, built in 1712 and still in use.

Return to route 4 south and **Portsmouth**. In 1630 when settlers stepped ashore from the Pied Cow on the west bank of the Piscataqua River they found the ground covered with wild strawberries, and so named it Strawbery Banke. That settlement grew into Portsmouth. Traders from the Laconia Corporation had already established settlements in 1623 upriver at Dover and 2 miles (3km) east at Odiorne Point, now a state park and virtually unchanged since then. Fishing and farming were the original mainstays of Strawbery Banke, but the abundance of timber and a natural harbour encouraged shipbuilding, and by 1653 when it changed its name to Portsmouth it was an important trading and commercial centre, as well as the seat of provincial government. It remained the capital of the colony until 1788 when New Hampshire became one of the original thirteen United States and the capital moved to Concord. It prospered as a shipbuilding town until the late nineteenth century, and now has a mixed economy, combing industry and tourism. The historic districts boast many fine old houses and the narrow, winding streets give it an old world charm. Many of the houses were built for wealthy merchants and sea captains. The warehouses which used to line the Old Harbor, especially Bow and Ceres Streets, are now fashionable boutiques, galleries and eateries, while the Portsmouth Academy of Performing Arts stages productions year round in the renovated brewery in Bow Street. There are also many fine Colonial and Federal buildings in The Hill and Deer and High Streets which are now offices. The oldest tombstone in the town's oldest cemetery, Point of Graves, off Mechanic Street, dates from 1682, and the 1766 Pitt Tavern was deeply involved in the Revolutionary War.

Portsmouth hosts many annual events including New England Clambake in June and waterfront Jazz Festival in June, the Arts Festival from late July to early August, and the Candlelight Tour of Historic Houses along the Portsmouth Trail in late August.

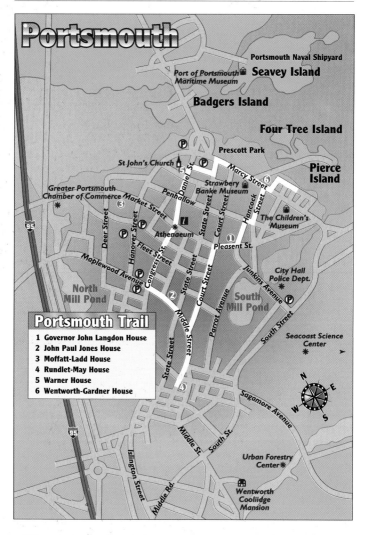

Portsmouth

Portsmouth Naval Shipyard

Port of Portsmouth Maritime Museum — **Seavey Island**

Badgers Island

Four Tree Island

Prescott Park

St John's Church

Strawbery Banke Museum

Marcy Street

Daniel St.

Penhallow

Greater Portsmouth Chamber of Commerce — Market Street

Pierce Island

State Street

Court Street

Hancock Street

The Children's Museum

Deer Street

Hanover Street

Fleet Street

Athenaeum

Pleasent St.

Congress St.

Maplewood Avenue

Middle Street

State Street

Court Street

Jenkins Avenue

City Hall Police Dept.

North Mill Pond

South Mill Pond

Parrot Avenue

South Street

Seacoast Science Center

Portsmouth Trail

1 Governor John Langdon House
2 John Paul Jones House
3 Moffatt-Ladd House
4 Rundlet-May House
5 Warner House
6 Wentworth-Gardner House

State Street

Sagamore Avenue

Middle St.

South St.

Islington Street

Middle Rd.

Urban Forestry Center

Wentworth Cooliidge Mansion

N E W S

    There are many guided tours of the town and area. Details are
available from the Seacoast Council on Tourism, 235 West Road,
Portsmouth NH 03801 and Greater Portsmouth Chamber of Commerce, 500 Market Street Portsmouth NH 03801. There are also
many harbour, river and sea cruises. There are five forts, the oldest
dating from the early 1600s, along the coast.

Warner House, Portsmouth, was built in 1716 and is a fine example of Colonial Georgian architecture

Portsmouth Harbor is now packed with boutiques, restaurants and galleries

✳ **Captain Whittaker's Isles of Shoals Steamship Company**, Barker Wharf, offers historic, natural history and sightseeing trips around the islands in replica late nineteenth-century steamboats. Sailings daily 11am and 2pm mid-June to early September. Charge. Allow 3 hours.

🏠 **Children's Museum**, 289 Marcy Street, has hands-on and interactive learning displays about earthquakes, the human body, different countries, space and lobstering. Open: Tuesday to Saturday 10am-5pm (Monday 10am-5pm during school holidays) and Sunday 1-5pm. Admission charge.

✳ **Athenaeum**, Market Square, is a Federal-style mansion built in 1803 and now housing more than 26,000 volumes and manuscripts, as well as portraits and ship models. Open: Tuesday and Thursday 1-4pm, Saturday 10am-4pm. Admission free.

✳ **Portsmouth Harbor Cruises**, offer boat trips of the harbour, river and islands. Sailings: Monday to Friday 12noon and 2pm, weekends 10am, 12noon and 2pm early June to October. Charge.

🚶 **Portsmouth Trail** takes in six of Portsmouth's most historic buildings. Brochures are available from the Chamber of Commerce. The six houses, which can be visited individually, are:

🏤 *Governor John Langdon House*, 143 Pleasant Street. This was built in 1784 by the three-time state governor, and one of the signatories of the Constitution. In 1789 George Washington described it as 'the finest house in Portsmouth'. The gardens include a 100ft (30m) long rose arbour. Open: Wednesday to Sunday 12noon-5pm June to mid-October. Admission charge.

🏤 *John Paul Jones House*, Middle and State Streets. This is a gambrel-roofed house which was built in 1758 by Captain Gregory Purcell and run as a boarding house by his widow. Its most famous guest was John Paul Jones who stayed there while overseeing the outfitting of the *Ranger* in 1777 and again in 1781 while the America was being built. Open: Monday to Saturday 10am-4pm, Sunday 12noon-4pm. Admission charge.

🏤 *Moffatt-Ladd House*, 154 Market Street, was built in 1763 by Captain John Moffatt and later became home of his son in law General William Whipple, a signatory of the Declaration of Independence. Noted for its panelling, splendid staircase, museum and formal gardens. Open: Monday to Saturday 10am-4pm, Sunday 2-5pm. Admission charge ☎ (603) 436-8221.

🏤 *Rundlet-May House*, 364 Middle Street, is a three storey Federal house built by merchant James Rundlet in 1807, with original decor and furnishings. Many of the pieces of furniture were made by Portsmouth craftsmen. Open: Wednesday to Sunday 12noon-5pm June to mid-October. Admission charge.

Warner House, Daniel and Chapel Streets, was built in 1716 in Georgian style with thick brick walls. Benjamin Franklin, a frequent visitor, is said to have supervised the installation of the lightning rod on the west wall in 1762. It is the finest example in New England of an early eighteenth-century brick mansion, and the oldest brick mansion in the US. Original painted murals include two life size Indian figures, believed to be two of the four 'Indian Kings' taken to London in 1710 to be presented to Queen Anne. Open: Tuesday to Saturday 10am-4pm, Sunday 1-4pm. Admission charge.

Wentworth-Gardner House, Mechanic and Gardner Streets, was built in 1760 and is one of the finest Georgian buildings in the country, noted for its fine doorway and carvings. Open: Tuesday to Sunday 1-5pm, mid-June to mid-October. Admission charge.

Prescott Park, Marcy Street, is between the Strawbery Banke Museum and waterfront. The gardens have fountains and a fishing pier, the All American Trail Garden and the 1705 Sheafe Warehouse where the *Ranger* was outfitted, and now a folk art museum. Open: park daily 5am-midnight, museum Wednesday to Sunday 10am-5pm June to early September. Admission free.

St. John's Church, Chapel Street, was built in 1807 on the site of the 1732 Queen's Chapel. It has many seventeenth- and eighteenth-century antiques, including a seventeenth-century French steeple bell captured by Colonial troops in Nova Scotia in 1745. It was damaged when the chapel burned down in 1806 and was recast by Paul Revere. The church has a rare 1717 'Vinegar ' bible, so called because in the parable of the vineyard, the word 'vinegar' appears instead of 'vineyard', and the Brattle Organ, the oldest known pipe organ in the US. Open: daily 8am-5pm. Donations.

Seacoast Science Center, Odiorne Point State Park, has cultural, marine and natural history exhibits. Open: Tuesday to Sunday 10am-5pm, Monday 12noon-5pm June to late October. Tuesday to Friday noon-5pm, weekends 10am-5pm rest of the year. Admission charge ☎ (603) 436-8043.

Strawbery Banke Museum covers a 10 acre (4 hectare) site between Marcy, State, Washington and Hancock Streets, which was a farm in the 1670s. Part of the land was sold in the 1690s and is now the Puddle Dock neighbourhood. This is a wonderfully well preserved historic waterfront and site of the original settlement, with more than forty restored buildings, the oldest dating from 1695. They include: the lavish Governor Ichabod Goodwin Mansion (1811) and the more austere Widow Rider's home, Chase House (1762); Captain Keyran Walsh House (1796); John Wheelwright House (1780); Thomas Bailey Aldrich House (1790); and Drisco

House (1790). They are furnished to reflect the various fines and changes in lifestyle over 350 years. The Abbott Little Corner store has war time groceries and prices from 1943. There are usually daily demonstrations by craftsmen including eighteenth-century cooking in the Wheelwright House. Open: daily 10am-5pm May to October. Admission charge.

✳ **Urban Forestry Center**, south on Elwyn Road has peaceful trails and gardens in a 170 acre (68 hectare) marshland, with wood and lake setting along Sagamore Creek. There are forestry and natural history programmes. Open: daily 7am-8pm. Admission free.

🏛 *USS Albacore*, **Port of Portsmouth Maritime Museum**, Albacore Park, was built at the Portsmouth Naval Shipyard in 1952 and commissioned in 1953 as a US Navy experimental submarine. Its revolutionary hull design enabled it to set an underwater sea record in the late 1960s, and transformed the role of naval submarines. The vessel was in service until 1972 although never fired a weapon. See the video in the visitor centre before taking the tour. The neighbouring Memorial Garden commemorates submariners killed in action. Open: daily 9.30am-5.30pm. Admission charge.

✳ **Water Country**, on US1, is a water theme park with pools, slides and attractions. Open: daily 9.30am-7.30pm July to early September, weekends 11am-6pm May and June. Admission charge.

🏚 **Wentworth Coolidge Mansion**, Little Harbor Road, was the official residence of Benjamin Wentworth, the first Royal Governor from 1741 to 1766. The oldest parts of the forty-two room mansion date from around 1695. Open: daily 10am-5pm late June to early September, weekends 10am-5pm May to late June. Admission charge.

New Castle is on Great Island in the bay off Portsmouth. It is a quaint fishing village founded on Great Island in 1693 which has retained its old world charm with narrow streets and old houses. The small park to the east of the square has the remains of Fort Constitution, formerly Fort William and Mary, the site of the first open act of rebellion against the British Crown. On 14 December 1774, following the heroic ride by Paul Revere, Portsmouth's Sons of Liberty, and patriots from Durham and New Castle, seized the fort and stole its munitions. The gunpowder was stored in Durham and used 4 months later against the British at the battle of Bunker Hill. The Great Island Common is the town's recreational heart with 31 oceanside acres (12 hectares).

A short detour from Portsmouth west on route 101 takes in **Greenland**, a residential community outside Portsmouth on the shore of Great Bay, with many eighteenth-century homes and colonial farmsteads. The spread of light industry along Ocean Road has not changed the character of this quiet town. There are many summer cottages along the bay, which offers boating, swimming, fishing, camping and walking. The green in the centre of town has a gazebo and bandstand, in the shadow of the white spired church.

From Portsmouth take route 1A south to the Rye area. **Rye** has been a settlement since the early 1600s on a dramatic stretch of coastline. Captain John Smith described it as 'an early paradise' in 1614. The historic fishing village covers 8 miles (13km) of the state's 18 miles (29km) of coastline, as well as three of the Isles of Shoals — Star Island, White Island and Lunging Island 6 miles (10km) offshore. The centre of Rye is 2 miles (3km) inland with tree lined boulevards and gracious estates, and many fine old homes. New Hampshire Seacoast Cruises, Ocean Boulevard, offer whale watching and sightseeing trips from Rye Harbor, and visits to the Isles of Shoals, with its White Island Lighthouse, marine laboratory and World War II Coast Guard installations. Cruises between May and October ☎ (603) 964-5545 for times.

Then take route 111 south-west through the Hamptons. **Hampton** was settled in 1638 and first called Winnacunnet, meaning 'Beautiful Place of Pines.' The first tax-supported public school was established here in 1649 for the education of both sexes. The Tuck Memo- rial Museum on Meeting House Green traces the town's history. The Green was established in 1638 and contains forty-two stones representing the town's earliest families. The Hampton Playhouse, Winnacunnet Road, is housed in a remodelled early nineteenth-century cattle barn, and noted for its summer theatre season. Open: Tuesday to Saturday at 8.30pm, matinees Wednesday and Friday 2.30pm. Sunday at 7pm, mid-June to late August.

North Hampton was first settled in 1639 as part of Hampton, it celebrated its 250th anniversary as a town in 1992. Situated on the coast roughly midway between Boston and Portland, Maine, made New Hampton a favourite resort for the rich families from both cities, who bought estates and built summer 'cottages' here at the end of the nineteenth and beginning of the twentieth centuries. Runnymede-by-the-Sea was the estate of Alvan T. Fuller, a former Massachusetts Governor and although the house has been demolished, the attractive gardens are a reminder of this elegant past.

Fuller Gardens, 10 Willow Avenue, were designed in 1939 to resemble the early twentieth-century Colonial Revival estate garden of Governor Fuller. The 2 acres (1 hectare) of gardens with fountains and statues, are at their best in June when the spring bulbs, azaleas, rhododendron and wisteria are in bloom, closely followed by the 1,500 rose bushes which flower until September. There is also a

Hosta display and Japanese garden. Open: daily 10am-6pm mid-May to mid-October. Admission charge.

Hampton Beach is a hugely popular seaside resort with long promenade, budget motels, fast food outlets and amusements. The granite New Hampshire Marine War Memorial on Ocean Boulevard and Nudd Avenue, commemorates American sailors lost at sea. To the north of Hampton Beach, Great Boars Head sticks out into the sea capped by a number of old summer cottages.

Hampton Falls is a major berry growing area. The Raspberry Farm, 3 miles (5km) west on SR84, has a 200-year-old barn and pick your own raspberries, strawberries and blackberries from July to mid-October.

Continuing south you arrive at **Seabrook**, a small coastal summer resort popular with families with safe beaches and lots of amusements. It is aso home of the Seabrook Station Nuclear Power Plant which opened in 1990. It runs the Science and Nature Center on SR1, with hands-on displays, models and audiovisuals on electricity, energy and wildlife. Bus tours visit the power plant and control centre simulator. There is also a self guiding nature walk along the Owascoag Trail. Open: Monday to Saturday 10am-4pm June to September, Monday to Friday 10am-4pm rest of the year. Admission free.

From Seabrook take route 107 north to route 108 and then north to **Exeter**, founded in 1638 by the non-conformist Reverend John Wheelwright close to the falls on the Squamscott River. Because of his views he was expelled from Boston and the settlement has a long history of dissent. It was one of the first towns to defy English rule and publicly burned effigies of the British Lords Bute and North. When war broke out, the capital moved from Tory-controlled Portsmouth to Exeter. Phillips Exeter Academy was founded as a preparatory school in 1781 and is still in existence. The town has many fine old buildings and a vigorous restoration programme.

The American Independence Museum, Governors Lane, is in the restored 1721 home of John Taylor Gilman, a Colonial Governor of New Hampshire. As Cincinnati Hall it was the state treasury between 1775 and 1789. It has original family furnishings, one of the three Purple Hearts awarded during the Revolutionary War, and an original copy of the Declaration of Independence with a working draft of the Constitution with notes by delegate Nicholas Gilman, a member of George Washington's staff. It also includes the 1775 Folsom Tavern. Open: Tuesday to Saturday 10am-4pm, Sunday 12noon-4pm May to October. Tours available. Tuesday and Saturday 12noon-3pm rest of year. Admission charge.

Gilman Garrison House, 12 Water Street, was built about 1690 as
a fortified garrison with huge sawn log walls and portcullis, and
remodelled in the eighteenth century. The logs came from two
nearby sawmills run by the Gilman family. It has seventeenth- and
eighteenth-century furnishings. Open: Tuesday, Thursday and
weekends 12noon-5pm June to mid-October. Admission charge.

Return south-west on route 111 through East Hampstead to
North Salem, a farming community in an area of rolling wooded
hills and lakes. America's Stonehenge, on Haverhill Road, is the
oldest known megalithic site in North America. Carbon testing
dates the site to around 2000BC, and there are several theories as to
what the stones were used for, suggestions ranging from a giant
astronomical computer to a ceremonial meeting place. Inscriptions
show that it was used between 800 and 300BC. Open: daily 9am-
5pm June to early September, daily 10am-4pm late April to May,
and early September to October, weekends 10am-4pm late March to
late April. Admission charge.

Take the country roads south to Salem and Canobie Lake Park, an
amusement park with rides, roller coasters and live entertainment.
Open: daily 12noon-10pm mid-June to early September. Times vary
mid-May to mid-June. Admission charge.

From Salem drive west to highway 93 and then north to **Derry**
named by Scottish-Irish protestant immigrants in the early eighteenth century, the settlers were soon using their linen making skills
and water power from the Beaver Brook. It rapidly became a major
linen producer and the industry flourished well into the twentieth
century when much textile manufacturing was moved to southern
states. Main industries today include circuit boards and giftware.
Commander Alan Shepard, the first American in space grew up in
Derry. About 4 miles (6km) east of town on Island Pond Road is the
water powered Taylor Up-and-Down Sawmill which last operated
commercially in 1865. Its operation is demonstrated during the
summer and at other times can be viewed from the outside. Robert
Frost Farm, on SR28, was the home of poet from 1900 to 1911, and the
inspiration for much of his work. The farmstead has been restored to
reflect life in the first decade of the twentieth century with family
furnishings and the poet's memorabilia. Open: daily 10am-6pm late
June to early September, weekends 10am-6pm late May to late June
and early September to October. Admission charge. From Derry it is
a short drive north back to Manchester.

Hampton Beach

*North Hampton
Town Hall which is
surrounded by the
summer homes of
the wealthy*

TOUR 2 • THE SOUTH-WESTERN CORNER

(125miles, 201km)

From Manchester take route 3 south to **Merrimack** with the ❄
Anheuser-Busch brewery at 221 Daniel Webster Highway. It offers
brewery tours, tastings, and the famous Clydesdale stables. Open:
daily 9.30am-5pm May to October, Wednesday to Sunday 10am-
4pm rest of the year. Admission free.

Continue south to **Nashua**, the southernmost of the three
Merrimack Valley cities that form the industrial backbone of New
Hampshire. Mills were established on the Nashua and Merrimack
rivers in the early nineteenth century, and the opening of the
Middlesex Canal in 1804 made Nashua the head of navigation on the
Merrimack with direct access to the markets of Boston. The town
rapidly became an important industrial and commercial centre.

Today more than 100 industries produce a huge range of products
from beer to computers, with an increasing emphasis on research
and development. The town also boasts more than twenty city
parks, with Silver Lake State Park, about 7 miles (11km) west,
offering extensive opportunities for outdoor activities. At **Milford**,
10 miles (16km) west off SR101, is a 500-seat theatre on the Souhegan
River, where the American Stage Festival stages Broadway plays
and children's shows between May and September.

Take 101A west through Milford to **Wilton** and Frye's Measure
Mill, off Burton Highway. Parts of the old mill dating from 1750
survive on the site which was originally a blacksmiths forge. Machinery imported from England in 1850 still produces handcards
used for spinning wool. There are also demonstrations of Shaker ❄
boxmaking. Open: Tuesday to Saturday 10am-5pm, Sunday
12noon-5pm May to mid-December. Mill tours at 2pm Saturday
June to October. Admission charge.

About 11 miles (18km) south-west of Wilton is **New Ipswich**, site
of Benjamin Pritchard's first unsuccessful cotton mill on the
Souhegan River. When the mill failed, he moved to Manchester and
opened the Amoskeag Mill in 1805, which later became the hugely
successful Amoskeag Manufacturing Company. There are many
early Colonial buildings in the town, which is now largely a trading
centre for surrounding farms.

Barrett House, Main Street was built in 1800 and is also known as
Forest Hall. The grand Federal-style home has a third-floor ball- 🏛
room and many well preserved examples of period furniture passed
down through the Barrett family. Open: for guided tours on the
hour Thursday to Sunday 12noon-4pm June to mid-October. Admission charge.

Then take route 123 north-west to **Peterborough**, famous as the home of the MacDowell Colony founded by composer Edward MacDowell in 1907. Over the years, the colony has attracted world famous award winning writers, artists, composers and filmmakers, and it is still an important centre for the arts, although only Clony Hall, the library and MacDowell's grave are open to the public, and visitors must register first at Colony Hall in the High Street between 1-4pm Monday to Friday. The Peterborough Playhouse started in a barn north of the colony in 1933. The professional company stages productions throughout the year at Stearns Farm, Hadley Road. ☎ (603) 924-7585. The New England Marionette Opera performs charming weekend puppet operas in the Opera House on Main Street ☎ (603) 924-4333.

Miller State Park covers 489 acres (196 hectares) 3 miles (5km) east off SR101, with a scenic drive and hiking trail to the summit of 2,288ft (698m) Pack Monadnock Mountain. The Wapack Trail also crosses the path. Open: daily 10am-6pm late June to early September, weekends 10am-6pm late May to late June. Admission charge. Peterborough Historical Society, Grove Street, has exhibits on local and state history, and two mill workers' homes, Victorian parlour, Colonial Kitchen and country store. Open: Monday to Saturday 10am-4pm July and August. Admission charge. Sharon Arts Center, 4 miles (6km) south on SR123, displaying hand made pottery, jewellery and furniture and working craftsmen. Open: Monday to Saturday 10am-5pm, Sunday 12noon-5pm. Admission free.

Take 101 west about 6 miles (10km) to **Dublin**. The settlement was established in 1753 by Scottish-Irish immigrants in dense forest away from major rivers which restricted growth and the town was not incorporated until 1771. Its isolation proved an asset in the 1800s and close to Mount Monadnock it became a popular summer resort area. Mount Monadnock is also popular with geologists and the name is now used to describe rock hard enough to resist glacial and other erosion and so stands out an otherwise eroded landscape. The area is largely covered by the Monadnock State Park.

The Friendly Farm, 13 miles (21km) west on SR101, has livestock and their young and visitors can feed and touch many of them. Open: daily 10am-5pm, May to early September, weekends 10am-5pm, early September to mid-October. Admission charge.

Then cut south through the Jaffrey Center to **Jaffrey**, originally part of the huge land grant made to Captain John Mason, and later sold to a group known as the 'proprietors,' one of whom was George Jaffrey who gave the area his name in 1775. In the mid-nineteenth century the area became a fashionable summer resort, and Ralph

Waldo Emerson, wrote the poem *Monadnoc* after scaling nearby Monadnock Mountain. It is now a charming, peaceful village built around the 1773 white clapboard Meeting House, site of the Amos Fortune Lectures, an annual public speaking contest which started in 1927. The lecture prizes come from a fund donated to the local school in the 1801 will of Amos Fortune, a former slave who prospered and bought both his freedom and his wife's. When the school closed in 1927, residents voted to use the money for the lectures.

Silver Ranch and Airpark, 1 mile (2km) east on SR124, is an activity park with scenic plane rides, carriage and sleigh rides. Open: daily.

Continue south to West Rindge and then take the country road south-east to **Rindge**, set in the Monadnock hills and a summer resort centre offering boating, fishing and walking. ✳

Cathedral of the Pines, north-east off SR119 is an outdoor shrine built from stones that come from every state and commemorates all Americans killed in war. The Memorial Bell Tower is specially dedicated to American women killed in war. Hilltop House has war relics dating from 1775 to the Persian Gulf. Open: daily 9am-5pm May to October. Donations.

Retrace your route to West Rindge, then take 119 west to **Fitzwilliam** which is a picture postcard New England village with its green surrounded by a meeting house, historic houses, antique shops and 1796 inn. Settled in the early 1760s, the town was incorporated in 1773 and became a manufacturing centre producing equipment for the textile mills. It now has industries producing hospital and surgical supplies.

Rhododendron State Park (294 acres/118 hectares), is just over ♣ 2 miles (3km) to the north-west, and noted for its 16 acres (6 hectares) of native *rhododendron maximum*, one of the biggest stands north of the Alleghenies. The bushes, some more than 20ft (6m) tall, usually bloom early to mid July. Open: daily dawn-dusk. Admission charge. From Fitzwilliam continue west on the 119 and then take route 10 north for Keene.

Keene is site of the 1762 Wyman Tavern on Main Street where in1770 the first trustees meeting of Dartmouth College was held. In 1775, Captain Isaac Wyman led twenty-nine Minutemen from the inn to Lexington at the start of the Revolutionary War. In the nineteenth century Keene was famed for the production of glass and pottery. Henry Schoolcraft's flint glass bottles are now prized collectors' items, as is the white pottery made between 1871 and 1926 by the Hampshire Pottery. The Keene State College Arts Center, on Wyman Way, stages plays, concerts and recitals during term time.

The Old Homestead is staged 3 nights in late July at the Swanzey Center, 4 miles (6km) south on SR32. It is an adaptation of the Prodigal Son parable set in Swanzey during the 1880s and first performed in 1886.

❄   There are six covered bridges on country roads off SR10 between Keene and Winchester. Five are on the Ashuelot River and can be located: south of SR119 at Ashuelot; west of SR10 a $^1/_2$ mile (1km) south-west of Westport; east of SR10 at Westport; east of SR10 at West Swanzey, and 1 mile (2km) north of SR32 at Swanzey Village. Another covered bridge crosses the South Branch of the Ashuelot River east of SR32, $^1/_2$ mile (1km) south of Swanzey Village. Main shopping areas is the Colony Mill Market Place, West Street, in a carefully restored wool mill.

🏠   Horatio Colony House Museum, 199 Main Street, was built in 1806 by Abel Blake, son of the first permanent settler in Upper Ashuelot. The house was later owned by Horatio Colony, grand son and namesake of Keene's first mayor. It has an eclectic collection of

Although Nashua is a major industrial centre, it has many fine old wooden buildings

family memorabilia and souvenirs of his world travels. The house is also noted for its ornamental tin ceilings and decorative tiles. Open: Tuesday to Saturday 11am-4pm, June to mid-October. Saturday 11am-4pm, mid-October to December. Admission free.

Horatio Colony Wildlife Preserve, on Daniels Hill Road, is a 450 acre (180 hectare) reserve for birds and animals with nature, hiking and cross-country skiing trails. Open: daily 24 hours. Admission free.

Take route 12 north-west from Keene to **Charlestown**, settled as a north-western outpost in 1744 by twelve families but abandoned in the winter of 1746 after repeated raids by Abenaki Indians. A team of fifty soldiers led by Captain Phineas Stevens returned in April 1747 and managed to hold off a 700 strong force of French and Indians. The settlement then flourished as a farming centre because of the fertile Connecticut River Valley. The town's main streets are so wide, it is said they were used as a training ground for soldiers under General John Stark, the hero of the Battle of Bennington. There are a number of buildings dating from the early nineteenth century.

Fort At Number Four Living History Museum, SR11, is a reconstruction of the 1744 fortified village of Charlestown rebuilt using original drawings, with stockade, watchtower, barns, and other buildings including the Great Hall. Furnishings and demonstrations illustrate eighteenth-century frontier life. Open: Wednesday to Monday 10am-4pm May to September (weekends only 10am-4pm first to third week of September). Admission charge. Allow 1-2 hours.

The Foundation for Biblical Research, Main Street, is in a 1774 mansion on a colonial estate, with antiques, Bible study library and artifacts from archaeological digs in Israel. Open: Tuesday to Saturday 10am-4pm May to September, Monday to Friday 10am-4pm rest of the year. Donations.

Continue north to Claremont. From here you can make a short detour west to the Connecticut River and then drive north for about 8 miles (13km) to **Cornish**, famous at the beginning of the twentieth century for its art colony dominated by sculptor Augustus Saint-Gaudens, Maxfield Parrish and others. The Saint Gaudens National Historic Site, off SR12A, was the home of the sculptor from 1848 to 1907, although the building was a tavern in the early 1800s. It contains the artist's furnishings, and the nearby Little and New Studios contains a collection of the artist's work. Contemporary work is exhibited in the Picture Gallery. Concerts are held on Sundays during the summer, and there are walks through the formal gardens. Grounds open: daily dawn to dusk, buildings open: daily 8.30am-4.30pm May to October. Admission charge.

❄ Just over 2 miles (3km) south of the historic site is one of the longest covered bridges in the country. It is 460ft (140m) long, was built in 1866 and crosses the Connecticut River linking New Hampshire with Windsor, Vermont.

You can either retrace your route back to Claremont or continue north along the river to Plainfield and then turn right to connect with 120 to take you south back to Claremont past Stowell Hill (2,142ft/653m) and Croydon Peak (2,781ft/848m) to the east.

Back in Claremont, take 103 east to **Newport** home of Sarah Josepha Hale, writer and editor of *Ladies' Magazine* and *Godey's Lady's Book*, among the nation's first women's magazines. As editor, she urged President Lincoln to declare Thanksgiving a national holiday, and perhaps more importantly, she wrote the nursery rhyme *Mary had a little lamb*, which was published in *Poems for Our Children* in 1830. Newport is now a commercial and industrial town. Take route 111 north the 3 miles (5km) to **Sunapee**, a year round resort on Lake Sunapee since the mid-nineteenth century. In 1869 Enos Clough invented an engine for a horseless carriage but it so terrified local livestock and horses that it was banned. He sold the invention and the engine ended up driving a boat. In August the town hosts two events, the New Hampshire Craftsmen's Fair at the beginning of the month, and the New Hampshire Gem and Mineral Festival at the end. There are a number of lake sightseeing trips and dinner cruises available.

♣ **Mount Sunapee State Park** is a scenic recreation area with a network of hiking trails in the summer and cross country skiing in the winter. There is swimming from the lake beach, and chairlifts which carry visitors to the 2,703ft (824m) summit where there is an observation platform. Open: daily dawn to 8pm. Chairlifts daily 8am-4.30pm mid-December to early April, Wednesday to Sunday 11.30am-8pm mid-June to early September, weekends 9am-5pm rest of the year. Admission charge.

Take route 103B south to Mount Sunapee, and access to the Mount Sunapee State Park, and then 103 south-east to Bradford. Continue on 114/77 south-east to route 202 just before Henniker. Follow this road south to **Hillsboro**, named after Colonel John Hill who was given a land grant along the Contoocook River in 1740. Hillsboro actually consists of a number of historic villages with many fine old homes. It is still mainly a farming and forestry centre with some light industry. It was the boyhood home of the fourteenth president of the United States, Franklin Pierce. **Fox State Forest**, on Center Road 2 miles (3km) north of Hillsboro, covers 1,445 wooded acres (578 hectares), and offers 20 miles (32km) of hiking paths and cross country ski trails and snowmobiling. Open: daily dawn to dusk.

Franklin Pierce Homestead, near the junctions of ŠR9 and SR31 is ⊞ a restored 1804 mansion which depicts the lifestyle of the wealthy in the nineteenth century. Open: Monday to Saturday 10am-4pm, Sunday 1-4pm July to early September, Saturday 10am-4pm and Sunday 1-4pm late May to June and early September and October. Admission charge.

From Hillsboro take the country road east through Deering to connect with the 149 east to South Weare, and then take the 114 east back to Manchester.

State And Other Major Recreation Areas

Bear Brook, 9,800 acres (3,920 hectares) 2 miles (3km) east of Allenstown, with camping, picnicking, hiking, boat rentals, fishing, swimming, winter sports and visitor centre.

Blackwater Dam, 18 miles (29km) north of Concord off SR127, with boating, fishing and winter sports.

Coleman, 1,605 acres (642 hectares). 12 miles (19km) east of Colebrook, with camping, picnicking, boating, fishing and winter sports.

Echo Lake, 396 acres (158 hectares), in North Conway, with picnicking, hiking, fishing and swimming.

Edward McDowell Lake, 1,198 acres (479 hectares). 4 miles (6km) west of Peterborough, with picnicking, boating, fishing and winter sports.

Franconia Notch, 6,440 acres (2,576 hectares). 5 miles (8km) north of North Woodstock, with camping, picnicking, hiking, fishing, swimming, cycle trails and winter sports.

Franklin Falls Dam, 2,800 acres (1,120 hectares). 2 miles (3km) north of Franklin, with boating, fishing and winter sports.

Greenfield, 401 acres (160 hectares). 1 mile (2km) west of Greenfield, with camping, picnicking, hiking, boating, fishing, swimming and winter sports.

Hopkinton Everett Lake, 7,992 acres (3,197 hectares). On SR127 near Dumbarton, with picnicking, hiking, boating, fishing, swimming, winter sports and visitor centre.

Lake Francis, 1,684 acres (674 hectares). 7 miles (11km) north of Pittsburg, with camping, boating, picnicking and fishing.

Monadnock, 699 acres (280 hectares). 4 miles (6km) north-west of Jaffrey, with camping, picnicking, hiking, winter sports and visitor centre.

Moore Reservoir, 3,500 acres (1,400 hectares). 8 miles (13km) west of Littleton, with picnicking, hiking, boating, fishing, swimming, cycle trails and visitor centre.

Moose Brook, 755 acres (302 hectares). 2 miles (3km) west of Gorham, with camping, picnicking, hiking, fishing and swimming.

Mount Sunapee, 2,174 acres (870 hectares). 3 miles (5km) south of Sunapee with picnicking, hiking, boating, fishing, swimming, winter sports and visitor centre.

Otter Brook Lake, 458 acres (183 hectares). 2 miles (3km) east of Keene, with picnicking, hiking, boating, fishing, swimming and winter sports.

Pawtuckaway, 5,500 acres (2,200 hectares). 4 miles (6km) north east of Raymond, with camping, picnicking, hiking, boating, fishing, swimming and winter sports.

Pillsbury, 3,702 acres (1,480 hectares). 3 miles (5km) north of Washington, with camping, picnicking, hiking, fishing and winter sports.

Rye Harbor, 63 acres (25 hectares). 10 miles (16km) south of Portsmouth, with picnicking, boating and fishing.

Silver Lake, 80 acres (32 hectares). 1 mile (2km) north of Hollis, with picnicking and swimming.

Surry Mountain Lake, 1,700 acres (680 hectares). 6 miles (10km) north of Keene, with picnicking, hiking, boating, fishing, swimming and winter sports.

Wellington, 183 acres (73 hectares). 4 miles (6km) north of Bristol, with picnicking, hiking, boating and swimming.

White Lake, 603 acres (241 hectares). 1 mile (2km) north of West Ossipee, with camping, picnicking, hiking, boating, boat rental, fishing, swimming and winter sports.

White Mountain National Forest, covers 77,000 acres (3,0800 hectares) with camping, picnicking, hiking, boating, fishing, swimming, cycle trails, winter sports and visitor centre.

Further Information

New Hampshire Office of Vacation Travel, PO Box 856-RC, Concord ☎ (603) 271-2666.

Greater Concord Chamber of Commerce, 244 North Main Street, Carrigan Common, Concord ☎ (603) 224-2508.

Greater Manchester Chamber of College, 889 Elm Street, Manchester ☎ (603) 666-6600.

Greater Portsouth Chamber of Commerce, 500 Market Street, Portsmouth ☎ (603) 436-1118.

Hampton Beach Area Chamber of Commerce, Lafayette Road, Hampton ☎ (603) 926-8717.

White Mountain National Forest, PO Box 638, Laconia ☎ (603) 528-8721.

Accommodation

The following Hotels (H) and Restaurants ® are recommended. A general price indicator is given: $ Inexpensive, $$ medium, $$$ expensive. * denotes an historic inn or hotel.

Ashland
The Common Man ® , Main St. ☎ (603) 968-7030 $$
Comfort Inn, 6 West St. ☎ (603) 968-7668 $
* *Glynn House B&B*, 43 Highland St. ☎ (603) 968-3775 $
Bartlett
Attitash Marketplace Motel, Route 302. ☎ (603) 374-2509 $
The Villager Motel, US302. ☎ (603) 374-2742 $
Bedford
* *Bedford Village Inn*, 2 Old Bedford Rd. ☎ (603) 472-2001 $$-$$$
Bethlehem
* *Adair B&B*, Old Littleton Road. ☎ (603) 444-2600 $$-$$$
* *The Mulburn Inn B&B*, Main St. ☎ (603) 869-3389 $-$$
Bretton Woods
* *Bretton Arms*, US302. ☎ (603) 278-3000 $$
Center Harbor
Red Hill Inn, SR25B. ☎ (603) 279-7001 $-$$
Concord
Brick Tower Motor Inn, 414 S. Main St. ☎ (603) 224-9565 $
Cat 'n Fiddle Restaurant, 118 Manchester St. ☎ (603) 228-8911 $$
Concord Comfort Inn, 71 Hall St. ☎ (603) 226-4100 $
Holiday Inn, 172 N. Main St. ☎ (603) 224-9534 $-$$
Conway
Conway Valley Inn, 850 White Mountain Hwy. ☎ (603) 447-3858 $
Darby Field Inn, SR16. ☎ (603) 447-2181 $$-$$$
Mountain Valley Manner B&B, 148 Washington St. ☎ (603) 447-3988 $
Dover
* *Silver Street Inn B&B*, 103 Silver ST. ☎ (603) 743-3000 $-$$
Exeter
Exeter Inn, 90 Front St. ☎ (603) 772-5901 $-$$
The Starving Chef ®, 237 Water St. ☎ (603) 772-5590 $$
Franconia
Bungay Jar Inn, Easton Valley Rd. ☎ (603) 823-7775 $
Franconia Inn, 1300 Easton Rd. ☎ (603) 823-5542 $
The Inn at Forest Hills B&B, SR142. ☎ (603) 823-9550 $
Sugar Hill Inn, SR117. ☎ (603) 823-5621 $$-$$$
Franklin
Maria Atwood Inn B&B, SR3A. ☎ (603) 934-3666 $
Neil Restaurant; 418 N. Main St. ☎ (603) 934-2557 $$

Glen
Bernerhof Inn, US302. ☎ (603) 383-4414 $-$$
Best Western Storybook Resort Inn, Glen Junction. ☎ (603) 383-6800 $-$$
Copperfield's ® US302/SR16. ☎ (603) 383-6800 $$

Gorham
Mount Madison Motel, 365 Main St. ☎ (603) 466-3622 $
Royalty Inn, 130 Main St. ☎ (603) 466-3312 $

Hampton
Curtis Field House B&B, 735 Exter Rd. ☎ (603) 929-0082 $
Inn of Hampton, 815 Lafayette Rd. ☎ (603) 926-6771 $-$$
Lamie's Inn, 490 Lafayette Rd. ☎ (603) 926-0330 $-$$

Hampton Beach
Bluefish Bar & Grill, 379 Ocean Blvd. ☎ (603) 926-1915 $$
Hampton House Hotel, 333 Ocean Blvd. ☎ (603) 926-1033 $$-$$$.
Ron's Beach House ®, 965 Ocean Blvd. ☎ (603) 926-1870 $$

Hanover
Daniel Webster Room ®, Main St. ☎ (603) 643-4300 $$
Hanover Inn, The Green, Dartmouth College. ☎ (603) 643-4300 $$-$$$

Holderness
* *Inn on Gold Pond*, US3. ☎ (603) 968-7269 $-$$
* *Manor on Gold Pond*, US3. ☎ (603) 968-3348 $$-$$$

Jackson
* *Christmas Farm Inn*, SR16B. ☎ (603) 383-4313 $-$$
* *Eagle Mountain Resort*, Carter Notch Rd. ☎ (603) 383-9111 $$
* *Inn at Thorn Hill*, Thorn Hill Rd. ☎ (603) 383-4242 $$-$$$
* *Nestlenook Farm B&B*, Dinsmore Rd. ☎ (603) 383-8071 $$-$$$
Thompson House Eatery, SR16A. ☎ (603) 383-9341 $$

Jaffrey
* *Benjamin Prescott Inn B&B*, SR124E. ☎ (603) 532-6637 $

Jefferson
* *Jefferson Inn B&B*, US2. ☎ (603) 586-7998 $

Laconia
* *Ferry Point House B&B*, SR3. ☎ (603) 524-0087 $

Lebanon
Days Inn, SR120. ☎ (603) 448-5070 $

Lincoln
Drummer Boy Motor Inn, US3. ☎ (603) 745-3661. $-$$
The Lodge, SR112. ☎ (603) 745-3441 $-$$
Mill House Inn, SR112. ☎ (603) 745-6261 $-$$
Profile Room ®, Indian Head Resort. ☎ (603) 745-8000 $$

Littleton
* *Beal House Inn*, 247 W. Main St. ☎ (603) 444-2661 $
* *Thayer's Inn*, 136 Main St. ☎ (603) 444-6469 $

Manchester
Center of New Hampshire (Holiday Inn), 700 Elm St. ☎ (603) 625-1000 $$
Days Hotel, 55 John E. Devine Drive. ☎ (603) 668-6110 $-$$
Renaissance Restaurant, 1087 Elm St. ☎ (603) 669-7000 $$

Nashua
Butcher Boy Restaurant, 1 Nashua Drive. ☎ (603) 882-4433 $$
Clarion Somerset Hotel, 2 Somerset Parkway. ☎ (603) 886-1200 $$
Comfort Inn, 10 St. Laurent St. ☎ (603) 883-7700 $
Green Ridge Turkey Farm Restaurant, Daniel Webster Hwy. ☎ (603) 888-7020 $$
New London
Millstone Restaurant, Newport Rd. ☎ (603) 526-4201 $$
* *New London Inn*, Main St. ☎ (603) 526-2791 $
North Conway
* *Cranmore Mount Lodge B&B*, 859 Kearsarge Rd. ☎ (603) 356-2044 $-$$
* *Eastman Inn B&B*, Main St. ☎ (603) 356-6707 $-$$
North Conway Mountain Inn, Main St. ☎ (603) 356-2803 $
The 1785 Inn, 3582 N. White Mountain Hwy. ☎ (603) 356-9025 $-$$
* *Stonehurst Manor*, US302/16. ☎ (603) 356-3113. $-$$
Snug Harbor Family Restaurant, US 302/16. ☎ (603) 356-3000 $$
North Woodstock
* *Woodstock Inn*, 80 Main St. ☎ (603) 745-3951 $-$$
Plymouth
Knoll Motel, US3. ☎ (603) 536-1245 $
Portsmouth
Comfort Inn at Yoken's, 1390 Lafayette Rd. ☎ (603) 433-3338 $
* *Dolphin Striker ®*, 15 Bow St. ☎ (603) 431-5222 $$
* *Governor's House B&B*, 32 Miller Ave. ☎ (603) 431-6546 $-$$
* *Inn at Christmas Shore B&B*, 335 Maplewood Ave. ☎ (603) 431-6770 $-$$
* *Martin Hill Inn B&B*, 404 Islington St. ☎ (603) 436-2287 $-$$
Oar House Restaurant, 55 Ceres St. ☎ (603) 436-4025 $$
* *Sise Inn*, 40 Court St. ☎ (603) 433-1200 $$-$$$
Salem
Park View Inn, 109 S. Broadway. ☎ (603) 898-5632 $
Sunapee
Dexter's Inn, Stagecoach Rd. ☎ (603) 763-5571 $-$$
Mount Sunapee Motel, SR103. ☎ (603) 763-5592 $-$$
* *Seven Hearths Inn*, 26 Seven Hearths Lane. ☎ (603) 763-5657 $-$$
Twin Mountain
Carlson's Lodge, US302. ☎ (603) 846-5501 $
Pleasant View Motel, US302. ☎ (603) 846-5560 $
Wakefield
* *Wakefield Inn*, Mt. Laurel Rd. ☎ (603) 522-8272 $
Whitfield
* *Maxwell Haus B&B*, 700 Parker Rd. ☎ (603) 837-9717 $-$$
Wolfeboro
Cider Press ®, 10 Middleton Rd. ☎ (603) 569-2028 $$
Lake Motel, SR28. ☎ (603) 569-1100 $-$$
Lakeview Inn and Motor Lodge, 120 N. Main St. ☎ (603) 569-1335 $-$$
Wolfeboro Inn, 44 N. Main St. ☎ (603) 569-3016 $$-$$$

Maine

4

Maine is the most north-easterly state of the US famed for its spectacular and rugged coastline and mountains, sparkling rivers and lakes, long and colourful history, and the huge range of activities and opportunities for the visitor. It is the largest of the New England states and often called the state of 10,000 lakes and 10,000 islands.

History

There are lots of legends about how the Vikings first explored this coastline around AD1000 followed by John Cabot's expedition at the end of the fifteenth century, but little evidence to support them. The British used the Cabot expedition, however, as their justification for claiming the territory.

Algonquian Indians were among the first inhabitants, and the Penobscot and Passam Aquoddy tribes were living along the coast and river valleys when the first European settlers arrived.

above: Whitewater rafting on the Allagash

It is known, however, that the coastline was explored on a number of occasions during the sixteenth century but attempts at settlements failed because of Indian resistance and hostility between the various nations trying to colonise the area.

By the beginning of the seventeenth century this hostility was largely between the English and the French. The French claimed Maine as part of Acadia in 1603, while Britain included it in land granted to the Plymouth Company in 1606. There were frequent periods of conflict, finally resulting in the French and Indian Wars. In 1763 the French were beaten and abandoned the region, leaving Maine and eastern Canada to the English. From 1652 until 1820 Maine was governed as a district of Massachusetts.

The imposition of the Stamp Act in 1765 brought renewed conflict, this time between the colonists and the British Government. British troops and vessels attacked Maine and held the colony for most of the Revolutionary War. The Maine patriots did score some victories, however, including the capture of the British warship *HMS Margaretta*.

The coastal towns fared little better during the war of 1812 and were often raided and bombarded by British warships.

Maine finally broke away from Massachusetts and became a state in 1820 when it entered the Union as part of the Missouri Compromise, but a border dispute between the British and the US led to the Aroostook War between 1838 and 1839. Forts were rapidly built although the war remained largely a local one, and escalation was averted by the Webster Ashburton Treaty of 1842.

During the Civil War Maine provided materials and troops, but there was no major engagement on its soils, and peace brought major problems for the state. Before the war, Maine flourished because of its timber, shipbuilding and fishing fleets. After the war, as western expansion gained pace, industrial growth was concentrated in states further west and south. Maine was hit hard and saw a significant population exodus.

Abundant timber and fast flowing rivers encouraged textile and paper manufacturing, and these two industries dominated the state's economy into the twentieth century until the Depression. Many mills were forced to close and the state in its search for other income sources, realised the potential of tourism, and Maine geared itself to becoming 'America's Playground'.

After World War II, Maine developed new industries, including space and communications research. In 1962 Andover became the ground base for the nation's first communications satellite. Maine is also noted for its pleasure craft boatyards, and is one of the world's most famous areas for lobster. Timber and shipbuilding still remain important industries, while others include textiles, leather goods and footwear. Farming, especially potatoes, is also important together with vegetable and horticultural holdings supplying the urban areas, mostly along the coast. Fishing for lobster, herring, cod, salmon, shrimp and clams is also a major earner and employer. Maine is the only state with a sardine cannery, and even herring scales are now used in the costume jewellery and cosmetic industries. Writers Longfellow, Harriet Beecher Stowe and Edna St Vincent Millay all lived in Maine, as did artists Winslow Homer and Andrew Wyeth.

The population is largely descended from English and Scots-Irish Protestants, and from French immigrants who left Quebec in search of work. About the half the population lives in rural areas, while few towns have populations larger than 25,000. More than half the population lives in the narrow coastal belt between Augusta and the New Hampshire border.

Today Maine has everything the holiday needs from stunning scenery, picture postcards towns and villages, beautiful coves and beaches, historic places, great hospitality and wonderful food.

Geography

Maine borders the Atlantic Ocean to the south and east, Canada to the north and north-west, and New Hampshire to the west. The state is 320 miles (515km) from north to south and 210 miles (338km) from east to west.

It is part of the Appalachian system and the undulating New England peneplain with rocky coast and mountainous hinterland.The highest peaks, rising to 5,268ft (1,606m) are in the northern half of the state. Northern slopes tend not to be steep and are often swampy because of poor drainage, while southern slopes are steeper with drainage by major rivers such as the Penobscott, Kennebec and Androscoggin.

The mountains have been heavily eroded by weather and glacial action, and the retreating ice sheet left thousands of inland lakes and hundreds of deeply scored inlets which explains why Maine has a shoreline almost 3,500 miles (5,635km) long even though as the crow flies it is only 228 miles (367km).

The northern two-thirds of the state is wilderness area, great for backpacking, fishing, water and winter sports. The largest lake in the northern wilderness is Moosehead, but there are hundreds of others to explore and enjoy. Forests cover 85 per cent of the land.

Some State Statistics

Population:	1,227,900
Area:	33,215 sq miles (86,096sq km)
Capital:	Augusta
Highest Point:	Mount Katahdin 5,268ft (1,606m)
Lowest Point:	Sea level
Taxes:	Statewide sales tax is 6 per cent
Official Nickname:	The Vacation State
Unofficial Nickname:	The Pine Tree State
State Gemstone:	Tourmaline
State Animal:	Moose
State Tree:	White Pine
State Bird:	Chickadee
State Cat:	Maine Moon Cat
State Insect:	Honey Bee

Things to See and Do

OUTDOOR ACTIVITIES

There are scores of coastal resorts and inland lakes offering a huge variety of water sports. There are great swimming beaches and white water rafting on the Kennebec and Penobscot Rivers. Canoeing is a great way to see the wilderness country with hundreds of miles of rivers and lakes to explore — even though you may have to carry your canoe and gear occasionally to the next stretch of water. The Allagash Wilderness Waterway stretches more than 90 miles (145km) from Lake Telos, west of Baxter State Park to close to the St John River. Some sections are recommended for experienced canoeists only.

There is great fishing throughout the state, both freshwater and offshore. Trout, salmon, perch, pickeral and other northern species can be caught in the lakes, while there is excellent sea fishing for bluefin tuna, striped bass and mackerel.

The Appalachian Trail ends at Mount Katahdin in Baxter State Park, but there are thousands of miles of other trails to walk, and wilderness campsites to stay in. Many of the more remote backwoods areas are only accessible by boat.

There is just as much to do during the winter months with several well developed ski areas around Auburn, Bethel, Bridgton, Camden, Caribou, Kingfield, Locke Mills, Presque Isle, Rangeley and Waterville. Other winter activities include ice skating, sledging, cross-country skiing and snowmobiling.

Getting Around

Maine is a very large state with a great deal to see and do. The south coast is the most populated and most visited area and route 1 runs conveniently along the coast before heading north along the western banks of the St Croix River and following the eastern border of the state with Canada. The northern part of the state is heavily wooded and mountainous, while the western part is an area of mountains and lakes, and both these areas are largely wilderness country where travelling off the beaten track is fun but time consuming.

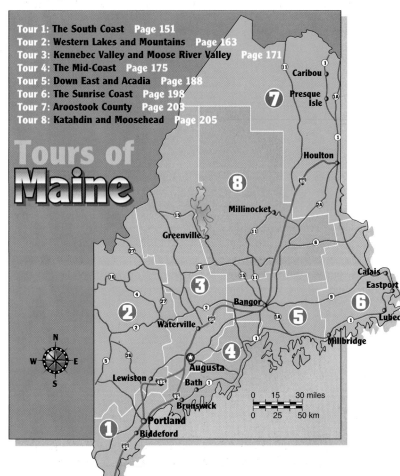

Tour 1: The South Coast   Page 151
Tour 2: Western Lakes and Mountains   Page 163
Tour 3: Kennebec Valley and Moose River Valley   Page 171
Tour 4: The Mid-Coast   Page 175
Tour 5: Down East and Acadia   Page 188
Tour 6: The Sunrise Coast   Page 198
Tour 7: Aroostook County   Page 203
Tour 8: Katahdin and Moosehead   Page 205

Tours of Maine

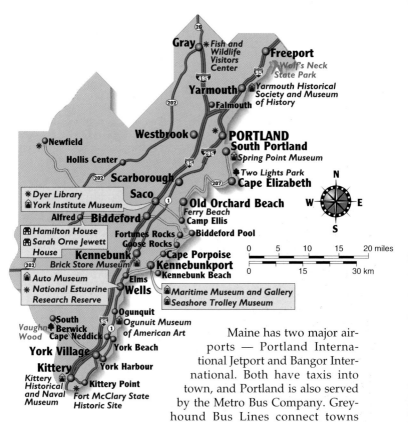

Maine has two major airports — Portland International Jetport and Bangor International. Both have taxis into town, and Portland is also served by the Metro Bus Company. Greyhound Bus Lines connect towns along route 1 with out of state destinations.

Many weeks are needed to explore the state thoroughly but the following tours suggested in conjunction with the Maine Publicity Bureau, will allow you to see most of what Maine's eight diverse tourists regions have to offer.

Tour 1 • The South Coast
140 miles (225km)

Start in **Kittery** and explore the town, founded in 1623 and an important shipbuilding and timber centre. The *Ranger*, the first ship to fly the Stars and Stripes was launched on 10 May 1777 under the command of John Paul Jones, and the first American submarine, the *L8*, was launched in 1917. The Portsmouth Naval Shipyard established in 1800 was was of the first owned by the Federal Government, and the town has many historic sites and nature trails, as well as nearby rocky beaches to relax on and explore. Fort Foster was built shortly after the Civil War on Gerrish Island, and is now a park.

✳ Fort McClary State Historic Site, on SR103 has a blockhouse built in the 1840s on the site of an early eighteenth-century fortification. Open: daily 9am-dusk May to September. Admission charge. Allow 1 hour.

Near the fort is the unusual Lady Pepperell House, designed by Sir William Pepperell, the first Amercian to be knighted by the British. The house is private.

🖼 Kittery Historical and Naval Museum, Rogers Road, has displays on the town's 350 year shipbuilding and maritime history. Open: Monday to Friday 10am-4pm, May to October. Admission charge. Allow 1-2 hours.

Visit Kittery Point across Spruce Creek Bridge. Follow 103 north
🏛 to 1A for **York Village**. York was first settled in 1624 and originally named Agamenticus after the abandoned Indian village on the site. In 1630 a group of wealthy nobles led by Sir Ferdinando Gorges from Bristol established a plantation and named it after their home town, and in 1642 the settlement was given city status and called Gorgeana, becoming the first chartered English city in America. Gorges died in 1647 and the citizens declared self-rule, but attacks by Indians and land disputes forced them to join Massachusetts in 1652. Massachusetts immediately downgraded the city to a town and named it York.

In January 1692 the town was attacked by a strong force of Abenaki Indians, many townspeople were killed and captured and most of the buildings destroyed in what has become known as the Candlemas Massacre. The town has many historic areas, postcard farmhouses and a host of outdoor activities on offer. Old York, Lindsay Road, contains many restored old shops and buildings depicting life from the eighteenth to twentieth centuries. Guided tours begin at Jefferd's Tavern. Open: Tuesday to Saturday 10am-5pm mid-June to September. Admission charge.

Historic buildings include the following: Colonial Revival Elizabeth Perkins House, near Sewall's Bridge; the 1742 Emerson-Wilcox House in the centre of town; Jefferd's Tavern off US1A built in 1750 in Wells and moved to York in 1939; John Hancock Warehouse on the river, one of the oldest surviving commercial buildings in Maine; the Old Goal built in 1719 and used as a prison until 1860; and the Old Schoolhouse, built in 1745. York Harbor has been a fashionable resort since the end of the Civil War because of its extensive beaches, with many luxury 'cottages' used as summer homes, and grand hotels. The harbour is now as busy with pleasure crafts and deep sea fishing boats as it was in the eighteenth and nineteenth centuries
✳ when it was a busy freight port. Of note are the restored Wiggley

suspension bridge over the York River. Cape Neddick Light, on a small island off Cape Neddick, was built in 1879, and is affectionally known to locals as Nubble Light.

Sayward Wheeler House, off Barrell Lane, was built in 1718 and contains family furnishings, and china 'liberated' during the attack on the French at Louisburg in 1745. Open: Wednesday to Sunday 12noon-4pm June to mid-October. Admission charge.

Follow Shore Road to **Ogunquit**, meaning 'Beautiful Place by the Sea'. Ogunquit is a popular summer resort with a 3 mile (5km) long sandy beach to the north and a rocky coastline to explore to the south. There is a trolley service around town from mid-May to mid-October. The 100ft (30m) sheer Bald Head Cliff juts out into the sea more than 300ft (91m), and the crashing sea can send spray 100ft (30m) into the air as it hits the rock. The area is popular with artists and there are many studios and arts and crafts shops. The Ogunquit Theater just south of town stages a summer programme, and art exhibitions are held in the Barn Gallery and Ogunquit Artists' Association Gallery. Perkins Cove is 1 mile (2km) away with galleries and eateries around the harbour where fishing boats can be chartered. Ogunquit Museum of American Art, Shore Road, displays the works of many notable twentieth-century American artists. Open: Monday to Friday 10.30am-5pm, Sunday 2-5pm July to mid-September. Donations. Allow 1 hour.

Continue on route 1 to **Wells**, settled in 1640 on the Webhannet River and with a mill operating by 1641. The settlement suffered repeated Indian attacks during its first 100 years. In 1692 fifteen soldiers barricaded in the Joseph Storer House fought off 500 Indians and French. The house still exists as a private home. The town then prospered as a trading port and fishing and farming centre, but tourism has become increasingly important in the twentieth century because of nearby Wells, Laudholm and Drakes Island Beaches. The Ocean View Cemetery has the grave of Colonel John Wheelright, whose tombstone, dating 1700, is one of the oldest in Maine.

Rachel Carson National Wildlife Reserve, SR9, covers 4,800 acres (1,920 hectares) of estuary salt marshes and upland habitat rich in native and migratory birds. There is an interpretive trail and brochure. Open: daily dawn to dusk. Donations. Wells Auto Museum, US1, has a large collection of antique and classic cars as well as Americana. Open: Monday to Friday 10am-5pm mid-June to September, weekends 10am-5pm May to mid-June and October. Admission charge. Wells National Estuarine Research Reserve, off Laudholm Farm Road, is based in a nineteenth-century saltwater farm with a Greek Revival farmstead, and 1,600 acres (640 hectares) of trails through beach, marsh and upland habitats. It is rich in wildlife and wild plants with visitor centre, slide presentations and guided nature walks. Open: daily 8am-5pm. Admission free. Parking charge.

From Wells Corner take route 9 east to the Kennebunks — Kennebunk, Kennebunkport and Kennebunk Beach — one of Maine's most popular tourist areas. **Kennebunk** originally part of Wells, grew up between the Mousam and Kennebunk Rivers in the mid-1600s and by the 1730s was an important shipbuilding centre, with a flourishing West Indies trade. The end of the Revolutionary War saw a period of industrial growth thanks to water power, although shipbuilding was still dominant. In the first half of the nineteenth century, the fifty or so shipyards along the Maine coast built more than 1,000 wooden vessels from clippers to cargo ships. This prosperity led to the many fine homes that can still be seen, particularly in the town's splendid historic district around Upper Main Street, Summer Street and parts of US1. There are architectural walking tours of the area between mid-June and mid-October starting at 10am on Wednesday and 1pm on Friday. The First Parish Church on Main Street has a bell cast by Paul Revere's foundry. Brick Store Museum, Main Street, is housed in four early nineteenth-century buildings, with art and local history exhibits. The museum also includes the Taylor-Barry House, 24 Summer Street, built in 1803 by master builder Thomas Eaton and noted for its stencilled hallway. Open: Tuesday to Saturday 10am-4.30pm. Admission charge. Allow 1-2 hours.

Kennebunkport is a very popular summer resort and haunt of artists and writers, with many galleries and crafts shops, especially in the well restored buildings around Dock Square. Parson's Walk runs from the square past Walker's Point, and off Cape Arundel, the former summer home of President George Bush, there is a water-spout just before high tide. The Kennebunkport Historical Society conducts guided walking tours of the historic district which leave from the White Columns House at 10.30am Wednesday and 1.30pm, Friday in July and August. There are cruises, whale watching and deep sea fishing charters availabe. There is a wonderful scenic drive along Ocean Avenue to the fishing village of **Cape Porpoise**. The Maritime Museum and Gallery, Ocean Avenue is housed in the renovated boathouse of author Booth Tarkington with the writer's memorabilia, paintings, ship models and maritime artifacts. Open: Monday to Saturday 10am-5pm, Sunday 11am-4pm mid-May to November. Admission charge. Allow 1 hour. The Seashore Trolley Museum, Log Cabin Road, is one of the world's oldest and largest collection of old electric trolley cars from around the globe, including the famous Streetcar named Desire. There is a video about the evolution of public transport. Open: daily 10am-5.30pm May to September, restricted opening rest of year, check times. Admission charge ☎ (207) 967-2800. Allow 1 hour.

Continue through Cape Porpoise, Goose Rocks Beach and Fortunes Rocks to scenic **Biddeford**, site of one of New England's first saw mills in 1662, and now a major textile, plastics, machinery and electronic manufacturing centre, closely tied to Saco, its sister town across the river. Its early French-Canadian connections are reflected in the annual La Kermesse Festival every June. Irish links are represented by the July St Mary's Festival, and the Lobster Festival is held in August. The beautifully restored 1895 Opera House is one of the finest examples of late nineteenth-century ornamental architecture, and is considered acoustically near perfect.

At **Biddeford Pool** you can visit the Point Sanctuary which has trails through 30 acres (12 hectares) of rocky coastal headland, and is one of the state's best birdwatching sites. Open: daily dawn to dusk.

Route 9 continues to **Saco**, settled in 1631 and sister town to Biddeford. It changed its name to Pepperelboro in 1762, and to Saco in 1805. Its prosperity was based on iron, and the first water powered iron works was built in the 1820s. There is excellent fishing in the Saco River, and Ferry Beuch State Park and Old Orchard Beach offer safe swimming. Aquaboggen Water Park and Cascade Water

Old Orchard Beach is one of the oldest and still one of the most popular seashore resorts in Maine with 7 miles (11km) of sandy beaches

and Amuseument Park, both on US1, have wave pools, water slides and other amusements. Both are open through the summer and charge admission.

❊ Visit Dyer Library and the York Institute Museum, Main Street. The library in the nineteenth-century Deering House has a collection of books, manuscripts and photographs on Maine history, while the ⛫ latter, founded in 1867, has displays of Maine furniture, decorative arts and paintings. Library open: Tuesday to Friday 10am-5pm, Saturday 9am-12noon. Museum open: Tuesday to Saturday 1-4pm, July and August, Tuesday to Friday 1-4pm May, June, September and October. Tuesday to Thursday 1-4pm rest of the year. Admission charge.

➤ Visit the Maine Aquarium, on US1N with tropical fish and marine life from round the world and shark, penguin and seal exhibits. Open: daily 9am-4pm. Admission charge.

Continue to Camp Ellis and Old Orchard Beach, and on to ❊ **Scarborough.** The Scarborough Marsh Nature Center on Pine Point Road covers more than 1,000 acres (400 hectares) ranging from mud flats to uplands, with nature trails and daily walking tours. Open: 9.30am-5.30pm mid-June to September. Admission free.

Turn right on to route 114 and then right again on 207 to follow the headland round through **Cape Elizabeth**, named in 1615 by Captain John Smith after Princess Elizabeth, sister of England's Charles I. The fishing and farming settlement, originally part of Falmouth, now Portland, survived many attacks by Indians and pirates, became a separate district in 1765 and a town in 1775. Now largely a suburb town of Greater Portland, the cape has a lot to offer with sandy beaches, cliff walks, two state parks and saltmarshes teeming ♣ with birdlife. Two Lights Park, 3 miles (5km) south on SR77 is next to Cape Elizabeth Light, while Crescent Beach State Park, 1 mile (2km) south of the town has good swimming beaches.

♣ Portland Head Light in Fort Williams Park, dates from 1791 and was built on the orders of President George Washington and was the ⛫ first to be built after the founding of the USA. It has a museum with nearby hiking trails. The park is open daily dawn to dusk. Museum open: daily 10am-4pm June to October, weekends 10am-4pm, April and May and November and December. Admission charge. Allow 1 hour.

⛫ In **South Portland** visit the Spring Point Museum on Fort Road. The museum is in a former repair shop of Fort Preble, has changing exhibits on local history, and a conservation laboratory where you can watch antiquities being restored. Open: Wednesday to Sunday 1-4pm May to October, or by appointment. Admission charge. ☎ (207) 799-6337.

The next stop is **Portland**, birthplace of Longfellow who de- ※
scribed it as 'the beautiful town that is seated by the sea'. It is now the
largest city in Maine, and a major industrial centre and distribution
hub for northern New England. The city, on Casco Bay and the
northern banks of the Fore River, works hard to retain much of its
Victorian charm with many well-restored old buildings, parks, tree
lined cobble stone streets, gaslights, historic district, and waterfront
areas. There is an ongoing city programme of restoration and preservation.

The Portland International Jetport is served by several US national carriers and a number of regional airlines. Greyhound, Concord Trailways and Vermont Transit bus lines link the city to the
nation, and the Metro Bus Service and South Portland Municipal
Bus provide in-city public transport. The great advantage of Portland, however, is that it is built on a peninsula and is small enough
to explore on foot which is the best way to get around downtown.

The city was officially established in 1632 although traders had
been operating from Casco Bay earlier. It was twice destroyed by
Indians in 1675, once by the British in 1775, and then by the Great
Fire in 1866, which explains why it largely consists of Victorian
architecture, and why its symbol is the Phoenix. Its location on hills
overlooking the sea, architecture and fine restaurants has also
earned it the name of 'The Little San Francisco of the East'. This is
one of many names it has had over the years. Originally called
Machigonne (Great Neck) by the Indians, it was called Casco by the
first settlers, then Falmouth in 1658, and finally Portland in 1786.

The Old Port Exchange was the heart of Portland's thriving
nineteenth-century business community, and many of the old waterfront buildings and warehouses have been converted to shops,
boutiques and restaurants. **Maine State Pier** on Commercial Street ※
has the near 1,000ft (305m) long 'Whaling Wall' mural depicting
marine life in the Gulf of Maine.

Portland is also the state's main cultural centre, and home to the
Portland Symphony Orchestra and Portland Performing Arts
Center with the Portland Stage Company, the contemporary Ram
Island Dance Company and the Center for Performing Studies, all of
which stage productions and concerts throughout the year. The city
also hosts many annual festivals including the Old Port Festival and
Waterfront Festival in June. Nearby there are Crescent Beach and
Two Lights state parks, and many islands that can be visited offshore, including the Calendar Islands (there were thought to be 365
of them), first visited by John Smith in 1614. There are many sea trips
available from short cruises and whale watching, to overnight
sailings for Yarmouth in Nova Scotia. A number of companies offer

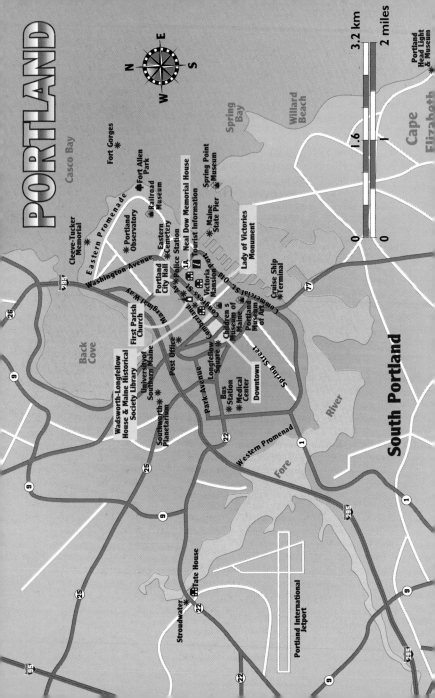

cruises such as Prince of Fundy Cruises and Bay View Cruises on Fisherman's Wharf and Casco Bay Lines from the pier at Commercial and Franklin Streets.

A self guiding walking brochure of the historic district is available from the Convention and Visitors Bureau, 305 Commercial Street, Portland ME 04101.

Historic buildings of interest include the following: Charles Q. Cladd House (1832), 97 Spring Street in Greek Revival style; City Hall (1909-12), Congress Street, in Second Renaissance Revival style; McLellan Sweat House (1800-1), 111 High Street, in Federal style; and the Old Port Library (1888), 619 Congress Street, an example of Romanesque Revival architecture. Western Promenade is one of America's best preserved Victorian residential neighbourhoods.

The **Children's Museum of Maine**, 142 Free Street has toys, models, space shuttle and hands-on science exhibits. Open: Tuesday to Saturday 10am-5pm (Friday to 8pm), Sunday to Monday 12noon-5pm. Admission charge. Allow 1 hour. **Cleeve Tucker Memorial**, was erected in 1833 on the Eastern Promenade in honour of the city's founders. **Eastern Cemetery**, on Congress and Mountfort Streets, was Portland's first cemetery and dates from 1688.

The **First Parish Church** Congress Street, is the city's oldest, dating from 1825. **Fore River Sanctuary** at the end of Rowe Avenue, is a 76 acre (30 hectare) city reserve with Jewel Falls, salt marshes, and trail to the towpath of the Cumberland and Oxford Canal. Open: daily dawn to dusk. Admission free. Allow 1 hour. **Fort Allen Park**, Fore Street and Eastern Promenade, is dedicated to Veterans of World War I. **Fort Gorges**, on Hog Island, is hexagonal fort built in 1858. It can be visited by private boat. **Fort Scala** is a Civil War fort on House Island and makes an interesting day out. In the early twentieth century the island was an immigration hospital for immigrants entering the US. The **Lady of Victories Monument** was erected in Monument Square in 1891 to commemorate Portland men who fought in the Civil War. **Harrington House Museum Store**, 45 Main Street, has museum reproductions, unusual arts and crafts and fine furniture. Open: daily. The **Longfellow Square** has a statue of the poet erected in 1888.

Maine Narrow Gauge Railroad Company and Museum, 58 Fore Street, is a working rail museum with shops and exhibits on Maine's 2ft (1m) trains. Open: daily 10am-4pm.

Neal Dow Memorial House, Congress Street, is in an 1829 late Federal-style built by politician, prohibitionist and abolitionist Neal Dow, with period furnishings and family memorabilia. It is also the headquarters of the Maine Woman's Christian Temperance Union, to whom the house was left. Open: Monday to Friday 11am-4pm.

Donations. Allow 1 hour. **Portland Head Light** and **Museum** are on Cape Elizabeth. The light was erected in 1791 and is the state's oldest. The museum has navigational aids and exhibits about the history of the light and Cape Elizabeth. Open: daily 10am-4pm June to October. Admission charge. **Portland Museum of Art**, Congress Square, exhibits classic and contemporary art, concentrating on artists associated with Maine. Open: Tuesday to Saturday 10am-5pm (Thursday to 9pm), Sunday 12noon-5pm. Admission charge. Allow 1-2 hours.

Portland Observatory, Congress Street, was built in 1807 overlooking the harbour to allow seamen's wives to look out for returning ships. Open: Wednesday, Thursday and Sunday 1-5pm, Friday and Saturday 10am-5pm, July and August, Friday to Sunday 1-5pm June, September and October. Admission charge. Allow 30 minutes.

Southworth Planetarium, University of Southern Maine campus, has exhibitions about space and solar system, astronomy and laser light shows. Open: Monday to Friday 9am-5pm. Exhibition admission free. Show admission charge. Allow 1-2 hours. **Spring Point Museum**, Southern Maine Technical College, has displays on the early history of Portland and area, and also features ongoing archaeological documentation and conservation of the Snow Squall, the last surviving American built clipper ☎ (207) 799-6337 for opening times. **Tate House**, 1270 Westbrook Street in Stroudwater, is a Georgian mansion, built in 1755 by George Tate, Mast Agent for the British Crown. Of note are the unusual roof, dogleg staircase, patterned floor, wood panelling and original cove ceilings. Open: Tuesday to Saturday 10am-4pm, Sunday 1-4pm July to early September, Friday to Sunday 10am-4pm early September and October. Admission charge. Allow 1 hour.

Victoria Mansion, 109 Danforth Street, is an Italianate villa designed by Henry Austin for the hotelier Ruggles Morse and built in the late 1850s with superb interior decor. The carpets were woven in Scotland. The mansion is also noted for the very ornate painted walls and ceilings, wood panelling and carved marble fireplaces. Open: Tuesday to Saturday 10am-4pm, Sunday 1-5pm June to early September, Friday and Saturday 10am-4pm, Sunday 1-5pm, early September to October. Admission charge. Allow 1 hour.

Wadsworth-Longfellow House, 485 Congress Street, was built in 1785 by General Peleg Wadsworth, grandfather of the poet who spent his childhood here. The bricks were brought by barge from Philadelphia and it was the city's first brick house. The third storey was added in 1815. The house has period furnishings and family memorabilia, and delightful gardens. Open: Tuesday to Saturday 10am-4pm June to October. Admission charge. Allow 1 hour. The

Maine Historical Society Library is in the grounds at the rear. Open: Tuesday to Friday and second and fourth Saturdays 10am-4pm. Admission free.

For further information contact Greater Portland Conventon and Visitor Bureau, 305 Commercial Street, Portland ME 04101 ☎ (207) 772-5800.

It is worth making the short detour north-east of Portland to **Falmouth**, declared a town in 1786, previously having been part of Portland. It has changed remarkably little over the years. A fishing, farming community, Falmouth also has several large estates and is home of the Portland Yacht Club.

Grisland Farm, on US1, is a 60 acre (24 hectare) coastal lowland ❄ reserve with nature trails and rich animal and bird life. There are animal and bird exhibits in the visitor centre. Grounds open: daily dawn to dusk. Centre open: Monday to Saturday 9am-5pm, Sunday 12noon-5pm. Admission free. Allow 1-2 hours.

You can then continue up the coast to visit **Yarmouth**, first settled in 1636 although Indian attacks drove away many of the early colonists and permanent settlement did not take place until 1713 when the four waterfalls along the Royal River were harnessed to power the timber mills. Farming, fishing and shipbuilding were also important industries. The area is now very popular in the summer with many scenic walks along the river and coast. The Yarmouth Clam Festival is held over the third weekend in July. Yarmouth Historical Society and Museum of History has exhibits, photographs and displays depicting local history. Open: Tuesday to Saturday 10am-5pm September to June, rest of the year Monday to Friday 10am-5pm. Donations.

The next coastal town is **Freeport**, known as the 'Birthplace of Maine' where the document was signed giving it independence from Massachusetts, which led to statehood in 1820. It is also the home of the legendary L.L. Bean sports store which never closes. The town is now a shopping and tourist centre, although there are still footwear and crab processing industries. The 40ft (12m) Big Indian statue is a famous landmark. There are many sea cruises offered, including trips to Eagle Island State Park where Robert Peary planned his North Pole expedition in his strange summer house. There are also lobster pot and seal watching cruises.

Desert of Maine, off Desert Road, is an area of sand dunes resulting from over intensive grazing of the grasslands. The top soil has been lost revealing sand deposited at the end of the Ice Age 8,000 years ago. The dunes, some 70ft (21m) high, cover 100 acres (40 hectares) and are spreading. Open: daily 9am to dusk. Admission charge. Mast Landing Sanctuary, Upper Mast Landing Road, is 140 acres (56 hectares) of land along the river, rich in animals and birds, with walking trails and the remains of an ancient mill. Open: daily dawn to dusk. Admission free. The North American Wildlife Expo, on US1, has dioramas of native species, many endangered. Open: daily 9am-9pm June to September. Admission charge. Allow 1 hour. Wolfe's Neck Woods State Park, has self-guiding nature trails. Open: dawn to dusk May to September.

From Freeport head inland on the country road to Pownal then turn left and after passing through the village of North Yarmouth turn right for **Gray**. The first settlement known as New Boston was often attacked by Indians and the people driven away. It was not until 1778 that Gray attained town status but the community then flourished as mills were built, including the first powered mill in the US. Gray is often called the 'Crossroads of Maine' as six major routes pass through the village. The Fish and Wildlife Visitors Center, on SR26, has native Maine wildlife, including moose and bear, many of them injured and not able to be returned to the wild. Open: daily 10am-4pm May to early November. Admission charge. Allow 1-2 hours.

Return to Portland and then head west on route 25 to **Westbrook** and Smiling Hill Farm, country road 781, a working dairy farm with petting zoo and animal exhibits and scale model farm equipment and pony rides for the children. Open: daily 10am-5pm May to September, 10am-4pm October. Admission charge.

Continue west on route 26 to Gorham, and then take route 4 west through Bar Mills and Hollis Center to Waterboro and then the country road north to **Newfield**, a farming district settled in 1778 and originally the Washington Plantation. It changed its name when the town was incorporated in 1794. The Willowbrook project has restored almost forty of the oldest buildings to recreate a nineteenth-century village with old vehicles, shops, tools and crafts. Open: daily 10am-5pm mid-May to September. Admission charge ☎ (207) 793-2784. Allow 2-3 hours.

Return south to connect with the 4/202 and continue south to **Alfred**, close to the Massbesic Experimental Forest. The Alfred courthouse holds records dating back to 1636. Take route 4A to Sanford where route 109 south connects with route 4 south for North and South Berwick, an early logging settlement providing masts for the British Navy with a sawmill operating before 1640. Mills and shipbuilding added to the prosperity which resulted in many fine Colonial homes gracing the town. The town is in the centre of a rich farming area and still has a manufacturing base. Hamilton House, Vaughan Lane, is a Georgian mansion built around 1785 by merchantman Colonel Jonathan Hamilton overlooking his wharves and warehouses on the Salmon Falls River. Noted for its murals, rustic

furnishings and gardens. Open: Tuesday, Thursday and weekends 12noon-4pm June to mid-October. Admission charge. Sarah Orne Jewett House, Portland Street, was built in 1774 and the home of author Sarah Orne Jewett born in 1849. The Georgian home is noted for panelling, early wallpapers and period furnishings. Open: Tuesday, Thursday and weekends 12noon-4pm June to mid-October. Admission charge. **Vaughan Woods**, off SR236, has woodland trails. Cow Cove is reputed to be where the *Pied Cow* landed in 1634 bringing the first cows to Maine. Later in the same year, the vessel also brought one of the country's first saw mills which was built nearby. Open: daily 9am-8pm May to September. Admission charge.

From here it is a short drive back to Kittery.

Tour 2 • Western Lakes and Mountains
225 miles (362km)

Start at **Auburn**, the sister town of Lewiston on the opposite banks of the Androscoggin River. It is about 30 miles (48km) inland from its mouth, and has a long history of textile and shoe production. Electronics and plastics have also become important. Together with Lewiston, the two town's are known as the 'industrial heart' of Maine, because of their early exploitation of water power. Auburn's shoe industry started in the 1830s and thanks to mechanisation, Auburn factories were making 2 million pairs of shoes a year by 1870. Lake Auburn, 3 miles (5km) north, offers fishing and there is cross country skiing at Lost Valley, 2 miles (3km) north-west. Androscoggin Historical Society Museum, County Building, has local history and natural history exhibits, including Civil War memorabilia. Open: Monday to Friday 1.30-5pm. Donations.

Lewiston, on the east bank of the Androscoggin, is the larger of the 'Twin Cities' and the state's second largest city. The first cabin was built in 1770 and a wood mill opened in 1819, but it was not until 1850 that the town really developed when the river was harnessed to power textile mills. French Canadians came to work in the many mills and contributed to the town's rich Franco-American heritage. A landmark is the rocky 340ft (104m) Mount David on the campus of Bates College, founded in 1864. The Lewiston Falls and Dam, which now power the city, are best viewed from Longley Bridge. Major annual events include the Maine State Parade in May and the Androscoggin Challenge Biathlon and Balloon Festival in August. Bates College Museum of Art, Olin Arts Center, Russell Street, has changing exhibits of eighteenth- to twentieth-century prints, drawings and paintings, and works by Lewiston native Marsden Hartley. Open: Tuesday to Saturday 10am-5pm, Sunday 1-5pm. Admission free. Thorncrag Bird Sanctuary is 200 acres (80 hectares) of woods and lakes and many species of native animals and birds. Open: daily dawn to dusk. Admission free.

Return to Auburn and head west on 11 to Mechanic Falls, then follow 11 south to **Poland Spring**, source of the widely distributed Poland Spring Water and one of the oldest resorts on the east coast. Outlet Beach offers good swimming and other water activities. Poland Spring Resort was destroyed by fire in 1975.

Maine State Building and All Souls Chapel, off SR26, was built to represent Maine at the 1893 Columbian Exposition in Chicago, and when it closed, was dismantled and rebuilt on its present site. The fine Victorian buildings contains exhibits and photographs about the area. The granite chapel is noted for its stained glass windows, Mason Hamlin reed organ and belfry with four Westminster chimes. Open: daily 9am-1pm July and August, weekends 9am-1pm May to June and September. Admission charge to museum, chapel free. The Shaker Museum, on SR26 is in the last active Shaker community in the US and was founded in 1782. Here you can visit many eighteenth- and nineteenth-century buildings of Shaker design, with Shaker furniture, handicrafts and workshops. Open: Monday to Saturday 10am-4.30pm May to October. Admission charge. Allow 1-2 hours.

Continue to Crescent Lake, then connect with route 302 and turn right for the short detour to **Naples**, on the north-western side of

Sebago Lake and noted for the the hand operated Songo Lock, part of the canal system which extended to Portland. The lock now connects Sebago and Long Lakes. This is an area of lakes and hills offering excellent walking, boating, windsurfing and fishing, and sightseeing lake cruises.

Head back east on the 302/35 and follow it as it swings south round the lake to **Sebago**, a holiday village in the hills to the west of Sebago Lake offering nearby fishing, walking and boating. The Jones Museum of Glass and Ceramics, off SR107, has more than 8,000 exhibits from around the world from the time of the Pharoahs to the present. Open: Monday to Saturday 10am-5pm, Sunday 1-5pm mid-May to mid-November. Admission charge.

Then take the 35 south for **Standish**. A landmark is the Old Red Church with its square towered belfry and brick red exterior. Marrett House, SR25, was built in 1789 and was the home of the Reverend Daniel Marrett whose descendents lived there until the 1950s. During the war of 1812, it was used to store gold from Portland banks. It has period furnishings and flower, kitchen and herb gardens. Open: Tuesday, Thursday and weekends 12noon-4pm mid-June to August. Guided tours on the hour. Admission charge.

Continue on 113 north-west to Steep Falls, and the 25 for Cornish and Kezar Falls. Head north on 160, then 113 for **Fryeburg**. The stone public library was once the schoolhouse, and has the books and gun collection of Clarence Mulford, creator of Hoplong Cassidy. The Soldiers Monument in Bradley Memorial Park stands on the site of the original Fryeburg Academy founded in 1791. The Hemlock Bridge, 3 miles (5km) north-east of town, is one of Maine's nine remaining covered bridges.

Take 302 east for **Bridgton**, a popular year round resort area with lakes offering waterside camping and cottage rentals, swimming, fishing and boating. Shawnee Peak at Pleasant Mountain is west of town and is a popular winter sports area.

Continue on the 37 and 35 north for **Bethel**. The town lies in the Oxford Hills along the Androscoggin River and was settled in 1774 as part of Sudbury, Canada. The remoteness and hostile Indians did not encourage settlement and by 1781, it had only ten families. It was renamed Bethel in 1796 and developed into a farming and timber town, and prospered further with the arrival of the railroad connecting Portland and Montreal. The railway also brought tourists wanting to visit the nearby White Mountains to the south-west. The area is now a popular year round resort, with hiking, cycling, swimming, fishing and rockclimbing popular in the summer, with cross country and alpine skiing in the winter at Mount Abram and Sunday River,

The County Building, Auburn, also houses the Androscoggin Historical Society Museum

opposite; The main church of Lewiston, the larger of the 'Twin Cities, of the Androscoggin

The Country Store in Poland Spring, one of the state's oldest and best known resorts

to the east. There is a free booklet from the Chamber of Commerce about self-guiding walks around the old town, especially historic Broad Street and Bethel Hill Village. PO Box 439, Bethel ME 04217. Dr Moses Mason House, Broad Street, is the 1815 home of prominent Main politician Dr Mason, with period furnishings and interesting landscape murals. Open: September to June Monday to Friday 10am-4pm, rest of the year Tuesday to Sunday 1-4pm. Admission charge. Allow 1 hour. Grafton Notch State Park is open from mid-May to mid-October and noted for its scenic drives. Points of interest include Screw Auger Falls, Spruce Meadows, Mother Walker Falls and Moose Cave.

Along this stretch of road you can detour to take in the White Mountain National Forest. From Bethel head north on 5/26 for Newry, east on 2 to Rumford Point, then north on the 5 to Andover with the Black Mountain of Maine on your right.

If you have time you can continue north from Andover to explore the lake country by taking the country road which connects with route 17 for Haines Landing and Oquossoc. You can then take highway 4 east to take in **Rangeley**. Visit the Hunter Cove Sanctuary on SR4 with trails through cedar swamps, woods and meadows. The area is rich in wildlife including bear, deer, bobcat and moose. Open: daily dawn to dusk. Admission free. The Wilhelm Reich Museum, Dodge Pond Road, is in memory of natural scientist Reich, a student of Freud. It contains memorabilia, paintings, tactile senses hands-on discovery room and nature trail. Open: Tuesday to Sunday 1-5pm July and August, Sunday 1-5pm September. Admission charge. Allow 1 hour. About 20 miles (32km) north of Rangely on route 16 is **Stratton**, originally a logging camp and and still reliant on timber based industries, but now a popular base for outdoor enthusiasts offering canoeing, hiking, camping, fishing, birdwatching and winter sports. The Dead River Historical Society Museum, has memorabilia about the town's early logging and hunting days, and a room dedicate to the 'drowned' towns of Flagstaff and Dead River. The road from Stratton to Canada is lined with markers describing the Arnold Trail, the route taken by Benedict Arnold's army marching on Quebec.

Take highway 27/16 south to **Kingfield**. The town is named after William King, Maine's first Governor, and was settled in 1806. Kingfield Historical Society maintains a wonderfully furnished home on School Street. The Stanley Museum, School Street is in honour of the inventive Stanley family, creators of the Stanley Steamer automobile. There are family memorabilia and other inventions, and early photographs taken by Chansonetta Stanley. Open: Tuesday to Sunday 1-4pm May to October and December to March.

Admission charge. Allow 1 hour. The historic Wire Bridge, 7 miles (11km) south in New Portland, was built in the 1850s, and is the oldest suspension bridge of its type in the country.

Take 142 south to **Phillips**, the base for the narrow gauge Sandy River and Rangeley Lakes Railroad. The Sandy River Railroad Park operates 1 mile (2km) rides over a section of the original track. Phillips Historical House Museum has a collection of railway memorabilia and Portland glass. The 40ft (12m) Daggett Rock, outside Phillips, is one of the world's largest glacier deposited boulders and is accessible from route 142 via a dirt track and then a third of a mile walk.

From Phillips take route 4 east to **Strong**, known as the toothpick capital of the world because it makes tens of millions of wooden toothpicks each year. The town is also the birthplace of the Maine Republican Party.

Then continue on route 4 to Fairbanks and then drive the 2 miles (3km) south to Farmington, to rejoin the main route.

If you do not want to take this detour, from Andover take 120 east to Mexico and Rumford and on to Wilton, before taking route 2 north to **Farmington**. Set in rich farming country, the town was settled with land grants issued after the Revolutionary War. The first school opened in 1788 and the town has had an association with education ever since. The University of Maine in Farmington stems from the Farmington Aacademy founded in the 1860s. In memory of the earmuff inventor, Chester Greenwood Day is celebrated in December. There are year round opportunities for outdoor activities, from summer boating and fishing to winter skiing.

The Art Gallery, Main Street, has works by Maine artists. Open: Sunday to Thursday 12noon-4pm, mid-September to mid-May. Admission free. Allow 1 hour. The Nordica Homestead Museum, Holley Road, is birthplace of opera singer Lillian Nordica. Exhibits about her career with costumes and jewellery. Open: Tuesday to Saturday 10am-12noon and 1-5pm, Sunday 1-5pm June to September or by appointment. Admission charge ☎ (207) 778-2042. Allow 1 hour.

Take route 2 and then 133 south from Farmington to **Livermore Falls**. Livermore is a farming and forestry community with 1,207ft (368m) Bear Mountain to the west. Norlands Living History Center, Norland Road, is a working nineteenth-century farm with restored homestead, stone library, schoolhouse, church and barn. Period tools, foods and crafts are featured in festivals throughout the year. Open for guided tours: daily 10am-4pm July and August. Admission charge. Allow 1-2 hours.

Take route 4 south to North Turner, then the 219 west to East and

West Sumner and West Paris. The West Paris area has prospered because of the rich minerals below ground. There have been mines and quarries for more than 100 years yielding gemstones such as beryl, rose, amethyst and aquamarine. A number of quarries are open to the public for free prospecting. The Maine Mineral Museum in **Perham's of West Paris**, has a huge display of local minerals. Open: daily 9am-5pm. Admission free. Snow Falls Gorge on SR26 allows access to the scenic waterfalls.

Take 26 south to **Norway**, noted for its manufacture of snow shoes, including a pair made for explorer Robert E. Peary. **South Paris** is the commercial centre for the district and Paris Hill is a charming residential area with eighteenth- and nineteenth-century homes. Hamlin Memorial Library, on Paris Hill Road in the old jailhouse was built in 1822. There is a collection of books and papers of Hannibal Hamlin, Abraham Lincoln's vice president. Open: Tuesday to Friday 11.30am-5.30pm (and Wednesday 7-9pm), Saturday 10am-2pm September to mid-June, Tuesday to Friday 10am-4pm, Saturday 10am-2pm rest of the year. Admission free. Allow 1 hour. Continue south on route 26 to Oxford, and then east through Mechanic Falls back to Auburn.

Naples; Canals and the historic Songo Lock allow vessels to cruise Songo and Long Lakes and Brandy Pond

Tour 3 • Kennebec Valley and Moose River Valley
150 miles (241km)

The tour starts in **Augusta**, capital of the state since 1827 and at the head of navigation on the Kennebec River. It is an administrative, commercial and industrial centre with paper manufacturing and meat processing, and computer industries. The Plymouth Colony established a trading post here in 1628 and John Alden and Captain Miles Standish, immortalised by Longfellow, were among the first settlers. Fort Western on the western bank, was built in 1754, and in 1797 the settlement, known to the Abenaki Indians as Cushnoc, was named Augusta, after the daughter of General Henry Dearnorn. Fort Western Museum of the Kennebec, Cony Street. The oldest surviving wooden fort in New England dating from 1754, with original garrison house and furnishings

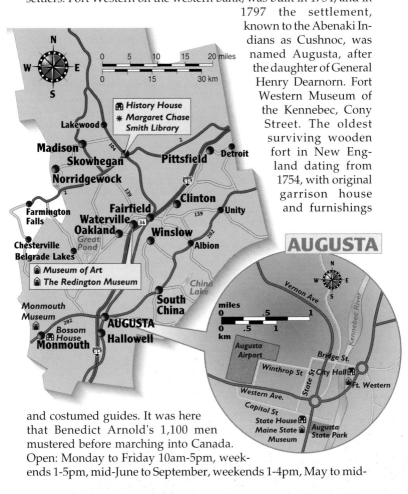

and costumed guides. It was here that Benedict Arnold's 1,100 men mustered before marching into Canada.
Open: Monday to Friday 10am-5pm, weekends 1-5pm, mid-June to September, weekends 1-4pm, May to mid-

June and October. Admission charge. Allow 1-2 hours. Main annual events include Whatever Week, in the 10 days before the 4 July, the highlight of which is the Great Kennebec River Whatever Race, in which any vessel that can float can take part. In mid-July, the city's French links are celebrated with the Le Festival de la Bastille. The Augusta State Park, Capitol Park, is noted for its many different species of trees and exotic shrubs and ferns, and the unusual triangular Maine Vietnam Veterans Memorial. Open: daily. Admission free. Allow 1-2 hours. Maine State Museum, in the Library Museum Archives Building in the State House complex, has exhibits about Maine's history dating back 12,000 years, and special display's about the state's manufacturing industry and Indian heritage. Open: Monday to Friday 9am-5pm, Saturday 10am-4pm, Sunday 1-4pm. Admission charge. Allow 2 hours.

The State House, designed by Charles Bulfinch and built from Hallowell granite in 1829 (although much added to over the years) is noted for its original portico, portraits and exhibit of battle flags. There is a self guiding tour with interpretive wall plaques. Open: Monday to Friday 8am-5pm. Admission free. Allow 1 hour.

From Augusta head east on 105 for Windsor, and then north on route 32 to **South China**, on the eastern shore of 8 mile (13km) long China Lake and the centre of a farming and summer resort area. China Village was known as Harlem until 1818, and the Albert Church Brown Memorial Library, in a nineteenth-century house on Main Street, has many artifacts from the town's earliest days.

Continue to Albion and Unity. Continue north on route 9 out of Unity then turn left on to the 220 for Detroit, then 11 west to Pittsfield. Travel south to explore Clinton, Fairfield, Winslow, Oakland and **Waterville**, a tribal council meeting place for the Abenaki Indians and now home of many childrens' summer camps. Also close by are the Ticonic Falls on the Kennebec River. Waterville was an important passenger and freight river port in the mid-nineteenth century but declined with the arrival of the railways. A dam was built at the falls in 1868 and many industries were established. Today it is an important industrial centre producing concrete and timber products, machinery and metals. The Waterville Theater Company stages productions in the Opera House. The Belgrade Lakes to the west include **Great Pond**, the inspiration for the play and film *On Golden Pond*, — the mailboat still operates daily. Colby College, founded in 1813, has the Miller Library with its collection of letters, manuscripts and books of Maine poet Edwin Arlington Robinson, and the Lorimer Chapel, with an organ designed by Albert Schweitzer. The Museum of Art has works from the eighteenth century to the present, including watercolours by prominent

American artists. Open: Monday to Saturday 10am-4.30pm, Sunday 2-4.30pm. Admission free. The Redington Museum, Silver Street, in one of the town's oldest buildings, has exhibits about the town's early history, plus Indian and Civil War artifacts, and a nineteenth-century apothecary. Open: Tuesday to Saturday 10am-2pm May to September or by appointment. Admission charge. The bridge crossing the Kennebec from Winslow to Waterville is just below the Ticonic Falls, and above the falls is the Two-Cent Bridge, the last known toll footbridge in the US. The tolltaker's house in on the Waterville side, but tolls are no longer charged.

Take the 139, then 104 north to **Skowhegan**, Indian for 'A Place to Watch' because this is where the Abenaki came to fish for salmon below the falls on the Kennebec River. The huge statue of an Indian sculpted by Bernard Langlais, commemorates these early inhabitants. The island's first European settlers arrived in 1771 and Benedict Arnold and his troops crossed the island in 1775 on their way to fight at Quebec. Timber has long been the town's mainstay and huge rafts of logs were floated down the river until 1976. There is still a large paper mill as well as many other manufacturing industries. The agricultural Skowhegan State Fair has been held annually since 1818 and is believed to be the oldest in the country, and the Lakewood Theater 6 miles (10km) north on Lake Wesserunsett, is Maine's state theatre. Founded in 1901 it stages productions throughout the summer. History House, Elm Street, was built in 1839 and has exhibits about local history. Open: Tuesday to Friday 1-5pm mid-June to mid-September. Donations. Margaret Chase Smith Library, Norridgewock Avenue, has exhibi- tions about the life and career of this prominent Maine politician. Open: Monday to Friday 10am-4pm. Donations.

Keep north on the 201, then turn left on the 148 west for Madison, then south to Norridgewock. Continue to Farmington Falls and then take the country road south through Chesterville to connect with route 17 south. Take route 133 west for 3 miles (5km) then route 106 south to highway 202, then head east for a short distance before turning off to visit **Monmouth**. The town was incorporated in 1792 and named after the Battle of Monmouth in New Jersey in which General Henry Dearborn, one of its first citizens, fought. The Victorian Cumston Hall opera house on Main Street has fine frescoes and murals and hosts a Shakespeare season in July and August. Monmouth Museum, Main Street, covers five buildings which re- flect nineteenth-century life in the town with blacksmiths forge, stencil shop, carriage house and warehouse with farm equipment. Open: Tuesday to Sunday 9am-4pm. Bossom House was built in the

One of the many fine old buildings in Augusta, founded in 1628

The weir at Skowhegan now blocks the Kennebec River where Abenaki Indians fished for salmon centuries ago

late eighteenth century. Open: Tuesday to Sunday 1-4pm May to September. Admission charge. Allow 1 hour.

From Monmouth take 135 east to Manchester and then take the road south to connect with **Hallowell**. In the early 1600s Abenaki Indians traded here with Plymouth merchants, and by the late 1700s, because of its position on the Kennebec River, the town had become a major port. Cruises now sail from the town docks, and Hallowell is noted for its antique shops along Main Street. From Hallowell it is a short drive north back into Augusta.

> **Note:** On this tour Madison is the most northerly point, and there is a huge area of wilderness country north of this which can be visited. The 201 is the main road north to Jackman and there are few roads off the main highway, but it is great country if you want to get off the beaten track.

Tour 4 • The Mid-Coast
200 miles (320km)

This is a delightful coastal area with a huge amount to see, islands to visit and beaches to laze on.

The tour starts in **Brunswick**, the main city of the eastern Casco Bay area and an industrial centre dating back to the 1620s, when an English trading post was set up to export salmon and sturgeon from the Androscoggin River. Originally known as Pejepscot, the settlement was frequently attacked by Indians and razed to the ground in 1690 and again in 1722. In 1714 the Pejepscot Proprietors bought the post, built Fort George and laid out the first town plan. Twelve Rod Road, now Maine Street, was 198ft (60m) wide, and one of the widest streets in New England. By the end of the eighteenth century, Brunswick as the settlement had been renamed, was a major lumbering, milling and shipbuilding centre. Bowdoin College, established in 1794, is the home of the Maine State Music Theater, where Broadway musicals are performed during the summer. Chamber music concerts are held on Friday evenings in the summer at the First Parish Church, and free open-air concerts are held on the Mall on Wednesday evenings in July. The inspiration for Harriet Beecher Stowe's *Uncle Tom's Cabin* is said to have come from a sermon given at the First Parish Church which opened in 1717. Governor Joshua Lawrence Chamberlain, famous for his defense at Gettysburg lived at 226 Maine Street. The Federal-style home with Victorian Gothic additions contains the Joshua Lawrence Chamberlain Museum. Open: Monday to Saturday. Main events during the year are

Topsham Fair with agricultural exhibits and harness racing, and the Maine Arts Festival, both held in August. Brunswick also hosts the Maine Highland Games on Thomas Point Beach on the third Saturday of August, and the Bluegrass Festival over the Labor Day weekend. Bowdoin College has as old boys Nathaniel Hawthorne and Henry Wadsworth Longfellow, Arctic explorers Robert Peary and Donald MacMillan, and President Franklin Pierce. Open for campus tours Monday to Friday 9-11am, 2-4pm and Saturday by appointment. Admission free. Allow 1 hour. Visit Bowdoin College Museum of Art, Walker Art Building, with European, Colonial and Federal paintings, the Warren Collection of classical antiquities and the Molinari Collection of medals and plaques. Guided tours available. Open: Tuesday to Saturday 10am - 5pm. Sunday 2-5pm. Donations. Allow 1-2 hours. Peary-MacMillan Arctic Museum, Hubbard Hall, has exhibits on the two explorers and the Arctic region. Open: Tuesday to Saturday 10am-5pm, Sunday 2-5pm. Donations. Allow 1 hour. Pejepscot Museum and Skolfield Whittier House, Park Row, is an Italianate 'double house' built by two sea captains in 1858. It is now a museum with changing local history exhibits, period furnishings and personal belongings of the two families exactly as they were left in 1925. Open: Monday to Friday 10am-3pm, Saturday 1-4pm. May to September, rest of the year Monday to Friday 10am-3pm. Donations. Allow 1-2 hours.

From Brunswick take highway 1 east then 201 north to Richmond Corner and 197 east into **Richmond**, on the Kennebec River 16 miles (26km) north of Brunswick and explored by the French in 1604 although the first permanent settlement was not established until 1776 with shipbuilding, textile and timber industries. It became a commercial city and port of call for vessels plying between Augusta, Portland and Boston. There are many fine old buildings and Slavic immigrants in the 1950s and 60s have introduced traces of Eastern European and Russian architectuture.

From Richmond head north to Gardiner and then cross the river to **Pittston** which flourished a century ago on its ice cutting business based on the Kennebec River. The Major Reuben Colburn House, built in 1765, and barn contain many exhibits about Benedict Arnolds march to Quebec, including some of the boats used by the troops to cross the rivers along the way. Open: daily or by appointment. Head south on route 27 to **Dresden Mills** and the Pownalborough Court House which dates from 1761. On route 128 is the town's brick schoolhouse, built in 1861, and museum. The one room schoolhouse has its original desks and exhibits about local history. Open by appointment.

Then head south on the 27 to **Wiscasset**, often called 'Maine's prettiest village'. It was once the state's chief port but declined rapidly after the 1807 Embargo Act, although its early gracious mansions remain. Also of note are the sad remains of the four masted schooners *Luther Little* and *Hesperus* slowly rotting in the harbour. Castle Tucker House Museum, Lee and High Streets, in an 1807 Georgian mansion with Federal, Victorian furnishings and paintings, and famous freestanding elliptical staircase can be visited. Open: Tuesday to Saturday 11am-4pm July and August, and by appointment in September. Admission charge ☎ (207) 882-7364. Fort Edgecomb State Historic Site is on the southern end of Davis Island, with 1809 octagonal oak blockhouse and earthworks. Open: daily 9am-5pm May to September. Admission charge. The Maine Coast Navigation and Railroad leaves from Wiscasset Pier on Water Street and offers train and boat rides along the Sheepscot River. The train makes a round trip to Newcastle. Both train and boat trips last about 1 hour 15 minutes, and operate between May and October ☎ (207) 882-8000 for times. The Maine Yankee Energy Information Center on SR144 has exhibits on nuclear power, hands-on display, and presentations about the plant. Open: Monday to Saturday 10am-5pm, Sunday 12noon-4pm. Admission free. Musical Wonder House, 18 High Street, has antique mechanical musical instruments from around the world. Open: daily 10am-5pm May to October. Admission charge.

Nickels-Sortwell House, on Main and Federal Streets, and the 1807 home of shipmaster Captain William Nickels with family memorablia and furnishings is open Wednesday to Sunday 12noon-4pm June to September. Admission charge. Old Lincoln County Jail and Museum, Federal Street, is an austere granite building with walls up to 41 inches thick and was a prison from 1811 to 1913. It still has the original cell graffiti. Exhibits include jailer's home and woodworking and farming tools. Open: Tuesday to Sunday 11am-4.30pm July and August, rest of the year by appointment. Admission charge ☎ (207) 882-6817. Pownalborough Courthouse, SR128, is the only remaining pre-Revolutionary courthouse in Maine built in 1761 with courtroom, judge's chambers, accommodation and tavern. Exhibits include old tools and machinery. The grounds contain a a Revolutionary cemetery. Open: Wednesday to Saturday 10am-4pm, Sunday 12noon-4pm July and August, by appointment rest of the year. Admission charge ☎ (207) 737-2504.

Take highway 1 east for 2 miles (3km) then take route 27 south on to the pensinsula to visit **Boothbay Harbor**, a delightful seaside resort and harbour which has retained much of its old New England charm, with its fishing boats, winding streets and old homes. Fishing and shipbuilding are still important, but the harbour also attracts many pleasure crafts and tourists. There are many cruises, fishing and whale watching trips available from the piers. The annual Windjammer Days Festival in late June commemorates the town's maritime past with antique boat parade and entertainments. Arts and crafts are featured in the Harbor Lights Festival each December. The Carousel Music Theater presents productions between mid-May and October.

Boothbay Railway Village, on SR27, resembles an 1890s village with antique cars and restored blacksmith shop, schoolhouse and general store, and narrow-gauge steam engine. Open: daily 9.30am-5pm, mid-June to mid-October. Admission charge. Allow 2-3 hours.

Visit Hendricks Hill Museum, on the island of **Southport**, with restored early nineteenth-century house and period household items and tools from the local fishing industry. There are also early fishing boats and tools used in the ice harvesting industry. Open: Tuesday, Thursday and Saturday 11am-3pm, July to September. Donations. Allow 1 hour.

Continue to **Newcastle** and the Maine Coast Railroad which offers an exciting train ride along the coast and then up to Martha Washington Pass, and an opportunity to see lots of wildlife. It

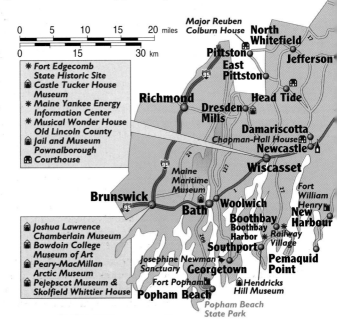

operates from mid-May to mid-October ☎ (207) 563-5252. St. Patrick's Church on SR215, was built in 1808, the oldest surviving Catholic church in New England, although the cemetery dates back to 1760. Open: daily dawn to dusk. Donations.

South-east of Newcastle across the river is **Damariscotta**. The settlement was founded by three families in 1730 although John Brown had lived in the area in the mid 1600s. Its position on the river with plentiful timber favoured shipbuilding, and it launched many vessels including the *Excelsior* in 1849, the first three decked ship built in Maine. The original model for the ship is in the Information Center on Main Street. The small community is now a shopping and commercial centre supplying the nearby resort towns. There are still many old homes, but fire destroyed most of the earliest buildings along Main Street in 1845. Chapman-Hall House, Main Street, was built in 1754, has period furnishings and original kitchen, plus shipbuilding exhibits and herb garden. Open: Tuesday to Sunday 1-5pm, mid-June to mid-September. Admission charge. Allow 1 hour. Round Top Center for the Arts, on US1, is an art gallery, with changing arts and crafts exhibits, concerts and plays. Many artists work on site. Open: daily 10am-4pm. Donations.

Outside the town along the river are 3 acres (1 hectare) of ancient oyster-shell dumps left by the Indians who summered here. In places the shells are 30ft

Map labels:
N
W E
S
Fort Knox
Prospect
Fort Point
Searsport
Moose Point State Park
Belfast
220
3
3
Matthews Museum of Maine Heritage
Union
Old Conway House and Museum
17
17
Camden
Maine Coast Artists Gallery
235
Rockport
Rockport Marine Park
Montpelier
Waldoboro
Museum
Rockland
Owls Head
Vinalhaven
South Warren
73
Transportation Museum
Thomaston
Vinalhaven Historical Society and Museum
Friendship
Museum
Farnsworth Art Museum and Homestead
Shore Village Museum
131
Port Clyde
Marshall Point Lighthouse Museum
Monhegan Boat Line
Monhegan
1
6
220

(9m) deep, and many artifacts found here suggest the Indians had frequented the site for around 2,000 years.

Head back into Newcastle and take 213 north and then the 218 to **Head Tide**, a tiny picturesque riverside community, now a National Historic District, with 1838 meeting house, 1860 school house, 1890 store and a number of eighteenth- and nineteenth-century homes. One of these was the birthplace of Pullitzer prize winning poet Edwin Arlington Robinson.

Continue north to North Whitefield and then take the country road east to **Jefferson** at the head of Damariscotta Lake in an area noted for hunting, fishing and outdoor pursuits. Nearby Haskell Mountain offers great views from the old lookout tower, and on route 126 there is an 1829 stone cattle pound used during round ups. Damariscotta Lake State Park has sandy beaches and trails.

Head north from Jefferson to route 17, then east to **Union** which hosts the Maine Blueberry Festival in late August which includes pie eating contests and the crowning of the Blueberry Queen. More than 5,000 pies are baked and given away free to visitors. Matthews Museum of Maine Heritage, Union Fairground, has memorabilia about the state's early settlers and local craftsmen demonstrate traditional arts and crafts. Open: Tuesday to Sunday 12noon-5pm July to early September, by appointment in June and rest of September. Admission charge ☎ (207) 785-3281.

From Union take routes 106 and then 131 to Searsmont and Belmont Corner, and then take highway 3 east into **Belfast**, a former shipbuilding town and home to many rich merchants and sea captains who built fine mansions. Belfast is now a popular artistic centre, attracting artists, artisans and writers. The 5 day Belfast Festival is held in the last weekend of July, and the Belfast Maskers stage theatrical productions year round. Many local cruises are available, and you can also take a ride on the Belfast and Moosehead Lake Railway. Free walking tour brochures are available from the Chamber of Commerce, PO Box 58, 31 Front St. Belfast, ME 04915 ☎ (207) 338-5900.

Follow highway 1 east along the coast to **Searsport**, one of Maine's main shipbuilding centres in the late eighteenth and nineteenth centuries, producing more than 250 sailing vessels. In 1870 it was said that one in ten of all the captains in the US merchant marines lived in the town. It is still a major deepwater port with a new container facility under construction able to handle five vessels at a time.

The town has many fine old mansions and is noted for its antique shops. Closeby is Moose Point State Park, and the 46 mile (74km) scenic drive along US1 between Rockland and Verona through the town is a must. The Penobscott Marine Museum, US1 and Church Street, has eight buildings including an 1816 captain's home and 1845 town hall. Exhibits on history of the area including shipbuilding, period furnishings and household effects, ship models, paintings and shipwright tool. Open: Monday to Saturday 9.30am-5pm, Sunday 1-5pm May to mid-October. Admission charge.

Continue to Stockton Springs, then head north on 1A for **Prospect** close to the granite quarries of Mount Waldo. The village is a farming and trading centre, and popular summer resort. The territory was contested by Maine and New Brunswick until 1839, and the granite pentagon-shaped Fort Knox was built in the mid-nineteenth century to protect the Penobscot River and prevent British warships reaching Bangor, although it was never threatened. Open: daily dawn to dusk mid-May to mid-September, 9am-5pm early May and mid-September to October. Guided tours available mid-June to early September. Admission charge. Allow 1 hour.

Continue to Frankfort, then take the country road west to connect with the 139 for Monroe and Brooks, then head south on route 7 back into Belfast to pick up highway 1 south along the coastline through Northport to **Camden**. This delightful small seaside resort and harbour, with old houses, attractive gardens and shaded streets, has long attracted writers and artists because of its beauty. There is a statue of poet Edna St. Vincent Millay at the harbour, and Millay memorabilia in the Whitehall Inn. The town is a year round resort offering a wide variety of water activities on the sea and inland lakes during summer, with cross country and downhill skiing and ice skating during the winter. The National Toboggan Championships are held every February as part of the Camden Snow Ball. There are scenic boat cruises year round, and great view of the area from Mount Battie in nearby Camden Hills State Park. Bok Amphitheatre and Marine Park, Atlantic Avenue has a number of concerts, art exhibitions and arts and crafts shows during the year. Musical events are also staged at the Camden Opera House. Old Conway House and Museum, 1 mile (2km) south off US1 is an eighteenth-century farmhouse with period furnishings and herb garden, a barn containing old vehicles and farm tools, blacksmiths forge, an 1820 maple sugar house and the Mary Meeker Cramer Museum with local history exhibits, costumes and models. Open: July and August Tuesday to Friday 10am-4pm. Admission charge. Allow 2 hours.

The next stop south is at **Rockport** formerly part of Camden but incorporated as a town in its own right in 1891. A harbour seal called Andre spent many summers off Rockport and became the subject of

The harbour in the heart of Damariscotta, founded in 1730 and noted for shipbuilding

Belfast prospered because of its harbour but now attracts tourists rather than ships

Camden attracts and caters for tourists year round and is also popular with artists and writers

Locomotives like this at Rockport used to transport lime to waiting ships in the harbour

a series of children's books. Concerts, the Festival of Maine storytelling and the Rockport Jazz Festival are held in the Opera House during the summer. Maine Coast Artists Gallery, Russell Avenue, exhibits local artists work. Open: daily 10am-5pm June to October. Donations. Rockport Marine Park, next to the harbour, has a statue to Andre the seal, and three restored lime kilns built in the early 1900s, plus a replica of one of the trains that used to haul the lime to the harbour. Open: daily dawn to dusk. Admission free.

Continue south to **Rockland**, a major fishing port, commercial and retail centre, and the birthplace of poet Edna St. Vincent Millay. It is called the Lobster Capital of the World and there are ferries and sea cruises to the many nearby islands.

Farnsworth Art Museum, Elm Street, has American and European art and concentrates on artists who have had ties with the state. Open: Monday to Saturday 10am-5pm, Sunday 1-5pm June to September, Tuesday to Saturday 10am-5pm, Sunday 1-5pm rest of the year. Admission charge. Allow 1 hour. Farnsworth Homestead, next to the museum, was built in 1850 in Greek Revival style and contains the original furnishings. Open: Monday to Saturday 10am-4.30pm, Sunday 1-4.30pm June to September. Admission with museum ticket. Owls Head Transportation Museum, SR73, has old planes, cars, motorcycles and carriages. Open: daily 10am-5pm April to October, Monday to Friday 10am-4pm, weekends 11am-3pm rest of the year. Admission charge. Shore Village Museum, 104 Limerick Street, has displays of Coast Guard relics, lighthouse and life saving equipment, Civil War artifacts, doll and costume collection and hands-on exhibits. Open: daily 10am-4pm June to mid-October and by appointment. Donations ☎ (207) 594-0311.

Vinalhaven Island is the largest of the Fox Islands in Penobscot Bay and an ideal day trip from Rockland. The Maine State Ferry Service operates a regular service on the 75 minute crossing. The village was incorporated in 1789 and was famous for its locally quarried granite used in many of the fine buildings in New York and Washington. The water filled quaries now offer excellent trout fishing. Lobstering is now the main industry, and the peaceful island has lots of opportunities for walking, birdwatching and rockpool hunting. The ferries carry cars for the less energetic.

Vinalhaven Historical Society Museum in the High Street, has exhibits about local history and the local fishing and quarrying industries. Open: daily 11am-3pm mid-June to early September or by appointment. Donations ☎ (207) 863-4318.

At **Thomaston**, a cross was planted in 1605 by Captain George Weymouth on Allen's Island in the mouth of the St. Georges River. It marked the first New England land claimed by an Englishman.

A trading post with the Indians was established in 1630 and settlers established what is now Thomaston in 1736. Many fine sailing ships were built here, and locally quarried lime was exported from the busy harbour. Fishing, boatbuilding and lobstering are still important industries. The town has many fine Colonial homes and also has the Maine State Prison with a shop where handcrafted items and furniture made by the inmates are sold. Montpelier, near the junction of US1 and SR131, is an elegant reproduction of the home of General Henry Knox, the first US Secretary of War. It contains original furnishings and family possessions. Open: Wednesday to Sunday 9am-5.30pm June to early September. Admission charge.

From Thomaston it is worth taking a detour south to Port Clyde and the ferry across to Monhegan Island. In **Port Clyde** visit the Marshall Point Lighthouse Museum, off SR131, in the keeper's house built in 1895 with local history exhibits. The lighthouse was built in 1857. Open: Tuesday to Sunday 1-5pm June to September, weekends 1-5pm March to May and October. Donations. Allow 1 hour.

The tiny **Monhegan Island** is 9 miles (14km) offshore and has been popular with artists for more than 100 years and still has many studios and galleries. The island has the tallest coastal cliffs in New England and a busy fishing harbour, which offers a number of cruises. It also has a rich wildlife. One reserve has 600 varieties of wild flowers and 200 species of bird recorded. There are many hiking trails to areas such as Cathedral Woods, the haunt of deer, and the 160ft (49m) Black Head and White Head cliffs. The small museum on Lighthouse Hill has maritime, local history and natural history exhibits. There are regular passenger sailings from Port Clyde throughout the year with greater frequency during the summer ☎ (207) 372-8848.

Return to Thomaston and continue west on highway 1. Make the short detour north to visit **Warren**, a good place to explore the Georges River Canal System, the second oldest in the US. The 28 mile (45km) canal was built in 1795 and there are many walking trails in the area. Open: daily dawn to dusk. Admission free.

Return to highway 1 and continue west to **Waldoboro**, a famous shipbuilding centre in the nineteenth century, especially of five masted schooners, and now a quiet farming and commercial centre on the Medomak River, with fishing for lobster and clams. Sauerkraut is also manufactured, an indication that many of the early settlers were of German origin. One gravestone in the cemetery bears the inscription: 'This town was settled in 1748 by Germans who immigrated to this Place with the promise and expectation of finding a prosperous city, instead of which they found nothing but wilderness'. The Old German Meeting House, built in 1772 is nearby. There are many galleries featuring the works of local artists, the renovated 1936 Waldo Theater and the popular Moody's Diner. Waldboro Museum, on SR220, is in three old buildings housing ship models, quilts and textiles, local history exhibits, a nineteenth-century farm kitchen, country store and schoolhouse. Open: daily 1-4.30pm July to early September, weekends 1-4.30pm rest of September. Donations.

Take route 32 south to drive round the pensinsula taking in **New Harbor** which offers lots of cruises to explore the coastline, visit nearby islands or view marine and birdlife, and **Pemaquid Point**. This historic promentory was the site of Maine's first permanent settlement in 1625 and the offshore naval battle in 1813 between the English brig *Boxer* and American brig *Enterprise*. The lighthouse was built in 1827 and can be reached by car. **Colonial Pemaquid State Historic Site**, off SR130, is the site of the seventeenth-century English settlement with museum displaying artifacts excavated in the area. Open: daily 9am-5.30pm May to mid-September, weekends 9am-5pm mid-September to October. Admission to the site free, museum charge. **Fort William Henry State Historic Site**, close to Pemaquid Beach, is the site of the British Fort Charles built in 1677, replaced by Fort William Henry in 1692 and destroyed by the French in 1696. Fort Frederick was built on the site in 1729 but was demolished by the Americans during the Revolutionary War to prevent the British capturing it. A reproduction now stands on the site. Open: daily 9am-5.30pm May to early September, weekends 9am-5pm early September to October. Admission charge. Allow 1 hour. **Lighthouse Park** covers 8 acres (3 hectares) and offers fine views. The lighthouse is not open to the public but the park contains the Fishermen's Museum and Art Gallery, displaying the work of local artists. The museum is open Monday to Saturday 10am-5pm, Sunday 11am-5pm May to September and by appointment the rest of the year. Donations ☎ (207) 677-2494. The gallery is open Monday to Saturday 10.30am-5pm, Sunday 1-5pm, July to early September, Friday and Saturday 10.30am-5pm, Sunday 1-5pm early September and October. Donations.

From Waldoboro, it is worth the detour south on route 220 to **Friendship** which overlooks Muscongus Bay and is a charming fishing village and summer resort. It is birthplace of the famous gaff-rigged *Friendship* sloop, noted for its seaworthiness. The Friendship Museum, in the old schoolhouse, has collections of local memorabilia.

Back on highway 1, continue west through Wiscasset to Woolwich and **Bath** on the Kennebec River and a shipbuilding centre and port since the early 1600s. It has built more than 4,000 over the centuries. Bath Iron Works now builds nuclear vessels and large merchant ships. There are a number of large old houses in the town, built during Bath's heyday as a major port. There are free brochures on walking and driving tours of historic Bath and area available from the Chamber of Commerce, 45 Front Street, Bath. ME 04530 ☎ (207) 443-9751. The Maine Maritime Museum, Washington Street, is on a 10 acre (4 hectare) site and is a tribute to the area's long shipbuilding history, with models, artifacts, paintings and interpretive displays. It also includes two old shipyards where wooden sailing ships were built, and where visiting vessels are docked. The Apprentice shop still teaches traditional boat building and repair skills. Open: daily 9.30am-5pm. Admission charge. Allow 2 hours. At **West Bath** you can visit the Hamilton Sanctuary, off Foster Point Road, which has trails through pine forests and meadows with views of the Maine coastline. It is also rich in birdlife. Open: daily dawn to dusk. Admission free.

From Woolwich you can also drive south on 127 to visit Southport and **Georgetown** with the Josephine Newman Sanctuary. A 119 acre (48 hectare) bird reserve of tidal mud flats, marsh and woodlands. Walking trails with swarms of mosquitoes. Open: daily dawn to dusk. Admission free.

From Bath take the 209 for West Point and **Popham Beach**, site of the first shortlived English settlement in 1607. Illness and Indian attack depleted their numbers and the following year the settlers built the *Virginia* and sailed home. The *Virginia*, a 30 ton pinnace, was the first American built sailing vessel. A local road leads to a memorial commemorating the site. The nearby Popham Beach State Park offers sandy beach, swimming, windsurfing and fishing. The fort at **Popham State Historic Site** was built of brick and rock in 1861 but never finished, and there is a second fort, built during World War II with three bunkers and tower which can be climbed. Open: daily 9am-dusk May to September. Admission free. Allow 1 hour.

On returning to highway 1 continue west to Cooks Corner, where you can again detour south to visit Orrs, Baley and Eagle Islands, or carry on back into Brunswick.

Tour 5 • Down East and Acadia
220 miles (354km)

❊ The figure of eight tour starts in **Bangor**, the principal city in northern Maine and a retail, commercial and administrative centre as well as a major industrial town and port. Timber, paper and spruce wood products, together with electronics, footwear and tourism are the main industries. It is also the home of novelist Stephen King. Bangor is at the head of tidewater on the Penobscot River and has long been heavily reliant on exporting its goods out of state. During the Revolutionary War this trade was virtually halted, and the town survived by blockade running and privateering. After the war the timber trade flourished and by the 1830s the town's population had tripled. For many years it was regarded as the timber capital of the world, and the port was so busy it became known as 'the Devil's Half-Acre' because of the number of drinking and gambling houses that sprang up. Of note are the statue of woodsman John Bunyan on Main Street, and the Veterans' Memorial in Norumbega Mall. Bangor Fair is the main annual event, held each summer, and one of the nation's oldest.

There is a self-guiding tour of the historic old town and maps and information are available from the Chamber of Commerce. There are also guided bus tours available between July and September ☎ (207) 947-0307 for details on both.

🏛 Bangor Historical Society Museum, 159 Union Street in the 1836 Greek Revival style Thomas A. Hill House, has period furnishings and paintings by local artists. Open: Monday to Friday 12noon-4pm, July to September, Tuesday to Friday 12noon-4pm March to June and October to mid-December. Admission charge. Allow 1 hour.

🏛 Cole Land Transportation Museum, Perry Road, has a collection of more than 200 vehicles with displays on the history of freight transportation. Open: May to November daily 9am-5pm. Admission charge. Allow 1 hour.

🏛 Isaac Farrar Mansion in Union Street, was the home of the timber baron and is a restored Greek Revival house with marble fireplaces, intricately carved woodwork, panelling and stained glass windows. Open: daily 9am-5pm. Admission charge.

From Bangor head west on route 100 through Damascus to Newport, then north on routes 7/11 to **Dexter**, a farming and manufacturing community on Lake Wassookeag. Woollen mills were founded in the nineteenth century, and textiles and footwear are still

🏛 major industries. The Grist Mill Museum is run by the Dexter Historical Society. It was built in 1853 and operated until 1966. Other exhibits include one-room schoolhouse, farm tools and old photographs. Open: Monday to Friday 10am-4pm, Saturday 1-4pm, June to August, Monday to Saturday 1-4pm September. Donations ☎ (207) 924-5721. Allow 1 hour.

Take 94 east to connect with route 43 which runs east to East Corinth, and continue on the 43 east through Hudson to **Old Town**, a timber and milling town since the early nineteenth century based on water power from the Penobscot River, and in 1836 became the northern terminus for New England's first railway which ran the 13 miles (21km) from the Penobscot Ironworks and Bangor. The town still has a strong manufacturing base and now straddles across several islands. The Old Town Cane Company makes a wide range of canoes but is most noted as one of the few remaining makers of traditional wood and canvas canoes. The Penobscot Indian Reservation takes in much of Indian Island and many of the uninhabited surrounding islands.

Old Town Museum, North Fourth Street, has exhibits about local history and the timber trade, and Indian artifacts. Open: Wednesday to Sunday 1-5pm early June to mid-August. Donations. Allow 1 hour.

Follow route 2 south to **Orono**, home of the University of Maine founded in 1868 with 12 students and now enrolling more than 11,000 annually. The town is also the centre for local farming and light industry. The university's Maine Center for the Arts includes the Hutchins Concert Hall and Hudson Museum, and astronomy programmes are presented in the Maynard F Jordon Planetarium. The university has a delightful campus with ornamental gardens and working farm ☎ (207) 581-3743.

Head back to Bangor then take 1A south to **Ellsworth**. Although settled as a lumber camp in 1763, industry developed because of water power from the Union River. Today it is quiet town with many inland lakes which makes it popular with boaters, canoeists, anglers and walkers. A wide range of birds and marine animals can be spotted from Ellsworth Marina Waterfront Park, off Water Street.

Black House, on SR172 dates from the 1820s and the interior furnishings have changed little since. Carriages and sleighs are exhibited next door. Open: Monday to Saturday 10am-4pm, June to mid-October. Admission charge. Allow 1 hour.

Stanwood Homestead Museum, on SR3 is the former home of ornithologist Cordelia Stanwood. The 1850 house has original furnishings and birdwatching and collecting exhibits, and is set in Birdsacre, a 130 acre (52 hectare) reserve with more than 100 native species. Museum open: daily 10am-4pm mid-June to mid-October,

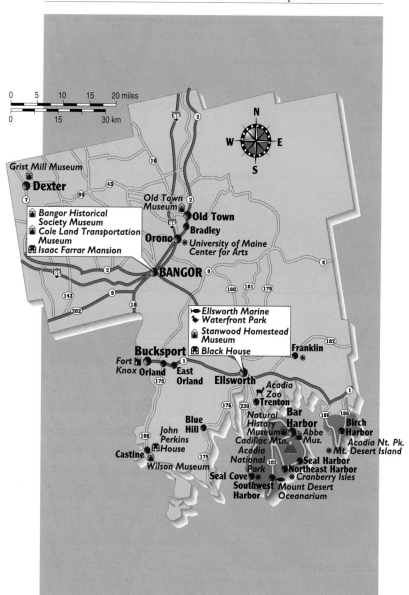

0   5   10   15   20 miles

0   15   30 km

Grist Mill Museum
Dexter
7
94
43
16
95 2

Old Town
Museum 2
Old Town
95 Bradley
Orono * University of Maine
Center for Arts

Bangor Historical
Society Museum
Cole Land Transportation
Museum
Isaac Farrar Mansion

BANGOR 9
95 2
143
202 2 9
1A
180 181 179

Ellsworth Marine
Waterfront Park
Stanwood Homestead
Museum
Black House

Franklin 182
*

Bucksport 1
Fort
Knox Orland East
175 Orland
Ellsworth
Acadia
Zoo
176 230 Trenton
Blue Natural Bar
Hill History Harbor 186 186
John Museum Abbe Birch
166 Perkins Cadillac Mtn. Mus. Harbor
House Acadia Acadia Nt. Pk.
Castine National 102 * Mt. Desert Island
175 Park Seal Harbor
Wilson Museum Northeast Harbor
Seal Cove * * * Cranberry Isles
Southwest Mount Desert
Harbor Oceanarium

Admission charge. Reserve open: daily dawn to dusk, donations
☎ (207) 667-8460. Allow 1-2 hours.

Using route 3 south drive to **Trenton** and Acadia Zoo, set in 30
acres (12 hectare) with native and exotic animals in natural settings.
Open: daily 9.30am-dusk July and August, 10am-4pm May, June,
September and October. Admission charge ☎ (207) 667-3244.

Then cross over to **Bar Harbor** on Mount Desert Island and
Acadia National Park. Bar Harbor stands at the entrance to Acadia
National Park, and because of its rugged beauty, a popular resort for
more than a hundred years. At the end of the nineteenth and
beginning of the twentieth century, it was a popular summer haunt
of the rich, and many wealthy families owned 'cottages', including
J.P. Morgan, Jospeh Pulitzer and John D. Rockefeler. The resort's
popularity waned with the Depression, and many of the estates
were destoyed by the fire which swept much of the island in 1947.

The town still makes a great base for touring the area and the park
with scenic drives and miles of hiking trails for the more energetic.
Glider rides over the area are also available,

Abbe Museum explores 4,000 years of the island's history, with
museum shop offering Indian baskets and crafts. Open: daily 10am-
4pm mid-May to mid-October, July and August 9am-5pm. Admission charge.

Acadian Whale Watcher sails from the pier at 60 West Street and
offers a 4 hour trip during which whales and other marine animals
can be seen. Trips leave at 8am, 12.15 and 4.45pm, July and August,
8.30am and 1.30pm, mid-June to 1 July and September. There are
also shorter wildlife trips between mid-May and mid-October.

Bluenose Cruises at the ferry terminal offers the chance to sail to
Nova Scotia for either full day or overnight visit. Sails: daily 8am late
June to late September. Charge ☎ (207) 288-3395. Allow 14 hours.

Jackson Laboratory, a national cancer research centre on SR3,
offers talks and audiovisual presentation about the work. Open:
Tuesday and Thursday 2pm mid-June to August. Admission free.

Mount Desert Oceanarium, about 8 miles (13km) west of Bar
Harbor on SR3 has a harbour seal colony, the Thomas Bay Marsh
Walk, Maine Lobster Museum and lobster boat trips. Open: Monday
to Saturday 9am-5pm, mid-May to late October. Admission charge.
Allow 2 hours.

The Natural History Museum on SR3 in the College of the Atlantic
exhibits mounted animals and birds, especially those of maritime
Maine with hands-on exhibits. Open: daily 9am-5pm July to September, rest of the year by appointment. Admission charge ☎ (207)
288-5015. Allow 1 hour.

➤ Oceanarium and Lobster Hatchery, Harbour Place has everything there is to know about lobsters. Open for guided tours every half hour Monday to Saturday 9am-8.30pm, July and August, 9am-5pm mid-May and June and September and October. Admission charge. Allow 1 hour.

The first mountains, perhaps as high as the Rockies, were thrust out of the sea millions of years ago, but massive erosion wore them down so that little remains today. The present mountains were formed as a result of uplifted seabed sediment and subterranean volcanic activity. Up to 30 ice sheets have covered the area over the past 2 to 3 million years, and fingers of the last ice cap, up to 9,000ft (2,744m) thick, carved out the deep valleys and fjords, such as Somes Sand, while trapped ice resulted in Eagle and Echo lakes. The glaciers smoothed and rounded the northern slopes of the mountains as it edged its way southwards before crashing over the peaks to leave the southern slopes jagged and steep. The huge rock near the South Bubble Mountain was a piece of debris carried by the glacier showing what force it had. As the ice melted, the sea rose and only the tips of mountains can now be seen as nearby islands. The new coastline was then subject to erosion from the sea, and Thunder Hole is one example of the power of the sea as boulders are continually being thrown into the cavern constantly enlarging it.

❋ **Mount Desert Island** can be reached year round by car on route 3. Start at the Hulls Cove Visitor Center, open between May and October, where there is information about the park and a half-hourly orientation film. Self guiding tape tours are also available.

There is a 20 mile (32km) loop road taking on most of the park's varied habitats and landscapes, partly closed in winter. It takes in Sand Beach, Great Head, Thunder Hole and the thickly forested Otter Cliffs. There is also a road to the 1,530ft (466m) summit of Cadillac Mountain. There are frequent turn-offs offering spectacular sea views, glacier carved valleys and lakes, and forests.

The park has two campgrounds. Blackwoods is open year round but reservations are required in the summer, while camping at Seawall, open May to September is on a first come, first served basis. There are also private campgrounds and accommodation in the neighbouring towns of Bar Harbor, Winter Harbor, Stonington, Northeast Harbor and Southwest Harbor.

🚶 Arcadia has more than 120 miles (193km) of walking trails ranging from lowland paths to rugged mountain routes, like the steep Precipice Trail. Bicycles are allowed on some carriage roads, but not walking trails, and can be rented in nearby towns, and carriage tours are available at Wildwood Stables. There are ranger-led walks and nature activities and evening campfire programmes.

Boats are available for rent, and there are also charters, cruises and ferries from nearby towns. Freshwater fishing requires a state license, but no permit is needed for sea fishing. During the winter, there are opportunities for cross country skiing, snow mobiling, ice fishing and winter hiking.

The Northern and Temperate zones overlap at Acadia which explains its rich and diverse wildlife. More than 300 species of birds have been recorded, 122 of them breeding species. There are seals and other marine mammals, rock pools rich in sea plants and animals, and a wealth of fish offshore, and more than 500 species of wild flowers within the park boundaries.

The Islesford Historical Museum and Blue Duck on **Little Cran-** **berry Island** to the south of Mount Desert Island and can be reached by ferry via Great Cranberry Island. The museum is open from mid-June to September and commemorates those who lived in the islands and preserves an important part of New England's maritime history. Hours vary according to the boat schedule and admission is free ☎ (207) 288-3338 for further information. The museum has rare early documents dating from the time when the area was New France and ship and shipbuilding artifacts, as well as domestic items from early island homes. The Blue Duck, named after the bird profile on the doorframe, was a ship's store in the 1850s and now houses island memorabilia

Isle au Haut was not settled in large numbers until the end of the Revolutionary War. In the 1880s a small summer community was established and in 1943, about half of the island was donated as part of Arcadia. The rest of the island is still privately owned. Passenger only access is by mailboat from Stonington and Town Landing. Between mid June and early September Monday to Saturday, the ferry also calls at Duck Harbor. The mailboat operates in a first come first served basis, and as the island has a limit on the number of visitors at any one time, access may not always be possible.

There are 18 miles (29km) of trails on the island, which can be rough and wet. Biking is discouraged. There is camping at Duck Harbor Campground in lean-to-shelters which can accommodate 6 people. A camping fee is charged and reservations are essential through the Isle au Haut Ferry Co. Stonington, Maine 04681 ☎ (207) 367-5193. For further information contact: Acadia National Park, PO Box 177 Bar Harbor, Maine 94609 ☎ (207) 288-3338.

Visit Seal Cove and Southwest Harbor before leaving the island. **Seal Cove** has a collection of more than 100 old and rare cars and motorcycles, plus motoring memorabilia. Open: daily 10am-5pm June to mid-September. Admission charge. **Southwest Harbor** makes a good base for visiting Acadia National Park and area. The

Acadia National Park

Locals say that if you have never tried doing nothing, Acadia is a good place to start. All you have to do is find your own rock ledge or piece of beach, sit down and do nothing because things will happen all round you.

Acadia National Park is 47 miles (76km) south-east of Bangor and includes part of the Schoodic Peninsula, more than 50sq miles (129sq km) of Mount Desert Island, the largest rock-based island on the Atlantic Coast, the Isle au Haut (High Island), and a number of smaller nearby islands.

The park is dedicated to preserving the natural beauty of Maine's rocky coast, with its coastal mountains and offshore islands. On fine days you can drive to the summit of Cadillac Mountain, the highest point, for the most spectacular views. Or better still, get out and walk or cycle the many historic and nature trails.

One entrance to the park is on the rocky, granite headland of the Schoodic Peninsula, and while most people head for the islands, the remote peninsula, about an hour's drive south of the visitor centre, is worth exploring. The park road is one way and follows the western shore of the peninsula to Schoodic Point and then north along the eastern shore past the Bueberry Hill parking area, with Little Moose Island offshore, and then on to Wonsqueak Harbor, Birch Harbor and access road route 186. There are frequent turn-offs to take in the view, and there is a 1 mile (2km) unmarked trail to Schoodic Head which can be driven or walked. Camping in this area of the park is not allowed but there are campgrounds nearby in Winter Harbor and Birch Harbor.

Huge shell heaps show that Indians inhabited Acadia National Park at least 6,000 years ago, but there are few other prehistoric remains. According to the records of the first European traders, the Abnaki Maine Coast Indians were hunters, fishers and foragers, and they referred to Mount Desert Island as 'Pemetic' — the 'sloping land'. They built bark-covered conical shelters and travelled in birch bark canoes.

On 5 September 1604 Samuel Champlain and his French expedition sailed into the bay. The first island they named Isle au Haut, and they ran aground on Pemetic, and named it 'Isles des Monts Desert'. It was 16 years before the Pilgrims landed at Plymouth Rock, and the area was originally known as New France, before it became New England. In 1613, French Jesuits established the French mission in America at Fernald Point, close to the entrance of Somes Sound, but it was destroyed by an English warship commanded by Captain Samuel Argall. For the next 150 years the island was disputed by the French who controlled Acadia to the north, and the English with their colonies to the south, but there was little attempt to settle the island. In 1688 a Frenchman, the self-styled Sieur de la Mothe Cadillac, received a grant of land along the Maine coast which included Mount Desert Island. The enterprise was short lived, however, and Cadillac moved west where he founded Detroit.

In 1759 following the French defeat in the north, Massachusetts received Mount Desert Island by Royal land grant, and in 1760 free land grants were offered to encourage settlers. Abraham Somes and James Richardson with their families were the first settlers and they established Somesville. After the Revolutionary War though, the western half of the island was ceded to Massachusetts and the eastern half to Cadillac's grand-daughter who sold their land to non-resident landlords who encouraged settlement. By 1820 farming, fishing, lumbering and shipbuilding were established industries, and by 1850 the island's economy was flourishing, and it was attracting writers and artists. Painters from the Hudson School exhibited their works and encouraged patrons and friends to flock there, and they returned summer after summer. By 1880 thirty hotels had been built and tourism had become a significant industry. In the 1880s and 1890s because of its remoteness and unspoilt beauty, the island attracted the rich and famous — the Rockefellers, Morgans, Fords, Vanderbilts, Carnegies and Astors. They transformed the island with elegant estates, and they held sway over the island for more than 40 years. In 1947 a devastating fire swept the island and many of the estates were destroyed. The fire started mysteriously on 17 October, was declared under control on 27 October but continued to burn until 14 November. Although the rich built extravagant homes, they also did much to preserve the natural beauty of the island, and in 1901, thanks largely to the effort of George Dorr, the Hancock County Trustees of Public Reservations was set up to protect land. By 1913 it had acquired 6,000 acres (2,400 hectares) which were offered to the federal government. In 1919 President Wilson established the Lafayette National Park, and Dorr became the park's first superintendant. There is a memorial to him at Sieur de Monts Spring, near Bay Harbor, where there is also the Abbe Museum of Stone Age Antiquities, and nature centre. The museum is open: daily 9am-5pm July and August, 10am-4pm daily mid-May and June and September to mid-August. Admission charge. Nature centre open: daily 9am-5pm July and August, daily 9am-2pm June and September. Gardens open daily year round. Admission free.

In 1929, the park's name was changed to Acadia and today, it covers 35,000 acres (14,000 hectares).

fishing village relies heavily on lobsters and tourists, with lots of cruises on offer. Bass Harbor Head Light, 3 miles (5km) south, is a much photographed spot. The Mount Desert Oceanarium, has unusual live coastal sea animals and exhibits. Open: Monday to Saturday 9am-5pm mid-May to mid-October. Admission charge. Wendell Gilley Museum, Main Street, has hundreds of bird models carved by Gilley and a resident woodcarver demonstrating his skills. Open: Tuesday to Sunday 10am-5pm July and August, Tuesday to Sunday 10am-4pm June, September and October, Friday to Sunday 10am-4pm, May, November and December. Admission charge.

You can detour from Ellsworth by taking highway 1 east to Hancock and then north to **Franklin**, a former timber, shipbuilding and granite quarrying town. It is now a blueberry processing and Christmas tree growing area. The Franklin Historical Society has established a 2 acre (1 hectare) Memorial Park featuring a galamander, a contraption used to haul large granite blocks. The former East Franklin Baptist Church houses the society's collection of photographs, tools and local history memorabilia.

You can continue through Hancock and Gouldsboro to **Milbridge** at the mouth of the Narraguagus River, a former shipbuilding centre and now noted for its sardine packing factory, blueberry processing plant and Christmas wreath works. Return to Gouldsboro and take the 186 to Winter Harbor and Schoodic Point, and explore the mainland section of the Acadia National Park.

From Mount Desert Island you can ferry across to explore the outlying islands, or return to Ellsworth, then head south-west on 172 to **Blue Hill**. The town is named after the 934ft (285m) Blue Hill, the summit of which offers extensive panoramic views. It was an important shipbuilding and timber town in the nineteenth century, and now a popular summer resort and crafts centre, noted particularly for its hand thrown pottery made from local clay. There are a number of potteries and art galleries. Parson Jonathon Fisher, is one of the town's most ingenious sons, and his home can be seen on SR3. He designed and built the house, made the paint to decorate it and built the furniture. He was also a prolific inventor building machines and a windmill to power them.

The Bagaduce Music Lending Library has sheet music for more than 620,000 titles, many of them very rare. The town hosts the traditional country Blue Hill Fair every Labour Day weekend, and the Kneisel Hall Summer Music School has a programme of concerts and recitals.

From Blue Hill take 177 north-west to Penobscot then 175 north to **Orland**, headquarters of the HOME (Home Workers Organised for

More Employment) cooperative which markets locally made products, and includes a wood mill, pottery, weaving shops and museum. Crafts demonstrations and guided tours.

From Orland it is worth detouring south on 175 and then 166A to **Castine**. The French built a fort in 1613 to protect the strategic harbour which was then fought over for 200 years by the French, British, Dutch and Americans. More than 100 plaques around town tell the story of these struggles. In 1760 the English established the first permanent settlement, and during the Revolutionary War the town was occupied by the British after trouncing the Colonial fleet offshore. The British built Fort George although it was handed over to the Americans in 1783. It was, however, the last site to be surrendered to the colonies at the end of the Revolutionary War. The Americans bought Fort Madison in 1811 and both forts were captured and occupied by the British in the 1812 war. Fort Madison was rebuilt during the Civil War and the earthworks and moat can still be seen. The partially restored Fort George can also be visited. The *State of Maine*, at Maine Maritime Academy Dock, is a 13,3000 ton training ship for the academy which trains cadets for the Merchant Marine, US Coast Guard and US Naval Reserves. Originally the *Upshur*, a luxury liner, it was converted into a troop ship during the Korean War and saw active service over the next 20 years. Open for tours when in port July and August. Admission free ☎ (207) 326-4311. Wilson Museum, Perkins Street, has prehistoric exhibits from around the world, Indian and Colonial artifacts, and the John Perkins House is fully restored pre-Revolutionary home with period furnishings, blacksmiths shop and funeral house. Museum open: Tuesday to Sunday 2-5pm, May to September. Donations. House open: Wednesday and Sunday 2-4.45pm July and August. Admission charge ☎ (207) 326-8753. Allow 2 hours.

Back in Orland take the 15 west to **Bucksport** at the head of Penobscot Bay and a great base for exploring the lovely unspoiled peninsula. The Waldo-Hancock bridge spans the river opposite Bucksport, and when built was considered the most beautiful of its time. Paper making is the town's main industry. Fort Knox across the river, is Maine's largest granite fortification, started in 1844 and never completed. It has underground stairways and elaborate stonework features. Open daily.

A local curiosity is the granite tombstone of Colonel Jonathan Buck on which the outline of a leg and arm can be made out. It is said this is the result of a curse from a women he condemned as a witch. Every attempt to clean the stone has failed to remove the image.

Then follow the road north to explore the Hampdens before returning to Bangor.

Tour 6 • The Sunrise Coast
210 miles (338km)

The tour starts in **Calais**, on Passamaquoddy Bay on the US-Canadian border and connected by the International Bridge to St. Stephen in New Brunswick. The first settlers moved in during the 1770s, attracted by the timber for homes and fuel, fertile soil and fishing. Within a short time Calais had become an important lumber town. In 1809 the town was renamed Calais by the Massachusetts Assembly in recognition of the role of the French during the American Revolution. There are close links between Calais and St. Stephen and the towns co-host the International Festival in late July and early August with street fairs, arts and crafts, parades and entertainments. The scenic drive on US1 between Calais and Bar Harbor is also noted for its wildlife, and nesting eagles can often be spotted. **Moosehorn National Wildlife Refuge** is in two parts, the 12,000 Baring Unit 3 miles (5km) south-west on Charlotte Road, and the 6,600 Edmunds Unit adjoining Cobscook Bay State Park. Both have thousands of migrant bird visitors, hiking trails and wilderness areas, and are open daily dawn to dusk.

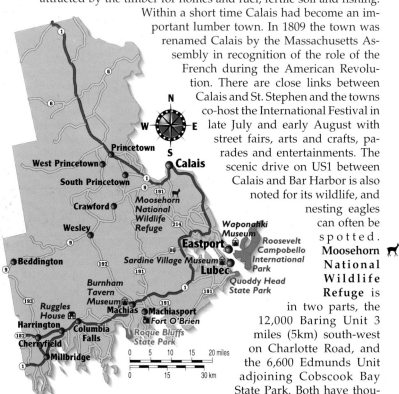

From Calais take highway 1 west and north to Princeton from where you can detour north to visit the lake and marshlands. Highway 1 runs north to Danforth while route 6 east goes to Lambert Lake and Vanceboro. There are few roads in this area and if you take this detour you will have to retrace most of the way along the same route.

opposite; Machias is Maine's oldest town, founded in 1763, and the market town for Washington County

*Calais on the banks of the Passamaquoddy Bay at he mouth of the
St Croix River on the US-Canadian border*

*Large prize bingo is allowed at Passamaquoddy. It is on Indian Reserve
land whose laws permit gambling*

At Princeton take the country road through West Princeton or South Princeton and continue until you meet highway 9. Turn right and travel west through Crawford and Wesley and on to Beddington, then south on 193 to Cherryfield, and south again to Millbridge. Then take highway 1A to Harrington, then 1 east through **Columbia Falls**, settled around 1780 with many fine old homes built during the shipbuilding and timber boom. Processing blueberries and clams are now the main industries.

Ruggles House off US1, was built in 1818 for Judge Thomas Ruggles, timber dealer and milita captain. The Adams-style house with period furnishings, has a flying staircase, and wonderful woodcarvings both inside and out, created only by penknife. Open: Monday to Saturday 9.30am-4.30pm, Sunday 11am-4.30pm June to mid-October. Admission charge. Allow 1 hour.

Continue through Jonesboro to **Machias**, settled in 1763 and keeping its Indian name which means ' bad little falls' because of the rushing water through the gorge off Main Street. Main industries are fishing, blueberry processing, timber and wood products, and the town is also a base for hunting and fishing trips to the many local lakes. **Roque Bluffs State Park** has a fine sandy beach. The naval battle in Machias Bay on 12 June 1775 was the first engagement of the American Revolution. A band of Machias residents led by Captain Jeremiah O'Brien planned their attack after learning that the British warship Margaretta was about to land to sieze timber supplies. The colonists sailed into the bay aboard the *Unity*, a small sloop, and captured the *Margaretta*. Burnham Tavern Museum, on Main and Free Streets, is where the colonials made their battle plans. It contains period furnishings, paintings and Civil War artifacts. Open: Monday to Friday 10am-5pm June to early September, by appointment rest of the year. Admission charge ☎ (207) 255-4432. Allow 1 hour.

Fort Machias was built at **Machiasport**, on the headland to protect the river during the Revolutionary War but was destroyed by the British in 1814. The remains that can now be seen are from earthworks from Fort O'Brien built in 1863. The site is open daily dawn to dusk. The fishing town is also popular with leisure boaters and many sea cruises are available. There is also good rockhunting on Jasper Beach, named after the mineral jasper which can be found.

Gates House, on SR92, is an 1807 Federal-style home with period furnishings and local history memorabilia including the offshore naval battle. Open: Monday to Friday 12.30-4.30pm mid-June to mid-September. Admission free. Allow 1 hour.

Continue to Whiting and from here detour east on 189 to visit **Lubec**, settled in 1780 and the first landfall in the US to be hit by the rising sun! Boats are available for charter and cruises along the spectacular coastline and to Machias Seal Island. The Sardine Village Museum traces the town's early history as a sardine packer. **Campobella Island** is across the Lubec Narrows in New Brunswick and connected to Lubec by the Franklin D Roosevelt Memorial Bridge. The island was owned by the Owen family from 1767 to 1881 and Admiral William Owen built his own quarterdeck on Deer Point looking out to sea. Franklin Roosevelt spent many of his summers on the island. **Roosevelt Campobello International Park** covers 2,800 acres (1,120 hectares) and includes the 34 room 'cottage' and estate, where Roosevelt stayed. Park open: daily 9am-5pm, Estate open: daily 9am-5pm late May to early October. Admission free. Allow 1-2 hours. **Quoddy Head State Park**, south of town is around 600 acres (240 hectares) of rocky cliffs around West Quoddy Lighthouse built in 1808 and remodelled in 1858. The lighthouse is not open to the public but the park is open daily 9am to dusk May to September. Admission free. Quoddy Village was built in the 1930s after the Passamaquoddy Bay tidal flow was harnessed to generate electricity. The average tide here is 18ft (5m) high but can also be as high as 27ft (8m).

Return to Whiting and head north on highway 1 along the western shore of Passamaquoddy Bay to Perry, then take route 190 south along the peninsula to **Eastport**. Fishing, timber and scallops are the main industries of Eastport on Moose Island first settled around 1880. In 1814 the capture of the town by the British led to the collapse of peace talks, and General Andrew Jackson's subsequent defeat of the British at the Battle of New Orleans. Largely as a result of this success he won the Presidency in 1829. The dockside is dominated by the deep water facility and the intensive salmon and trout farms. The US record tidal variations, up to 26ft (8m), have been recorded here, and Old Sow, believed to be the world's second largest whirlpool can be seen about 2 hours before high tide from Dog Island. Inland, the moors are full of blueberries and cranberries. The area is rich in wildlife and there are many cruises available from the town.

Waponahki Museum, on SR190, has exhibits on the Passamaquoddy Indians. Open: Monday to Friday 8.30-11am and 12.30-3.30pm. Donations. Allow 1 hour. Return to Perry and continue north back to Calais.

The small picturesque town of Danforth is surrounded by spectacular woodland and hills

Eastport has a number of galleries and shops, but it is mainly a busy fishing port

Tour 7 • Aroostook County
260 miles (418km)

The tour starts in **Houlton**, originally a timber town and now the centre of and shipping point for the Aroostook potato industry. There is an unusual 1916 cast iron drinking fountain in Pierce Park. The sculptor of 'the boy with the leaking boot', is unknown but almost identical statues exist in Italy and Germany. A.E. Howell Wildlife Conservation Center is on Lycette Road. More than 60 acres (24 hectares) are dedicated to conservation and recreation with trails and a wide range of birds and animals, including occasional bears and moose. There is also fishing and winter skiing. Open: daily 9am-dusk. Admission charge. Allow 1-2 hours. Aroostook Historical and Art Museum, 109 Main Street, has displays of old tools, clothing and historical artifacts. Open: Monday to Friday 12noon-3.30pm June to mid-September, rest of the year by appointment. Donations ☎ (207) 532-4216. Allow 1 hour. Lieutenant Gordon Manuel Wildlife Management Area, Linneus and Cary Plantation, at Hodgdon covers more than 6,000 acres (2,400 hectares) of woodland and water for hunting and fishing. Open: daily 24 hours. Admission free.

From Houlton head north on highway 1 through Monticello and Mars Hill to **Presque Isle**. The town also has perfumes and cosmetic industries. The *Double Eagle* II took off from here on 11 August 1978 to become the first hot air balloon to cross the Atlantic, landing in France after 5 days. A replica of the balloon stands in Double Eagle II Park off Spragueville Road. The small city is an industrial and commercial centre in farming country, and the University of Maine has a 375 acre (150 hectare) experimental farm nearby investigating better ways of producing potatoes and other crops. The University's Pioneer Playhouse stages productions in June and July. A statue by Bernard Langlais, of an owl, the university's symbol, overlooks South Main Street. Aroostook State Park, 4 miles (6km) south, offers summer and winter sports.

The Tante Blanche Museum is named after Marguerite Blanche Thibodeau who during the Black Famine in 1797 gathered food to give to the poor and hungry. She is remembered as 'the angel of mercy'.

Continue north to **Caribou**, centre of one of the world's largest potato producing areas, with lots of facilities for year round outdoor sports and activities, especially fishing in the Aroostook and Little Madawaska Rivers, noted for salmon and trout, which run through town. The town was settled between 1838 and 1839 by soldiers sent to the frontier for the Aroostook War who stayed on to log or farm, but it was not until the arrival of the railway in the 1890s that the town prospered with produce, including potatoes, being distributed quicker. In mid-February the eleven day Winter Carnival is held, and on the third Sunday of July the 12 mile (19km) Roostook River Raft Race is held between the town and Fort Fairfield. The area north of Caribou was largely settled by Swedes in the 1870s, thus names such as Sweden, New Sweden and Stockholm. They still celebrate Midsummer Day with Scandinavian festivities. The Nylander Museum, Main Street, houses the mineral, geological and Indian artifact collection of naturalist Olaf Nylander, plus wildflower, butterfly and bird exhibits. Open: May to September Wednesday to Sunday 1-5pm, weekends 1-5pm March and April and October to December. Donations. Allow 1 hour.

Detour to take in Fort Fairfield to the east. Keep on highway 1 from Caribou for **Van Buren**, settled by refugee Acadians in 1789, the town has strong French Canadian links and is connected by bridge to St Leonard in New Brunswick. Many signs in the area are bilingual. The town is surrounded by farmlands, growing mostly potatoes and the countryside offers hunting and fishing, and swimming and boating at Long Lake. Acadian Village on US1 has sixteen reconstructed buildings, including forge, country store, schoolhouse and museum tracing the early history of the town and valley. Open: daily 12noon-5pm mid-June to mid-September. Admission charge.

Then follow the St John River north-westwards to St David and **Madawaska**, settled from Nova Scotia refugees in 1785 and the Acadian Cross Historic Shrine off US1 commemorates the first Acadian landing in the St John Valley. The weeklong Acadian Festival in late June also commerates the town's heritage. The town is named after the Indian word for 'porcupine'. There are tours of the Fraser Paper Works Monday to Friday 9-11am and 1-3pm but cameras are not allowed. Admission free.

Continue to **Fort Kent**, the northern terminus of US1 which runs south to the Florida Keys. It is a farming area and linked by bridge to Clair, New Brunswick. It can also act as a base for those wishing to explore the huge northern Aroostook wilderness area.

The town of Fort Kent overlooks Canada on the St John River and was settled by French Acadians deported from Nova Scotia in 1755 by the British. The fort was built between 1839 and 1840 when the territory was contested by the British and Americans and the Webster Asburton Treaty of 1842 settled the dispute peacefully. There is a duty free shop on West Main Street. Fort Kent Historic Site, off Main Street, contains the timber blockhouse. Open: daily 9am-dusk, May to September. Donations. Allow 1 hour.

Then take route 11 south through spectacular scenery and Eagle Lake, Portage, Ashland to Knowles Corner and Sherman, and then east on route 212 to Smyrna Mills and then back east to Houlton.

If you have time you can continue south from Knowles Corner to Sherman Mills and then take the country road about 3 miles (5km) east to connect with route 2 south to Macwahoc, and then take alternate route 2 north-east back through Haynesville to Houlton.

Tour 8 • Katahdin and Moosehead
240 miles (386km)

This is another huge area to explore but access is restricted by lack of roads in many areas. From Medway take route 11 north through Sherman to **Patten**, a timber town for almost 200 years with mills and wood product industries and also a centre for walking, hunting and fishing. Lumberman's Museum, close to the northern entrance to Baxter State Park, spreads over nine buildings and tells the history of lumbering in the town and area. Open: Monday to Saturday 9am-4pm, Sunday 11am-4pm July and August, Tuesday to Saturday 9am-4pm, Sunday 11am-4pm, May, June and September, Saturday 9am-4pm and Sunday 11am-4pm October, and by appointment. Admission charge ☎ (207) 528-2650. Allow 2 hours.

Houlton Court House, in the heart of Aroostook County, the largest in the state and larger than Rhode Island and Connecticut combined

The very unusual but attractive iron steeple of Fort Kent's Catholic church

Then take route 159 to Shin Pond. This road continues as a country road beyond the town and bears westwards into **Baxter State Park**. The park is north of Millinocket in northern Maine and accessed by a country road off route 11. The country road travels through the park exiting in the north-east corner close to the Matagamon Wilderness Campgrounds and Camps just outside the park boundary. All visitors are advised to report to the park headquarters at 64 Balsam Drive, Millinocket, before setting off into the park, especially if planning to stay overnight. Travel permits are required to enter the park. Roads are gravel, narrow and winding.

The park is a wilderness area covering 20,000 acres (8,000 hectares) offering camping, hiking and fishing, and was a gift to Maine by former Governor Pervcival Baxter. There are 46 mountain peaks and ridges, 18 of them above 3,000ft (915m) and the highest is 'mile high' Baxter Peak at 5,267ft (1,606m) with its spectacular 4,000ft (1,219m) vertical drops. The peak also marks the northern end of the Appalachian Trail. There is a fee for park use. There are several campgrounds in the park and early reservations are recommended. The park is open from mid-May to mid-October for general use, from mid-May to 1 December for day use only, from 1 December to 1 April for winter use, and from 1 April to mid-May for day use only.

The road snakes its way south through this spectacular area. After exiting the park, one can continue south to **Millinocket**, the southern gateway to Baxter State Park and home of one of the country's largest manufacturers of newsprint and paper.

Return to Medway, or if you have the time, turn right when exiting the park and take the country road west to the Ripogenus Dam, and then south through incredible scenery to Kokadjo and Lily Bay to **Greenville**, at the southern end of Moose Lake. This is a tourist town with year round outdoor activity opportunities. There is swimming, fishing, boating, canoeing, hiking, mountain climbing, white water rafting and riding in the summer, and skiing and snow mobiling in the winter around Squaw Mountain. There is also shooting for deer, bear and partridge in the autumn. Lake cruises to Mount Kineo, an ancient Indian meeting place, are available.

Katahdin, in the town centre, is a restored 1914 lake steamboat which cruises the lake in summer, and displays exhibits about logging and steamboat operations.

Moosehead Marine Museum has exhibits about vessels which have operated on the lake. Open: Tuesday to Sunday 9am-5pm, Monday 10am-3pm June to September. Donations.

Follow route 6/15 south to **Monson**, built on a slate ridge with extensive quarrying and mining in the area. The Monson Historical Society's Museum has exhibits the town, slate quarrying and the local narrow gauge railroad which used to operate.

The next community is **Guildford**, an agricultural and manufacturing area on the Piscataquis River. It has a large woollen mill, and there is excellent fishing in the Sebec Lake area to the north. To the east is Low's Covered Bridge over the Piscataquis River between Guildford and Sangerville, the birthplace of Hiram Maxim, the inventor of the machine gun, smokeless gunpowder, and a gas headlight for trains.

Then take route 6 east to **Dover-Foxcroft**, a commercial and residential community with a new regional hospital and YMCA facility. On the northern outskirts on route 153 is the Blacksmith Shop Museum, a restored Civil War farrier's shop with much of its original equipment. Open: daily. Further along the road is Peaks Kenny State Park on the shore of Sebec Lake with a sandy beach and good fishing.

Continue east to Milo and then take the country road north to the Brownville district. Close to the small rural towns of Brownville and Brownville Junction is a 6 mile (10km) gravel track to the former **Katahdin Iron Works** founded in 1843. For 50 years it was the major industry in the area. Fourteen kilns were needed to produce enough charcoal to fire the blast furnaces. The blast furnace and charcoal kiln have been restored and now produces 2,000 tons of raw iron.

You can then either return via routes 16 and 6 to Howland, and then on highway 95 back to Medway; or take route 6/16 south through Boyd Lake to Lagrange and then 6/155 north to connect with route 95 which runs north back to Medway.

State And Other Main Recreation Areas

State parks are usually open from mid-May to mid-October and during the winter if offering winter sport facilities. An admission charge is made.

Allagash Wilderness Waterway, almost 100 miles (161km) of connected waterways in north-west Maine, offering camping, boating, fishing, swimming and winter sports.

Aroostook, 577 scenic acres (231 hectares), south-west of Presque Isle, with camping, picnicking, hiking, boating, fishing, swimming and winter sports.

Baxter, 201,000 acres (80,400 hectares) over ten separate areas, north of Millinrocket off SR159, with canoeing, camping and wilderness sites, picnics, hiking, fishing, swimming and winter sports.

Bigeow Preserve, 29,000 acres (11,600 hectares) north of New Portland off SR27, with camping, picnicking, hiking, boating, fishing, swimming and winter sports.

Bradbury Mountain, 272 acres (109 hectares) north-west of Freeport off SR9, with camping, picnicking, hiking and winter sports.

Camden Hills, almost 5,500 acres (2,200 hectares) 2 miles (3km) north of Camden, with camping, picnicking, hiking, winter sports. Very scenic.

Cobscook Bay, 868 acres (347 hectares) 2 miles (3km) south-east of Dennysville, with camping, picnicking, hiking, boating, boat rental, fishing and winter sports.

Crescent Beach, 174 acres (70 hectares) 1 mile (2km) south of Cape Elizabeth on SR77, offers picnicking and swimming.

Damariscotta Lake, 17 acres (7 hectares) in Jefferson off SR32, with with picnicking, fishing and swimming.

Ferry Beach, 117 acres (47 hectares) in Saco off SR9, with nature trails, hiking, picnicking and swimming.

Gafton Notch, 3,100 acres (1,240 hectares) 16 miles (26km) north of Bethel on SR26, with picnicking, hiking and swimming.

Gero Island, 3,000 acres (1,200 hectares) north-west of Millinocket of SR11, with camping, picnicking, boating, fishing, swimming and winter sports including ice fishing.

Lake St George, 360 acres (144 hectares) 2 miles (3km) west of Liberty on SR3, with camping, picnicking, boating, boat rentals, fishing, swimming and winter sports.

Lamoine Beach, 55 acres (22 hectares) 6 miles (10km) south of Ellsworth on SR184, with camping, picnicking, boating and fishing.

Lily Bay, 925 acres (370 hectares) 8 miles (13km) north of Greenville, with camping, picnicking, boating, fishing, swimming and winter sports.

Mahoosucs, 2,100 acres (840 hectares) near Bethel off SR26, with camping, hiking, picnicking, boat rentals and winter sports.

Mount Blue, 1,273 acres (509 hectares) in two areas north of Weld, with camping, picnicking, hiking, boating, boat rentals, fishing, swimming and winter sports.

Outlet Beach on Outlet Road 1 mile (2km) east of SR26 on Lake Sabbathday, with picnicking, boating, boat rental, fishing and swimming.

Peacock Beach, 100 acres (40 hectares) north-west of Richmond off SR210, with picnicking and swimming.

Peaks-Kenny, 839 acres (336 hectares) 6 miles (10km) north of Dover-Foxcroft, with camping, picnicking, hiking, boating, fishing and swimming.

Popham Beach Park, 529 acres (212 hectares) west of Popham Beach, with windsurfing, picnicking, fishing and swimming.

Rangeley Lake, 691 acres (276 hectares) south-west of Rangeley, with camping, picnicking, boating, fishing, swimming and winter sports.

Range Ponds, 750 acres (300 hectares) in Poland off SR122, with picnicking, boating, fishing and swimming.

Reid, 768 acres (307 hectares) 2 miles (3km) east of Georgetown on SR127, with picnicking, fishing and swimming.

Roque Bluffs, 275 acres (110 hectares) 7 miles (11km) east off US1 from Machias, with picnicking, fishing and swimming.

Scarborough Beach, 5 acres (2 hectares) 3 miles (5km) south of Scarborough with picnicking, fishing and swimming.

Scraggly Lake, with 10,000 acres (4,000 hectares) off Grand Lake Road, north-west of Mount Chase, with camping, hiking, picnicking, boating, fishing, swimming and water sports.

Sebago Lake, 1,300 acres (520 hectares) 3 miles (5km) south of Naples off US302, with camping, picnicking, boating, fishing, swimming, winter sports and a programme of natural history activities.

Swan Lake, 67 acres (27 hectares) north of Swanville, with picnicking, fishing and swimming.

Warren Island, 70 acres (28 hectares) in Penobscot Bay, with camping, picnicking and fishing.

Maine's Covered Bridges

Bab's Bridge (1843) off River Road north of South Windham over the Presumpscot River. Burned down in 1973 and rebuilt.

Bennett Bridge (1901) off route 16 south-west of Wilsons Mills Post Office over the Magalloway River.

Hemlock Bridge (1857) on route 302 in Fryeburg over the Saco River.

Lovejoy Bridge (1883) South Andover over the Ellis River.

Low's Bridge (1857) north-east of Sangerville over the Piscataquis River. Carried away by flood waters in 1987 and rebuilt in 1990.

Porter Bridge (1876) route 160, south of Porter over the Ossipee River.

Robyville Bridge (1876) in Corinth over the Kenduskeag Stream. The only completely shingle covered bridge in Maine.

Sunday River Bridge (1872), north-west of North Bethel over the Sunday River. 'The Artist's Bridge'.

Watson Settlement Bridge (1911) off route 1 between Woodstock and Littleton over the Meduxnekeag Stream.

SOME SUGGESTED FALL FOLIAGE TOURS
1 From Sanford 85 miles (137km). Allow 2 hours
Head east on US202 through Alfred to Hollis Center, north on 35 to Standish, west on 25 through Kezar Falls to Porter, south on 160 to Limerick, and finally south on 11 back to Sanford.

This trip takes in the southern corner of Maine and includes orchard country, Porter Covered Bridge, the restored nineteenth-century Willowbrook village, and many scenic stretches. Allow 2 hours.

2 From Fryeburg 130 miles (209km). Allow 3-4 hours.
Take US302 east through Bridgton to Naples, north on 35 to Harrison, north on 117 to just before Norway, then west on 118 for about 1 mile (2km) to take the local road north along the shores of

Lake Pennesseewassee to Greenwood, east on 219 to the 26, north on the 26 to Bethel, west on US2 to Gilead, south on 113 to Stow, east on the local road around the west side of Lake Kezard to north Lovell, then south on 5 through Lovell back to Fryeburg.

This trip passes through peaceful west Maine and includes the Hemlock covered bridge, Lake Sebago with lake cruises, the scenic White Mountain National Forest and many scenic stretches.

3 From Rumford 108 miles (174 km). Allow 3 hours.

Head west on US2 to Newry, north on 26 to Errol just across the border in New Hampshire, east on 16 to Oquossoc, west on 4, then south on 17 to Mexico, then US2 west across the bridge back to Rumford.

This trip is through undisturbed mountains and forests and takes in the Sunday River covered bridge, also known as the Artist's Bridge, Screw Auger Falls, Moose Cave and Mother Walker Falls in Grafton Notch State Park, where you can go hiking or rock hunting for semi-precious stones, Angel Falls, and the scenic overlook Height of Land on route 17.

4 From Wiscasset 141 miles (227km). Allow 4 hours.

Head east on US1 to Newcastle, south on 130 to New Harbor and Pemaquid Point, then return on the 130 to New Harbor and take 32 north to Waldoboro, turn right on Main Street to the 220, then head south on the 220 to Friendship, north-east on 97 and then country road through Cushing to Thomaston, north on US1 through Rockland and Camden to Lincolnville, west on 173 to Lincolnville Center, south on 235 to Hope, north-west on 105 to 131, then south on 105 and 131 through Appleton to 17, west on 17 to Stickney Corner, south on 220 to 126, south-west on 126 to Jefferson, south-west on 213 to 215, north-west on 215 to 194, north-west on 194 to Head Tide, then bear left and cross the river on local road to 218, then south on 218 back to Wiscasset.

This takes you along the coast and includes many picture post-card fishing villages and includes Pemaquid Lighthouse and Fishermen's Museum, Fort William Henry and Museum, Colonial Pemaquid, Farnsworth Museum in Rockland, Shore Village Museum, Camden and Mount Battie.

For Further Tourist Information:

Calais, 7 Union Street ☎ (207) 454-2211. Year round.

Fryeburg, US route 302 ☎ (207) 935-3639. Late May to late October.

Hampden, 1-95 north ☎ (207) 862-6628. Year round.

Houlton, Jct 1-95 and US route 1. ☎ (207) 532-6346. Year round.

Kittery, Between 1-95 and US route 1 ☎ (207) 439-1319. Year round.

Yarmouth, Between I-95 exit 17 and US route 1 ☎ (207) 846-0833.
Year Round.
Maine Nordic Ski Council
PO Box 645, Bethel, Maine 04217. ☎ (207) 824-3694.

Accommodation

The following Hotels (H) and Restaurants ® are recommended. A
general price indicator is given: $ Inexpensive, $$ medium, $$$
expensive. * Denotes an historic inn or hotel.

Auburn
Coastline Inn, 170 Center St. ☎ (207) 784-1331 $
No Tomatoes ®, 1 Auburn Center. ☎ (207) 784-3919 $-$$
Augusta
Best Western Senator Inn, 284 Western Ave. ☎ (207) 622-5804 $
Holiday Inn, 110 Community Drive. ☎ (207) 622-4751 $
Bangor
Best Western White Horse, 155 Littlefield Ave. ☎ (207) 862-3737 $
Comfort Inn, 750 Hogan Rd. ☎ (207) 942-7899 $
Country Inn By Carlson, 936 Stillwater Ave. ☎ (207) 941-0200 $-$$
Greenhouse Restaurant, 193 Brod St. ☎ (207) 945-4040 $-$$
Hampton Inn, 10 Nabgor Mall Blvd. ☎ (207) 990-4400 $
Miller's Restaurant, 427 Main St. ☎ (207) 942-6361 $-$$
Ramada Inn, 357 Odin Rd. ☎ (207) 947-6961 $$
Bar Harbor
Anchorage Motel, 51 Mt Desert St. ☎ (207) 288-3959 $
Bar Harbor Inn, Newport Drive. ☎ (207) 288-3351 $$-$$$
Brick Oven Restaurant, 21 Cottage St. ☎ (207) 288-3708 $$
Castlemaine Inn, 39 Holland Ave. ☎ (207) 288-4563 $$
Cromwell Harbor Motel, 359 Main St. ☎ (207) 288-3201 $
* *Graycote Inn B&B*, 40 Holland Ave. ☎ (207) 288-3044 $$
* *The Kedge B&B*, 112 West St. ☎ (207) 288-5180 $$
* *Manor House Inn B&B*, 106 West St. ☎ (207) 288-3759 $$
Quarterdeck Restaurant, 1 Main St. ☎ (207) 288-5292
Quimby House Inn, 109 Cottage St. ☎ (207) 288-5811 $$
Wayside Inn B&B, 11 Atlantic Ave. ☎ (207) 288-5703 $-$$
Bethel
Bethel Inn, on SR5. ☎ (207) 824-2175 $$-$$$
Blue Hill
Jonathan's ®, Main St. ☎ (207) 374-5226 $$
Boothbay Harbor
Brown's Wharf Hotel, 105 Atlantic Ave. ☎ (207) 633-5440 $$
Fisherman's Wharf Inn, 40 Commercial St. ☎ (207) 633-5090 $-$$
Rocktide Inn, 45 Atlantic Ave. ☎ (207) 633-4455 $$

Welch House Inn B&B, 38 McKown St. ☎ (207) 633-3431 $-$$
Brunswick
The Atrium Motel, SR24. ☎ (207) 729-5555 $
Captain Daniel Stone Inn, 10 Water St. ☎ (207) 725-9898 $$
Viking Motor Inn, 287 Bath Rd. ☎ (207) 729-6661 $
Bucksport
Best Western Jed Prouty Motor Inn, SR15 ☎ (207) 469-3113 $
* *Jed Prouty Inn*, SR15. ☎ (207) 469-7972 $-$$
* *L'Ermitage* ®, 219 Main St. ☎ (207) 469-3361 $$
Calais
Calais Motor Inn, 293 Main St. ☎ (207) 454-7111 $
The Townhouse Restaurant, 84 Main St. ☎ (207) 454-8021 $$
Camden
The Belmont, 6 Belmont Ave. ☎ (207) 236-8053 $$
Blue Harbor House, 67 Elm St. ☎ (207) 236-3196 $$
* *Camden Harbor Inn*, 83 Bayview St. ☎ (207) 236-4200 $$-$$$
Capy's Chowder House, 1 Main St. ☎ (207) 236-2254 $$
* *Hawthorn Inn B&B*, 9 High St. ☎ (207) 236-8842 $$
* *Lord Camden Inn B&B*, 24 Main St. ☎ (207) 236-4325 $$
Castine
The Castine Inn, town centre. ☎ (207) 326-4365 $-$$
The Manor, Battle Ave. ☎ (207) 326-4861 $-$$
East Boothbay
* *Five Gables Inn*, Murray Hill Rd. ☎ (207) 633-4551 $$
Smuggler's Cove Motor Inn, SR6. ☎ (207) 633-2800 $-$$
Ellsworth
Crazy Girls ®, White Birches, US1. ☎ (207) 667-3621 $-$$
Ellsworth Motel, 24 High St. ☎ (207) 667-4424 $
Hilltop House Restaurant, SR3. ☎ (207) 667-9368 $-$$
Farmington
Farmington Motel, US2. ☎ (207) 778-4680 $
Mount Blue Motel, US2/SR4. ☎ (207) 778-6004 $
Freeport
Casco Bay Motel, US1. ☎ (207) 865-4925 $
Cottage St. Inn B&B, 13 Cottage St. ☎ (207) 865-0932 $-$$
Harraseeket Inn, 162 Main St. ☎ (207) 865-9388 $$-$$$
* *181 Main Street B&B*, 181 Main St. ☎ (207) 865-1226 $
Maine Dining Room, 162 Maine St. ☎ (207) 865-9377 $$
Fryeburg
The Oxford House Inn, 105 Main St. ☎ (207) 935-3442 $-$$
Greenville
Cabbage Patch Restaurant, SR 6/15. ☎ (207) 695-2252 $
Evergreen Lodge B&B, route 15. ☎ (207) 695-3241.
Greenville Inn, Norris St. ☎ (207) 695-2206 $$

Houlton
Scottish Inns, Bangor Rd. ☎ (207) 532-2236 $
Kennebunk
*Arundel Meadows Inn B&B, US1. ☎ (207) 985-3770 $$
English Meadows Inn B&B, 141 Port Rd. ☎ (207) 967-5766 $$
Hennessey House Restaurant, Western Ave. ☎ (207) 967-4114 $$
* The Kennebunk Inn, 45 Main St. ☎ (207) 985-3351 $$
Topher's Restaurant & Piano Bar, 27 Western Ave. ☎ (207) 967-5009 $-$$
* The White Barn Inn, Beach St. ☎ (207) 967-2321 $$-$$$
Windows on the Water ®, 12 Chase Hill Rd. ☎ (207) 967-3313 $$
Kennebunk Beach
* Sundial Inn B&B, 48 Beach Ave. ☎ (207) 967-3850 $-$$
Kennebunkport
* Captain Fairfield Inn, 8 Pleasant St. ☎ (207) 967-4454 $$
* Captain Lord Mansion B&B, off Ocean Ave. ☎ (207) 967-3141 $$-$$$
1802 House B&B Inn, Locke St. ☎ (207) 967-5632 $$
*Maine Stay Inn B&B, 34 Maine St. ☎ (207) 967-2117 $$-$$$
* Old Fort Inn B&B, Old Fort Ave. ☎ (207) 967-4547 $$-$$$
* Old Grist Mill ®, Mill Lane. ☎ (207) 967- 4781 $$
Kingfield
* The Inn on Winter's Hill, Winter Hill. ☎ (207) 265-5421 $$
Kittery
Coachman Motor Inn, US1 ☎ (207) 439-4434 $-$$
Warren's Lobster House ®, 11 Water St. ☎ (207) 439-1630 $$
Lubec
* Peacock House B&B, 27 Summer St. ☎ (207) 733-2403 $
Naples
* Augustus Bove House B&B, routes 302/114. ☎ (207) 693-6365 $
* Inn at Long Lake B&B, Lake House Rd. ☎ (207) 693-6226 $-$$
Ogunquit
The Anchorage By the Sea, Shore Rd. ☎ (207) 646-9384 $-$$
Arrows ®, Berwick Rd. ☎ (207) 361-1100 $$
Clay Hill Farm ®, Agamenticus Rd. ☎ (207) 646-2272 $-$$
Gorges Grant Hotel, US1 ☎ (207) 646-7003 $-$$
Hurricane Restaurant, Perkins Cove. ☎ (207) 646-6348 $$
Joanathan's Restaurant, Bourne Lane. ☎ (207) 646-4777 $$
Milestone Motor Inn, 333 Main St. ☎ (207) 646-4562 $-$$
Sea Chambers Motor Lodge, 37 Shore Rd. ☎ (207) 646-9311 $-$$
Old Orchard Beach
* Atlantic Birches Inn B&B, 20 Portland Ave. ☎ (207) 934-5295 $-$$
Joseph's By The Sea ®, 55 W Grand Ave. ☎ (207) 934-5044 $$
Ocean Walk Hotel, 195 E Grand Ave. ☎ (207) 934-1716 $-$$
The Village Inn ®, 213 Saco Ave. ☎ (207) 934-7370 $$

Portland

Back Bay Grill, 65 Portland St. ☎ (207) 772-8833 $$

The Inn at Portland, 1150 Brighton Ave. ☎ (207) 775-3711 $$

* *Inn on Carleton B&B*, 46 Carleton St. ☎ (207) 775-1910 $

Jordon's Lobster House, 202 Larrabee Rd. ☎ (207) 856-2284 $

* *Portland Regency Hotel*, 20 Milk St. ☎ (207) 774-4200 $$-$$$

South Portland Marketplace Restaurant, 101 Maine Mall Rd. ☎ (207) 772-3754 $

* *West End Inn B&B*, 146 Pine St. ☎ (207) 772-1377 $$

Rangeley

* *Northwoods B&B*, Main St. ☎ (207) 864-2440 $

Rockport

Glen Cove Motel, US1 ☎ (207) 594-4062 $

Samoset Resort, 220 Warrenton St. ☎ (207) 594-2511 $$-$$$

Saco

Cascade Inn Family Restaurant, 941 Portland Rd. ☎ (207) 283-3271 $-$$

Classic Motel, 21 Ocean Park Rd. ☎ (207) 282-5569 $

Lord's Motel, 720 Portland Rd. ☎ (207) 284-4074 $

Searsport

* *Brass Lantern Inn B&B*, 81 W Main St. ☎ (207) 883-3401 $$

* *The Nickerson Tavern* ®, US1. ☎ (207) 548-2220 $$

South Portland

The Channel Crossing ® 231 Front St. ☎ (207) 799-5552 $$

Costline Inn, 80 John Roberts Rd. ☎ (207) 772-3838 $

Hampton Inn Hotel, 171 Philbrook Ave. ☎ (207) 773-4400 $-$$

Portland Marriott Hotel, 200 Sable Oaks Drive. ☎ (207) 871-8000 $$-$$$

Snow Squall Restaurant, 18 Ocean St. ☎ (207) 799-2232 $$

Southwest Harbor

* *Lamb's Ear Inn B&B*, 9 Clark Point Rd. ☎ (207) 244-9828 $-$$

Waterville

Holiday Inn, 375 Main St. ☎ (207) 873-0111 $-$$

John Martin's Manor Restaurant, 54 College Ave. ☎ (207) 873-5676 $$

Waterville Motor Lodge, 320 Kennedy Memorial Drive. ☎ (207) 873-0141 $

Wells

Billy's Chowder House, Mile Rd. ☎ (207) 646-758 $-$$

Litchfield's Seafood Restaurant, US1. ☎ (207) 646-5711 $$

Ogunquit River Plantation, US1. ☎ (207) 646-9611 $-$$

Seagull Motor Inn, US1. ☎ (207) 646-5164 $-$$

Yarmouth

Down-East Village Motel, US1. ☎ (207) 846-5161 $

Muddy River Restaurant, US1. ☎ (207) 846-3082 $$

York
York Commons Inn, US1. ☎ (207) 363-8903 $-$$
York Beach
Lighthouse Inn, US1A. ☎ (207) 363-6072 $-$$
Sunrise Motel, US1A. ☎ (207) 363-4542 $-$$
Union Bluff Hotel, 8 Beach St. ☎ (207) 363-1333 $$-$$$
York Harbor
Bill Foster's Down East Lobster and Clambake ® Axholme Rd. ☎ (207) 363-3255 $$
* *Edwards Harborside Inn B&B*, Stage Neck Rd. ☎ (207) 363-3037 $-$$
Inn at Harmon Park B&B, 415 York St. ☎ (207) 363-2031 $
* *Riverbank on the Harbor B&B*, 11 Harmon Park Rd. ☎ (207) 363-8333 $$
Stage Neck Inn, Stage Neck Rd. ☎ (207) 363-3850 $$-$$$
* *York Harbor Inn*, York St. ☎ (207) 363-5119 $$

The area of Peacham is surrounded by beautiful Churches and countryside

Fact File 5

Accommodation

There is a huge range of accommodation to suit all tastes and pockets from international hotels in the major cities, to historic inns and bed and breakfast rooms in the countryside. Motels generally provide good value rooms if all you want to do is shower and sleep after an exhausting day's exploration. There are inns and lodges, campgrounds and RV hook ups, and many campgrounds also offer cabins as well.

Most modern hotels and motels usually offer two double beds in each room, and as you pay for the room, this can work out very reasonably if you are travelling as a family or with friends. As rooms tend to be large, an extra single bed or cot can also usually be obtained for a small additional fee, provided the management receive adequate notice. Most rooms have en suite bathroom and telephone, air-conditioning and cable/satellite television is standard. Older hotels often offer rooms with just a single or double bed.

Because competition is intense prices are generally much lower than comparable accommodation in the UK and mainland Europe — and there are usually added incentives to tempt you. These can range from free breakfasts to free shuttle buses to take you to and from the attractions.

Prices vary according to season and standard of service offered. Most hotel chains offer vouchers which if pre-paid, offer substantial discounts so it is worth checking with your travel company. Before buying vouchers, however, make sure the hotel offers the standard of service you require. There are also substantial discounts for senior citizens, and members of the American Automobile Association.

If you are visiting during peak seasons, around Christmas, Easter, during the summer or around fall foliage time, it is advisable to book accommodation. At other times, you may want to cruise around and hunt out the best bargains if there is a choice. All hotels and motels clearly advertise their room rates as well as other perks on offer, and you can always pop in and check the room out before deciding. If you feel up to it, you can always haggle over the price and see if you can get a few extra dollars knocked off for staying several nights, paying cash or whatever.

Many restaurants and motels have their own restaurants, and will usually offer American Plan (full board) or Modified American Board (half-board). If the establishment has no restaurant, there is usually coffee available in the lobby at most times, with free doughnuts often available in lieu of breakfast. Ice machines and soft drinks dispensers are generally available. Many hotels and motels also provide cooking facilities in rooms, and these establishments are advertised as 'efficiencies'. The cooking facilities provided, however, can vary from a single hot plate to a fully-fitted kitchen, so if you plan to do a lot of cooking, check out the facilities on offer before agreeing to take the room.

Most hotel and motel chains have toll-free numbers to ring from within the US for information and reservations. Always check to see what discounts are available and if there are any restrictions concerning children and pets.

Best Inns 1-800-237-8466
Best Western 1-800-528-1234
Budgetel Inns 1-800-4-BUDGET
Budget Host Inns 1-800-BUD-HOST
Clarion-Choice Hotels:
Comfort Inns 1-800-228-5150
Clarion Inns 1-800-CLARION
Econo Lodges 1-800-55-ECONO
Friendship Inns 1-800-453-4511
Quality Inns 1-800-228-5151
Rodeway Inns 1-800-229-2000
Sleep Inns 1-800-62-SLEEP
Days Inns 1-800-325-2525
Economy Inns of America 1-800-423-3018
Embassy Suites 1-800-528-1100
Hilton Hotels 1-800-HILTONS
Holiday Inn 1-800-HOLIDAY
Hospitality International Inns 1-800-251-1962
Howard Johnson 1-800-654-2000
Hyatt Hotels International 1-800-228-9000
Marriott Hotels 1-800-228-2800
Ramada Inns 1-800-2-RAMADA
Sheraton Hotels, Motor Inns and Resorts 1-800-325-3535
Super 8 Motels 1-800-800-8000
Travelodge 1-800-255-3050

Bed and Breakfast and Guesthouses
These are worth hunting out if you want a taste of real country living. They are often more expensive than a cheap motel or hotel, but they do allow you to stay in a family home, and are often delightfully furnished. Local tourist offices have lists of homes offering bed and breakfast accommodation, and guest houses, otherwise known as boarding houses.

YMCA & Youth Hostels
For inexpensive accommodation, these make ideal bases, although

advance booking is essential for both during peak periods. If travelling from abroad and wanting to stay in a youth hostel, you must be a member of your own country's hostelling association.

Babysitting

Most hotels offer baby sitting facilities, and there are a number of registered companies that will send baby sitters to your hotel room or villa, or take the children off your hands by escorting them to the attractions. Most hotels and resorts also have special events and areas for children, from infants to teens, with trained staff to supervise them.

Canoeing

Canoe rentals are available in most locations near water including many national and state parks, and provide an excellent way of exploring, as you can gently paddle down backwaters often inaccessible in any other way.

Caravans and Camping

Caravans and motor homes (known as RVs — recreational vehicles) also make excellent bases. Caravan and RV parks are usually equipped to a high standard, and apart from electricity and water hook-up, usually have on-site shop, restaurant, bar and club house, as well as many other facilities. Most parks rent out mobile homes, and if you want to travel about you can rent a car and caravan, or an RV.

Camping and backpacking is very popular in national and state parks. Most have official campgrounds with many facilities as well as wilderness sites where you have to carry everything in, including water. In many parks, camping is free in the remoter areas but you will have to hike in, and you may require a wilderness permit. These are usually obtained locally from the information centre. Always check first. If moving on foot in remote areas always try to travel in groups of at least three. In that way if someone is hurt, one person can stay and look after the injured, and another can go for help.

Warning. Off-road camping, even when permitted, is not recommended.

Climate

New England enjoys warm to hot summers and cold, snowy winters. Each season has its own weather patterns and the only common factor is how quickly the weather can change — so be prepared. Cold air from the Canadian north often sweeps south while hot air from the tropics rushes north; the result can be

Climate in New England

Temperature

Rainfall

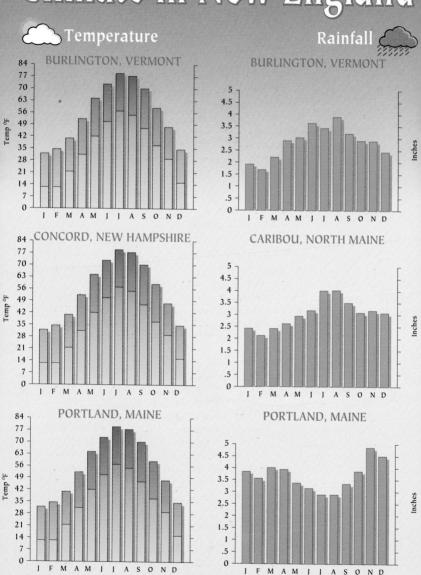

rapidly changing conditions with hot mornings, cold, foggy afternoons and torrential rain in the evening. Temperatures are warmer throughout the year in south-eastern New England because of the warming influence of the Atlantic.

Winters are long and cold with temperatures often many degrees below zero. In the north thick snow can lay from late November to April, but in the south-east standing snow before Christmas is unusual as are sub-zero temperatures. Spring brings warm weather but is known locally as the 'mud season' because of all the melting snow. Summer day temperatures range from 70-90°F (21-32°C) but can be foggy and wet. The Connecticut River valley in central Massachusetts has the hottest summers.

Autumn not only offers fabulous fall foliage colours but sunny days. Indian summers are a regular feature although evenings and nights can be chilly.

If you are driving during a summer downpour, turn on your headlights and windscreen wipers, and reduce your speed. Exercise the greatest caution because roads often flood, and there can be blinding spray and the risk of aquaplaning.

Crime

There is no evidence to show that holidaymakers face any greater risk in the US than they do in many other places around the world. Millions of visitors travel to this part of the US every year and never see any signs of trouble. If basic sensible precautions are taken, there is no reason why you should. Do not wave money about, wear as little jewellery as possible and keep money, credit cards and passport separate.

Before leaving the airport, make sure you know where you are going and how to get there. If it is very late and you are tired, take a taxi to an airport hotel and stay overnight so that you can continue your journey the next day refreshed and in daylight.

If staying in a hotel or motel, use their safe for valuables such as passports and tickets. Carry a photocopy of your passport in case you are officially asked for identification.

When travelling in a car keep the doors locked and the windows up, and when leaving the car parked, make sure there is nothing visible that might tempt a thief. Never sleep in the car overnight, find a cheap motel or hotel. Ask hotel staff or the tourist centre if there are any areas to avoid, and make sure you do not stray into them, especially at night.

It is quite safe to walk around during the day, but there is always the outside chance of a bag snatcher, or someone trying to grab your video camera, so be careful. If you are stopped and threatened, do not resist. Most thiefs only want cash or easily disposable items, and most will make their getaway as soon as you hand them over.

If you are robbed, report it to the police immediately. Report the theft of credit cards and traveller's cheques to the appropriate organisations, and if your passport is stolen, report it as soon as possible to your Embassy or Consulate.

Currency and Credit Cards

The American dollar comes in denomination of $1, $2 (rare), $5, $10, $20, $50 and $100. In practice, it is not a good idea to have higher denomination bills and some establishments refuse to accept $50 and $100 dollar bills because there are forgeries about. Always keep a few $1 bills in your wallet for making up tips.

It is easy to confuse the various denominations because they are all the same size and colour, the only difference is their face value. Always check that you are handing over the right note, and check your change.

The dollar is divided into cents with the following coins: 1c (penny), 5c (nickel), 10c (dime) and 25c (quarter). There are 50c and $1 dollar coins but these are rarely found in circulation.

Most major credit cards are widely accepted, particularly American Express, Diners Club, Visa and Mastercard. There may be problems occasionally in submitting foreign Access cards, but these are usually overcome if you point out that it is part of the Mastercard network. There is little point in taking all your credit cards with you so pick one or two that will be most useful, and leave the others in a secure place at home. If taking traveller's cheques, make sure they are dollar cheques, which can be handed over in lieu of cash in most places.

Customs

There are strict Customs and Department of Agriculture laws governing what can and cannot be imported into the United States. Drugs, dangerous substances, firearms and ammunition are banned, as are a wide range of foods, such as meat, dairy products, fruit and vegetables in order to maintain the disease-free status of the country's agriculture. The US has rabies and pets should be vaccinated against the disease.

While there are no restrictions on how much cash you can take into the US, all amounts over $10,000 must be listed on your customs declaration form. This is part of the authorities fight against drug trafficking. All gifts taken into the country and their value, should be listed on the declaration, and should not be wrapped so they are available for inspection if required.

You are allowed to import duty-free into the USA, 200 cigarettes, 50 cigars, 2kg of tobacco, or proportionate amounts of each; 1 litre of alcoholic drinks (if aged 21 or over), and gifts up to the value of $100.

If arriving by air from outside the US, you will have to hand in your customs declaration after clearing immigration.

You can buy duty-free goods at the airport before leaving the US, but you generally cannot pick up your purchases until just before you board the plane. After paying for your goods you will be given a receipt, and you must remember to collect your goods from the duty-free staff who will be somewhere in the tunnel between the exit gate and plane.

Driving

A valid UK or other national driving licence is needed if you want to hire a car and you must be 21 years of age or over. Many overseas automobile clubs are affiliated with the American Automobile Association (AAA) and proof of membership of one of these entitles you to a range of services, including breakdown assistance, free maps and discounts for car hire, hotels and attractions. Driving in the US is a pleasure once you have got used to driving on the other side of the road and familiarised yourself with traffic signs and so on.

Because of the lower speed limits and generally good lane discipline, you should not have any problems driving in towns and cities, and it can be positively therapeutic in the countryside. It assists navigation wonderfully if you can remember that even numbered roads generally run east to west, while highways with an odd number, usually run north to south.

If you want to get from A to B in a hurry, take an Interstate road or a turnpike. Interstate roads are multi-lane highways with a maximum speed limit of 55mph (88kmph) except in some rural areas where it increases to 65mph (104kmph). Interstates also often have minimum speed limits, usually 40mph (64kmph).

While no charge is levied for travelling on Interstate highways, a toll is due if you travel on turnpikes. These roads are privately maintained and you either pay a toll to go on to a particular stretch of road, or you take a ticket and pay when you turn off, the toll depending on how far you have travelled. The same speed limits apply as for Interstates. On both turnpikes and interstates there are frequent pull in areas for food and petrol (gas).

US Highways are slower, often running through towns where delays can occur at traffic lights and because of lower urban speed limits. You will find, however, far more roadside cafés, restaurants, and overnight accommodation and other services along US Highways. Speed limits vary between 45mph (72kmph) and 55mph (88kmph) in rural areas to 15 to 40mph (24 to 64kmph) in urban areas. The lowest speed limits are usually found in areas around schools.

A freeway is a road running through the heart of an urban area, designed to get traffic quickly through the built up area.

Country lanes are like country lanes everywhere. They can be narrow with few overtaking or passing points and care needs to be exercised when driving along them. They do, however, provide an opportunity to see the countryside off the tourist routes. Roads in National Parks are often narrow and winding, and speed limits must be observed. Parking on the road is not allowed and frequent pull offs are provided. Drivers must be alert for other traffic and wild animals on the road, especially at night. Many popular park roads are one-way to ease traffic flow. Often park roads are not suitable for large vehicles or trailers and there is usually a parking area where trailers can be left.

Rules of the Road
- Drive on the right and pass on the left
- Observe the posted speed limits: 55-65mph (88-104kmph) on highways, 25-40mph (40-64kmph) in urban areas, and 15mph (24kmph) in school zones
- All traffic accidents must be reported
- School buses. If a school bus has stopped to board or unload passengers traffic in both directions must stop. The only exception is when oncoming traffic is separated from the bus by a central reservation
- Do not park near a fire hydrant. If you do you will be fined and your vehicle may be towed away
- Always give way to emergency vehicles

Traffic Signals
Red light - you must stop
Amber light - signal is about to change, or it is a warning light
Green - go
Green arrow - follow the direction of the arrow
Flashing red light - you must stop but may then proceed with care
Flashing yellow light - slow down and then proceed with care

Maps

Free maps are available from car hire companies, tourist information offices and the American Automobile Association if you belong to an affiliated association or club. Before setting out on a journey plan your route and allow plenty of time to reach your destination without speeding. If arriving in the US by air for the first time, ask your car hire company to indicate on their free map, the best route to take to reach your first destination.

Breakdown

If you breakdown in a rural area, move across on to the hard shoulder, lift the bonnet (hood), and then get back into your vehicle, lock the doors and wait for help. If it is at night, you must use your emergency flashers. Police cars patrol the highways and will come to your assistance.

If you are driving a rental car, contact the company at once and ask for a replacement vehicle. Members of affiliated overseas automobile associations can also contact the American Automobile Association. You can find the AAA number in the telephone directory,or in the event of a breakdown, you can ring toll-free 1-800-AAA-HELP.

Accidents

If you are involved in any road accident, exchange particulars with other drivers and get the names and addresses of any witnesses. You must report to the police any accident that involves personal injury, or significant damage (anything other than a minor bump). Never admit liability or even say 'I'm sorry'. Some insurance companies will not honour a policy if a driver has admitted liability. If you are driving a rented car, notify the hire company as soon as possible. If people are injured, no matter how hard it seems, leave medical assistance to those who are qualified to administer it. If you try and help and something goes wrong, you could face a massive bill for damages.

Driving Under the Influence of Alcohol or Drugs

Even having an open container of alcohol in a car is illegal, and it is just not worth the risk of drinking and driving as the penalties are very severe, including imprisonment and vehicle confiscation. Driving under the influence of drugs is also a serious crime and you could end up in prison.

Parking

When parking in urban areas at night, choose a spot that is well lit and ideally in a busy area. Lock all doors and make sure that no luggage is visible.

Petrol (Gas)

Most new cars take unleaded fuel, but always check before filling up.

Getting petrol can be confusing because petrol pumps operate in a number of different ways. Usually the nozzle has to be removed and then the bracket it rests on, moved into an upright position to activate the pump.

Some petrol filling stations require pre-payment and smaller stations will often not take credit cards, while others may charge a fee if a credit card is offered.

Speeding

Police can impose on the spot fines for speeding, and you can even spend a night in jail for going too fast. Be careful on turnpikes as your ticket is time-stamped and if you get to a payment booth too fast, you may be fined for speeding.

Electricity

Electrical appliances operate on a 110 volt alternating current. Adapters can be used but if you have a dual volt appliance such as a battery charger for a video camrecorder, make sure the voltage is set correctly and that you alter it back on your return to the UK.

Embassies

UK - 5 Upper Grosvenor Street, London W1A 2JB
☎ 071 499-7010
Canada - 1155 Saint Alexandra, Montreal, Quebec H22 122
☎ 514-398-9695
Australia - 36th floor, Electricity House, Park & Elizabeth Streets, Sydney NSW 2000 ☎ 02-261-9200
New Zealand - 4th floor, Yorkshire General Building, CNR Shortland & O'Connell, Aukland ☎ 09-303-2724

Emergencies

The emergency telephone number is 911, and if that fails, dial 0 for the operator who will put you through to the appropriate service.

Fishing

Fishing is almost a way of life in rural US. People fish for both food and sport. State saltwater and freshwater fishing licenses are needed for all anglers aged 16 and older. All fees collected are used specifically for improving and restoring fish habitats, building artificial reefs, researching marine life and habitats, enforcement and education.

Licenses are obtained from local fishing and bait shops, visitor centres and often hotels. Fishing charters and cruises are widely available throughout the south-west. It is usually best to go in a group or be prepared to join others as this cuts the cost down. Most charters include the cost of boat, equipment, bait and guides. There are also many fishing camps.

Handicapped Travellers

The US leads the world in the provision of facilities for the handicapped. By law, all public buildings, national and state parks must provide access facilities for the handicapped, and most hotels and attractions mirror this with superb access and facilities. They also have special provision for the totally or partially blind or deaf. Most national parks have some trails suitable for wheelchairs.

Many of the major car rental companies can provide specially adapted cars and vehicles with special controls, if given advance notice.

Horse Riding

There are many opportunities for riding. Many of the national and state parks have horse riding trails and local tourist offices, hotels and the telephone directory will give you the numbers of nearby stables.

Illness and Injury

It is absolutely essential to have adequate insurance cover if travelling within the US. It is a good idea to carry a photocopy of your insurance policy with you, and keep the original in your room or in another safe place.

While medical service is first rate, it is expensive. If you need to seek a doctor while staying in a hotel, motel or rental home, the staff will normally be able to recommend someone to call. If you are injured away from your base, there are 24-hour emergency clinics and hospitals. Procedures for payment vary but you will most probably be asked to pay by credit card or cash, so make sure you get all receipts so that you can reclaim on your insurance. If you need a dentist, you will find a list of the names in the telephone directory, and again expect to have to pay on the spot and reclaim for treatment later.

In an emergency dial 911, keep calm, explain the problem and help will be sent.

If bitten by an animal, wild or domestic, seek medical help as rabies is endemic.

It is always worth travelling with a small first aid kit, and you will need sun screen and insect repellant, although these are best bought locally. If you are taking medication, make sure you have enough to last throughout the trip, and a letter from your doctor explaining why the medication was prescribed, may prevent a difficult situation if questioned about the drugs.

Immigration

If flying from abroad into the US you will have to clear US Immigration and Naturalisation formalities. You must have a valid passport and appropriate visa or visa waiver document. You will be directed to an immigration line (queue) once you enter the terminal building. When you are called by the immigration officer, present your passport and other necessary forms which you will have been given to fill in on the plane. Provided you have a return ticket, you should have no problems and your passport will be stamped with a date in the future allowing you time to complete your holiday or business. You must leave the country by this date, or seek an extension from an immigration office. A portion of your immigration form is stapled to your passport, and this is surrendered when you leave the country, so do not lose it. This portion is used to tell the computer that you have left the country, and without it, you may be classified as an illegal alien, and have a lot of explaining to do next time you try to go back into the US.

Insurance

It is essential to take out insurance before travelling to the US. Make sure that the cover is adequate to meet any claims that might have to be submitted in the event of an accident or health problem. Remember that medical care and hospital bills are likely to be much higher than in many other parts of the world, and awards in the court for damages as a result of an accident can be astronomic. Make sure the insurance covers you against third party law suits, and carry a copy of your insurance cover with you. It is always worth shopping round for holiday insurance because cost and cover can vary enormously.

Language

English speaking visitors should have few problems visiting the US. The language is largely the same although some words are spelt differently. Words that may confuse are:

British	American
air	air conditioning
biscuit	cookie
car boot	trunk
car bonnet	hood
car bumper	fender
chips	french fries
cot	crib
crisps	chips
eggs fried one side only	sunny side up
both sides over easy	(soft yolk)
both sides over hard	(hard yolk)
fizzy drink	soda
refuse	garbage trash
grilled	broiled
ground floor	first floor
layby	pullover
lift	elevator
motor caravan	RV - recreational vehicle
pavement	sidewalk
post	mail
petrol	gas
public school	private school
public toilet	rest room
reverse charge call	collect call
road	pavement
scone	biscuit
single bed	cot
sweet	candy
tap	faucet
tights	pantyhose

Photography

All types of film are freely available in the US and often cheaper than at home. Always ask for a discount if buying large quantities of film because you can normally get a reduction, especially if paying by cash.

One hour developing is also widely available but it costs more than the normal turn round for film processing. If it very sunny, it is often best to use high speed film, and if your camera permits, it is worth buying a suitable filter to reduce glare. It is important to prevent your camera from getting too hot because the film may be damaged.

Post Offices and Mail

Many shops sell stamps but it is often advisable to avoid stamp machines which can work out more expensive. Post offices can handle all your mailing requirements and will hold letters sent to you for up to 30 days provided they are clearly marked with your name and the words 'c/o General Delivery'. You will be asked for identification before any letters are handed over.

American Express card holders can also have mail sent to them c/o the local Amex office. Again, it is usually held for 30 days. Mail should be clearly addressed with the recipient's name and marked 'Client Mail'.

US Mail boxes are not always immediately obvious but can be found in most shopping areas, and there are usually facilities in hotels and so on, for posting mail.

Postcards need a 30c stamp and letters a 50c stamp for mailing to the UK and mainland Europe.

Public Holidays

Major public holidays are:

New Year's Day	January 1
Martin Luther King Day	January 16
President's Day	Third Monday in February
Memorial Day	Last Monday in May
Independence Day	July 4
Labor Day	First Monday in September
Comlumbus Day	Second Monday in October
Veteran's Day	November 11
Thanksgiving	Last Thursday in November
Christmas	December 25

Halloween, while not an official public holiday, is a time for major celebrations.

Sales Tax

Sales tax causes a lot of confusion among foreign visitors who find that they are asked to pay more for goods than the amount printed on the price tag. Each State has its own sales tax which is added automatically when you pay. It is usually between 6 and 7 per cent. Most goods are subject to the sales tax but groceries and medicines are exempt.

Telephones

All telephone numbers have a three-digit area code followed by the number. For long distance calls within your particular area code, dial 1 + the number; for outside the area code, dial 1 + area code + number.

For the operator — for collect calls (transfer charge), credit card calls and person to person dial 0 + the number given for the operator, or 0 + area code = operator's number for operator calls outside your area code.

International calls for direct dialling 001 + country code + area code + number. Full dialling instructions are printed beside all pay phones.

It is cheaper to make long distance and international calls between 5-11pm and at weekends, and if you want to make an international call using cash from a public call box, you will need a bucketful of change.

Theft and Lost Property

If luggage or property is lost or stolen report it to the police and the relevant authority (i.e. airport, car hire company, hotel, park ranger) as soon as possible, and try to contact your insurance company for permission to replace stolen items and keep all receipts.

Times and Dates

New England is in the Eastern Time Zone which is 5 hours behind Britain, and 6 hours behind most of mainland Europe. The Americans put their clocks forward in April and back in October but not at the same time as Europe, so there is a further 1 hour time difference during these overlap periods.

Tipping

Generally tip $1 to porters for each piece of luggage carried. Elsewhere tips of 15 per cent are considered normal in bars, restaurants, taxis and so on. Wages in the catering sector are low and staff aim to boost their take home pay by tips. For exceptional service you may inspired to tip 20 per cent. If dining in a restaurant which adds an automatic service charge, this is normally paid in lieu of tips. If the service was not up to expectations, however, complain and refuse to pay the service charge.

Toilets

Better known as the rest room, bathroom, men's room or lady's room. Public toilets are found almost everywhere. There are frequest rest areas with toilets along major highways, and you will find them in most shopping malls, visitor centres, attractions and so on. You will even find them in stores. If you need the toilet, ask for the men's or lady's room or the restroom.

Tourist Information Offices

USA: US Division of Tourism,1667 K. Street NW. Suite 270 Washington DC 20006 ☎ (202) 293 3707

UK: US Division of Tourism, 2 Cinnamon Row, Plantation Wharf, York Place, London SW11 3TW ☎ (0171) 978 5262

Canada: US Division of Tourism, 33 Niagara Street, Toronto M5V IC2 ☎ (416) 362 8784

Australia: US Division of Tourism, Suite 6106, MLC Centre King & Castlereagh Streets, Sydney, NSW 2000 Australia ☎ 02 233 4055

Travel

Air

Most foreign visitors arrive by air flying into international airports such as New York or Boston. After clearing immigration there are many opportunities for catching an internal flight, to get you closer to your final destination. Air fares are highest at peak times — Christmas, Easter and the summer holidays. At other times of the year, however, there are usually bargain air tickets to be found if you look around for them but check the details. The fare might sound cheap but it might mean long stop overs between connecting flights and a very late arrival, which could be a problem with young children. Package deals generally afford the best value. If you want the freedom to roam or pick your accommodation, go for fly-drive. Always check with your travel agent what special offers, hotel discounts and so on are available.

If you fly on a regular basis, it is worth joining the free 'frequent flyer' schemes operated by most airlines.

Car Hire

It is usually cheaper to arrange your car hire through your travel company or as part of a fly-drive package. Although it is optional, you are strongly advised to have collision damage waver (CDW) and it is often cheaper to pre-pay this as well.

The car hire companies are either situated on the airport or a short drive away. If off the airport, courtesy buses shuttle to and from the car pick-up point.

You will need a valid driving licence and be 21 years old or over. You will need to give the address at which you will be staying. If planning to tour, give the address of where you will be spending your first night. You will also be asked to give a contact telephone number, and you may be asked to produce your passport and return airline ticket. If paying by pre-paid voucher, you will also be asked for a credit card to pay for incidentals such as airport tax, additional drivers and so on.

When you check in to collect your hire car, do not be persuaded to upgrade or take out extra insurance unless you want to. Cars available range from economy models to limousines, and some rental companies will urge you to upgrade simply because they have run out of vehicles in the category you ordered. If they can persuade you to upgrade they will charge you the difference, but if you refuse they must still give you a bigger car because they are obliged to provide you with a vehicle. If they have run out of models in the category you ordered, you will finish up with something bigger but at no extra cost.

Train
If you like train travel, get an Amtrak USA Rail pass, which offers unlimited travel and as many stopovers as you like, for 45 days. Some routes carry restrictions and you will have to pay extra for sleeping car accommodation. For further details ask your travel agent, or write to Amtrak at 60 Massachusetts Ave NE, Washington DC 20002, or ☎ US 202-383-3000 from outside North America, or use freephone 1-800-USA-RAIL from within the USA or Canada.

Buses
The Greyhound service is almost legendary, and a Greyhound Ameripass is a very cheap and interesting way to travel around, especially city to city, and to meet a lot of people. The scheme incorporates Greyhound and a number of other private bus and coach companies, and is fine for medium and long distance travel. Problems can occur when you get off the Greyhound bus and then have to find public transport to take you to your final destination.

Taxis
Local public transport can be erratic outside towns and cities, and rental cars or taxis are the best ways of getting around. Taxis are not expensive and offer a safe way of travelling around late at night.

Travel Documents

All visitors to the USA must have a valid passport with at least 6 months to run from the day they are scheduled to return home.

Under the Visa Waver Program, visitors from the UK, most EC countries and Japan, arriving by air or sea aboard a carrier participating in the programme, do not require a waver, provided they do not plan to stay for more than 90 days. If travelling under this programme, you must complete a green 'visa waiver' form, which is handed in to immigration on arrival.

Visitors making frequent trips to the USA or planning to stay for more than 3 months should have a valid visa. You obtain a US visa by filling in the application form (obtainable from Embassies and some travel companies) and sending it, together with your passport and other documents required, to the visa section of the United States Embassy in your country. Allow at least 21 days for processing, although the visa is often returned earlier than this. Some travel companies, because of special arrangements with the US Embassy, can get the visa within 48 or 72 hours. In emergencies, it may be possible to visit the visa section personally, but always check first.

The normal tourist visa allows multiple entries to the US and is valid indefinitely. Even if you have to renew your passport, the visa is still valid in the cancelled passport, provided you present both at immigration.

Further information can be obtained by writing to the United States Consulate General, Visa Branch at the United States Embassy in your country. See page 229 for addresses.

Weights and Measures

Americans still use the Imperial system of weights and measures, although metric measures are becoming more common. Road distances are always in miles while petrol (gas) can be in either gallons or litres, or both.

The major difference is that a US gallon = .833 of an Imperial gallon = 3.8 litres.

Women's clothes sizes in the US are two sizes less than the UK equivalent (i.e. a size 12 dress in the UK would be labelled size 10 in the US), while women's shoe sizes in the US are labelled two sizes larger (i.e. a size 6 in the UK would be size 8 in the US).

Index